(RE)THINKING ORIENTALISM

minding the media

CRITICAL ISSUES FOR LEARNING AND TEACHING

Shirley R. Steinberg and Pepi Leistyna
General Editors

Vol. 12

The Minding the Media series is part of both
the Peter Lang Education list and the Media and Communication list.
Every volume is peer reviewed and meets
the highest quality standards for content and production.

PETER LANG
New York • Bern • Frankfurt • Berlin
Brussels • Vienna • Oxford • Warsaw

RACHEL BAILEY JONES

(RE)THINKING ORIENTALISM

Using Graphic Narratives to Teach
Critical Visual Literacy

PETER LANG
New York • Bern • Frankfurt • Berlin
Brussels • Vienna • Oxford • Warsaw

Library of Congress Cataloging-in-Publication Data

Jones, Rachel Bailey.
(Re)thinking orientalism: using graphic narratives to
teach critical visual literacy / Rachel Bailey Jones.
pages cm. — (Minding the media: critical issues for learning and teaching; vol. 12)
Includes bibliographical references and index.
1. Orientalism. 2. Islamophobia. 3. Oriental literature.
4. Graphic novels—Social aspects. 5. Visual literacy.
6. Cross-cultural studies. I. Title.
DS61.85.J66   303.48'2182105—dc23   2014033081
ISBN 978-1-4331-2229-3 (hardcover)
ISBN 978-1-4331-2228-6 (paperback)
ISBN 978-1-4539-1414-4 (e-book)
ISSN 2151-2949

Bibliographic information published by **Die Deutsche Nationalbibliothek**.
Die Deutsche Nationalbibliothek lists this publication in the "Deutsche
Nationalbibliografie"; detailed bibliographic data are available
on the Internet at http://dnb.d-nb.de/.

© 2015 Peter Lang Publishing, Inc., New York
29 Broadway, 18th floor, New York, NY 10006
www.peterlang.com

TABLE OF CONTENTS

CHAPTER ONE

Introduction: Bringing Theory to Practice

The purpose of this text is to present the context of the representation of difference and the way that students in American schools learn about those who are different from them. To confront and challenge stereotypical understanding, I argue that educators need to first present the problematic, stereotypical images and text for analysis to understand how and why more authentic representations can counteract bias and lead to change. The first four chapters of the book establish the theoretical and historical context for the analysis of media and graphic narratives that follow in Chapters 5 through 10. This introduction lays the framework for the media and texts that are analyzed in later chapters. This also presents the theoretical and analytical foundation for the rest of the text, including comics theory, critical visual analysis, critical visual literacy, critical race and feminist theory and pedagogy. The first chapter gives the historical context of colonialism, postcolonialism, and Orientalism that explicitly or implicitly informs all of the graphic narratives in the text. Chapter 2 goes into more depth about visual modes of representation of difference and the encoding of visual language in the service of narrative. The third chapter traces the fundamental impact of the terrorist attacks on September 11th on the representation of Muslims in the United States and global relationships. This dovetails into the fourth chapter that begins the analysis of contemporary works of fictional and nonfictional representations of difference, in the form of television shows, independent film, and comics that challenge the stereotypical tropes of Islamophobia. I choose to separate the graphic narratives into chapters based on the geographical setting of the text but also considering the relationship of the author to the narrative. In Chapter 5, I analyze several texts that are memoirs about the authors' own experience in their cultural homeland(s) and the negotiation of identity and culture from their own perspectives: *Persepolis* (Satrapi 2003, 2004), *Nylon Road* (Bashi, 2009), and *A Game for Swallows* (Abirached, 2012). The texts analyzed in Chapter 6 are accounts of Western journalists who describe the experience of "other" with the intention of relating the real lived experience of others through graphic journalism: *The Waiting Room* (Glidden, 2011), *Palestine* (Sacco, 2001), and *The Photographer* (Guilbert, 2009). Chapter 7 focuses entirely on one fictionalized account of a distant and "exotic" land full of beautiful visual and verbal art along with problematic stereotypes and representations of gender: *Habibi* (Thompson, 2011). Other graphic narratives (in Chapter 8) are accounts of the author's homeland in the form of fictionalized or true stories of the experience of others in their own culture: *The Tunisian Awakening* (Hussein, 2011), *Rise* (Shahin, 2011), and *Zahra's Paradise* (Amir & Khalil, 2011). Chapter 9 broadens the scope of my analysis to texts that involve the complex representation of difference in multiple forms: *American Born Chinese* (Yang, 2008a), *Pyongyang* (Delisle, 2007), *Burma Chronicles* (Delisle, 2010), and *Fun Home* (Bechdel, 2007). The final chapter draws conclusions about the use of these narratives to teach critical visual literacy to students who are steeped in assumptions and flattened representations of difference.

Graphic Representations of Difference

Graphic representations of difference are communicated visually and verbally, though it is the visual nature of the graphic narrative and the inextricability of the images from the narrative that make it a powerful tool for teaching critical visual literacy. Historically grounded images have been used to propagate racism, anti-Semitism, Islamophobia, sexism, homophobia, and other forms of oppressive relationships. The power of bigoted images involves the relating of two or more people (often implicating the viewer) and highlighting the supposed normalcy and superiority of one while dehumanizing and degrading the other. Some derogatory imagery relies on taking a supposed physical characteristic of one group of people and exaggerating the feature to make them appear ridiculous and subhuman. The illustrations from *Vaught's Practical Character Reader* (Vaught, 1902) include pages devoted to various types of facial features, including noses and what the length, size, and slope of a nose means about the nature and character of the person. Noses that were pointed downward, bumped, or "hooked" were labeled as "pessimistic" and "cunning" (Vaught, 1902, p. 9). An example of this from popular culture is the use of a pronounced hooked nose in the villains of Walt Disney. Playing off anti-Semitic stereotypes of Jewish noses, Disney started to illustrate his villains with large noses that had a bump and turned sharply downward. Infamous villains including Captain Hook (*Peter Pan;* Disney, Geronimi, Jackson, & Luske, 1953), Governor Ratcliffe (*Pocahontas;* Pentecost, Gabriel, & Goldberg, 1995), and Jafar (*Aladdin;* Clements & Musker, 1992) showcase the connection in Disney animation between evil and nose shape. The noses of villains subtly recall anti-Semitic stereotypes that young viewers may not consciously understand.

In one of the most infamous examples of the popular curriculum about difference, Disney created *Aladdin* in 1992, loosely based on the tales of the *Arabian Nights*. The film has been criticized as a prime example of how Orientalism (the fantastical Western creation of the Middle East as an exotic, savage land) is communicated to children. The introductory song "Arabian Nights" originally included the lyrics, "Oh, I come from a land, from a faraway place where the caravan camels roam. Where they cut off your ear if they don't like your face. It's barbaric, but hey, it's home" (Fox, 1993, para. 4). After the film was released in theaters in 1992, the American-Arab Anti-Discrimination Committee protested the clear racism and Orientalism of the lyrics. In a rare act of contrition, Disney rewrote the lyrics for the film's video release. The revised lyrics were, "Where it's flat and immense and the heat is intense. It's barbaric, but hey, it's home" (para. 5). Though the offensive lyrics were changed, the inherent racism of the film was not altered. The world of Disney's *Aladdin* was full of racist stereotypes of Arabs, including conniving merchants, overly sexualized harem girls, violent punishment, and genies in bottles. Aladdin, the hero of the film, has an American accent, lighter skin, and more Westernized features, while the other characters (especially the evil Jafar) have darker skin, hooked noses, and vaguely foreign accents. The world of the film was an American fantasy of the Arab world that is part of a long history of flattened, stereotypical representations that both sensualize and vilify the Arab people. These animated motion pictures relate to the world of comics, though they reach a wider audience and have much larger budgets.

Comics as a Medium, Graphic Narrative as a Form

Many people of my generation were introduced to comics in the newspaper, especially the full color Sunday edition. Comics were short, sometimes funny, and sometimes part of an ongoing narrative that continued on the newspaper pages from week to week. Others were introduced to comics through the comic book, often associated with the masculine superhero that saves the damsel in distress and the world from evil. The medium of comics is vast, diverse, and made up of many different genres. Graphic narratives are a form of comics that are book-length narratives and that combine image and text in unique and creative ways. I choose to use the term graphic narrative rather the more widely used graphic novel because I analyze fictional and nonfictional texts (and others that blur the line between fiction and non-fiction).

Though the field of comics studies and theoretical approaches to reading comics is relatively new, some interesting work is being done on how to apply the theoretical perspectives of postcolonialism, multiculturalism, and border theory to graphic narratives. In adapting theoretical approaches that were originally used to analyze traditional text-based books, it is important to highlight the unique qualities of production, representation, and reception that are possible with graphic narratives; these are not simply books with pictures added in. The work is to determine how visual and verbal codes that are culturally and historically contingent function to create and disturb meaning in graphic narratives. The extended length of the narrative form and its visual storytelling over space is unique; most of our encounters with the visual are presented in still photos or artwork or predigested in film and television. Though certainly there are stories and visual codes present in all of these media, the graphic narrative must be experienced and read over a greater length of time; the visual codes repeat and evolve throughout the text. They involve a significant commitment on the reader's part to decode text and image and to make meaning of difference.

The visual language of comics varies based on the individual voice and hand of the creator, generally ranging from realistic to iconic. Realistic images use a lot of detail that tries to copy elements of the real object world in the panels of a comic world. Iconic images use basic shapes and lines to suggest reality without trying to copy it directly. In realistic comics, the creator does most of the work in translating the images from reality to the page, while the iconic style leaves more interpretive and translational work to the reader. The relationship between realistic comics and the real world of objects is closely aligned; therefore the images are read as images rather than as mental concepts. McCloud (1993) lays out a triangular matrix of the visual language of comics with "the picture plane," "language," and "reality" with all comics images fitting along these matrices. In the recent history of comics, the cutting edge, underground comics tend toward the more iconic, language point of the triangle. The comics that tend to strive for greater realism are the mainstream superhero and dramatic comics.

There has been a recent surge of interest in graphic narratives as pedagogical tools and in comics theory as a means of analysis, but the field is still emerging. In "Workshop I: Toward a Toolbox of Comics Studies," Kukkonen and Haberkorn (2010) attempt to collect a set of analytical tools that could be used to approach the wide variety of comic forms. They critique much existing comics theory as too reductive, "the hammer of simplification," which focuses on one element of comics as central; either the words are central while the images function simply as illustrations or the images are primary and the words are mere caption. The authors suggest moving away from a single, catchall approach and urge scholars to create a useful set of analytical tools and approaches to analyze comics. The first lenses for inclusion are production and reception, examining the context of production of the comic and how the audience/readers receive the comic. As cultural artifacts, comics are written, produced, and reproduced by a range of authors and artists, published by small and large comic and literary publishing companies that have stakes in the content and context of the comic. Authors and publishers have cultural positions and background knowledge and values that inform the production and distribution of the work. Once published and distributed, looking critically at audience involves analysis of who reads certain comics, how they are read, and what reaction or learning takes place as a result of the consumption. The second pair of tools in the analytical box are form and content, intertwined elements in comics. Many theorists in the field (including Groensteen, 2007) focus on the form of the comic panel elements and the formal sequencing of panels to create a narrative flow. The formal elements clearly impact the content and the reception of the comic's audience, with some authors purposefully manipulating the formal elements to drive their content while others consciously keep the form standardized to fade out of discussion of content. The final elements for toolbox inclusion are poetics and rhetorics. "Both have established a catalogue of devices used, in literature and oratory respectively, to achieve certain effects and to express certain contents" (p. 241). These traditional devices are useful in analyzing elements of discourse, character, and expression. The toolbox is broad enough to capture the variety of approaches to scholarly analysis of comics while not prescribing certain ways of reading or writing about comics.

Comics Terms

Though the manner in which authors combine image and text to create graphic narratives is diverse, there are a few terms that cut across the texts, and (almost) all work in comics. "The frames—which we may understand as boxes of time—present a narrative, but that narrative is threaded with absence, with the rich white spaces of what is called the gutter" (Chute, 2010, p. 6). Images and text in comics are generally broken into different frames on each page, which traditionally are rectangular in shape and contain an image and may include text that is dialogue between characters in the frame or is descriptive of the action that is taking place. There is also some space around and between these frames that is called the gutter. All of the authors that are discussed in this book use the frame and gutter convention but play with, alter, and change the shape and sequence of frames to further the narrative. The authors also utilize the gutters, the visually empty spaces, to pace the narrative flow and add meaning and drama to the text.

The gutter, the empty space around the panels, is unique to comics as a medium of expression. The sequential nature of the panels means that readers must fill in the action that happens between panels and in the gutters. If one panel shows an open eye and the next shows a closed eye, the reader mentally visualizes the steps of the closing eye without it being drawn on the page. "Nothing is *seen* between the two panels, but *experience* tells you something *must* be there!" (McCloud, 1993, p. 67). McCloud (1993) called this "closure," and it is the visual grammar that allows the language of comics to create and communicate meaning. He argued that the medium of comics requires a high level of participation from the reader. "Closure in comics fosters an intimacy surpassed only by the *written word*, a *silent, secret contract* between *creator* and *audience*" (p. 69). McCloud laid out six categories of transition between panels:

1. The moment-to-moment sequence that connects two images closely related in time and requires the least amount of closure.
2. The action-to-action transition shows images that follow closely due to a sequence of action, like striking a baseball.
3. The subject-to-subject sequence is a more abrupt transition between two related but different subjects.
4. The scene-to-scene transitions "transport us across *significant distances* of *time* and *space*" (p. 71).
5. The aspect-to-aspect transition does move through time but shows a different viewpoint of the same scene.
6. The non sequitur transitions between two unrelated images require a great deal of work to create meaning.

Most Western comics fall in the range of 2–4, though many Japanese comics use a much broader set of transitions and require more work from the reader to decode the transitions.

The transitions of comics relate to the passage of time in the narrative of comics. As the readers move through the space of panels and gutters, they also move through time in the story. The movement through time is not necessarily consistent between different frames in the same comic and most certainly not the same as in other comics. One panel can represent a single instant in time like a photograph, but one panel could also represent a significantly longer period of time, depending on whether there is speech in the panel and how the action is portrayed. "The few centimeters which transport us from *second to second* in *one* sequence could take us a *hundred million years* in *another*" (McCloud, 1993, p. 100). The time-space of comics separates it from other media; the visual nature of the panel structure allows for several ways to manipulate the perception of time through the use of space. The physical length of a frame can affect how long the time represented within the frame feels to the reader. Size of panels can also indicate relative importance; an especially vital, moving, or significant part of the story may be placed in a full-page or large panel. The panel and gutter conventions can be manipulated in various ways to affect the reader's experience of the story. *Bleeding* is a term used to describe the way an image can extend past the borders of a panel or if there is an image in a comic with no panel frames at all. In the West, we are trained to read all images and text from left to right and from top to bottom. We also assume that time moves in a linear fashion from the first page of a book to the last. All of these assumptions are tested in comics, especially the more experimental or underground comics. Comics play with ideas of space-time movement between panels and they also use various visual codes to indicate movement within a single panel.

The communicative elements of panels and gutters are unique to comics, but the use of art elements and written language function in complementary ways. The language of images in comics includes the traditional elements of visual art: texture, space, shape, color, tone/value, and line. Each of these elements affects the way that meaning is communicated to the reader, expressing emotion, context, and mood and combined with words to create complex narrative structures. The element of line can be used to represent very different concepts that are both visible and invisible. McCloud (1993) used the example of a series of three curved lines that can represent visible smoke wafting out of a pipe or the invisible stench emanating from a garbage can. Straight, choppy lines evoke different senses and emotions in the viewer than smooth, curving lines. The quality of lines in the drawings, their thickness, character, curve, angle, and pattern affect the emotional quality and the meaning of each panel and sequence of panels. In black and white graphic novels, the use of line is especially important in creating tone and mood and moving the reader's eye through the story. The lines could be solid or wispy, thick or thin, softly curving or sharply angled; each of these variables alters the visual impact of the panel and the sequence of panels on the page. Graphic weight refers to the impact of graphic elements in the panels, which panels draw the focus of the reader's eye through use of contrast, negative space, or unique use of line, shading, color, or texture. In using black and white, some authors like Satrapi and David B. use only black and white without shades of gray. This starkly graphic use of black and white lends impact to the contrast and pattern created without the use of color or shading. Other authors who work in black and white, as in *Stitches* by Small (2010), use more painterly approaches to their work, utilizing shades of gray to convey meaning and tone.

The visual elements of color, shade, tint, line, and shape affect the story and the way that authors illustrate difference in time, space, and people. The use of darkness and light, open and closed spaces carry great symbolic meaning in the panels and gutters of graphic narratives. Most of the graphic narratives that are analyzed in this book are presented in black and white, although a few utilize a limited color palate. Both color palettes offer varying levels of dark and light, highlight and shadow, but the added element of color can add an additional source of meaning. Color is an important element in some graphic narratives, but many authors work only in shades of black, white, and gray. The few graphic narratives that are presented in full color use the emotional and symbolic meaning of various colors to add meaning to the story. Color carries culturally specific meaning, and in work like *American Born Chinese* (Yang, 2008a), authors use the difference in color significance to highlight cultural differences. The mainstream American meanings of colors include the following: white can symbolize purity and innocence, red could mean passion and love or blood and violence, and green may be interpreted as relating to nature or jealousy. Meanings assigned to colors are culturally constructed, and the effect of color on the narrative of graphic novels can shift and change based on the cultural identity of the author, characters, and readers. Red is a color that has diverse and powerful cultural meaning. In Chinese tradition, red symbolizes good luck and celebration and is used as a focal color in wedding ceremonies and New Year's festivities. In the United States, the meaning of red can vary from love and passion (omnipresent in Valentine's Day celebrations) to danger and warning (on stop signs, color coding warning signs of danger). While symbolizing purity and celebration of weddings in the West, white is the color of unhappiness and sorrow in India, death and mourning in China. Colors also carry gendered cultural meaning, although meaning is contested and changing globally. The color associated with masculinity in the United States is blue, while black is for young boys and yellow represents masculinity in China.

In a classic text of comics theory, *The System of Comics*, Thierry Groensteen (2007) analyzed the way that formal elements in comics affect the meaning of narrative. Rather than analyzing the distinct pictorial and textual elements within a panel or even the transitions between panels, Groensteen analyzes the page layout as a whole. He introduces the hyperframe as a way to discuss the page margin as unique to the field of comics. The hyperframe defines the limits of content on a page of a graphic narrative, but the margin outside the hyperframe is not always empty or blank. Some authors change the color or measurements of the margin to delineate shifts in narrative structure. Others, like Sacco and Thompson, use the hyperframe and margins in places but also create pages where the images and text extend to the edge of the page, leaving no hyperframe or space for margin. Within the page or hyperframe, one panel or multiple panels are located to direct the reader in some way. The site of each panel on the page refers to its location relative to the hyperframe and to other panels. Groensteen also accounted for the double page, the full spread of a book that is available for the reader's gaze. At any point in reading a graphic narrative in printed form, two pages are adjacent and form a visual relationship that affects the perception of the narrative.

One of Groensteen's (2007) major contributions to the field is the delineation of the six "Functions of the Frame," the readerly function, expressive function, structural function, rhythmic function, separative function, and closure function. The function of closure is the visual limiting of space that the frame offers. The author makes a conscious choice to create frames of certain sizes and shapes and to enclose drawing and text within that space. The delineation of space within the page (gridding) is the first step in crafting the narrative for most comics authors. Groensteen contrasted the use of framing in comics, where the author chooses what information to include in the frame without having to consciously exclude anything, to the framing of film, where every choice of what to include in the visual frame necessitates the exclusion of other information. The separative function of the frame is related to the closure; the frame contains the image/text within its boundaries and it also separates one panel from the surrounding panels. "In this consideration, the panel frame plays an analogous role to that of punctuation marks in language...these signs that divide within a *continuum*, the pertinent units, thus allowing—or facilitating—the comprehension of the text" (p. 43). Distinct lines usually separate frames, although that is not always the case. Some frames are not bounded by lines but are separated by white spaces; other frames merge together without a physical separation.

The rhythmic function of the frame relates to the way the reader's eye moves through the page and thus the narrative. The frames offer "progression/retention" (Groensteen, 2007, p. 45) by both holding the eye in one place and then asking it to move on to the next frame. Often, the frame's size correlates to the amount of time the events depicted within the frame take and with the time spent reading it. If there are many, small frames on a page, they suggests quick movement from one frame to the next, while larger frames suggest lingering and slow movement. This relationship of size of frame and time is not a rule, and there are many authors who play with and subvert expected rhythms. A related function of the frame is the structuring function, describing the organization and shape of frames on a page. The standard shapes for frames are rectangles and squares, due to their relationship to the rectangular hyperframe of the page and the ease of lining up those shapes in sequence. If an author experiments with alternative frame shapes, like circular frames, it disrupts either the gutter surrounding the frame or the adjacent frames to which it must relate. The structure of the frames also relates to the movement of the eye and to dynamic action on the page. In Western tradition, the eye reads from left to right and moves through the narrative image/text of each panel from left to right as well. Groensteen (2007) described how most Western comics authors use this left-to-right movement when they illustrate movement on the page. Elements in the frame generally move from a starting position on the left toward the right edge of the frame, for instance, characters walking to the right. If the author chooses to depict movement from right to left, "it will aim to make the reader feel something that shares the same sense of disequilibrium, dread, or exultation attributed to the characters" (p. 48). This use of action within a frame to express disequilibrium or emotional disturbance leads into Groensteen's description of the expressive function of frames. The size, shape, and order of frames can influence the emotive power of the narrative, especially when these elements confound expectations or offer a surprise. In narratives such as *Burma Chronicles* (Delisle, 2010), the frames are consistently placed and shaped throughout the text and therefore neither add to nor detract from the flow of the narrative. In *Habibi* (Thompson, 2011), the frames shift in size, shape, and position, along with shifting borders and gutters, and impact the dramatic and expressive qualities of the sweeping narrative. The final of the six elaborated functions, the readerly function of the frame, points to the fact that by virtue of being contained within a frame, the content is to be examined, read, and decoded by the reader. An interesting example of this readerly function comes from *Habibi* in the chapter entitled "Orphan's Prayer." In this chapter, there are several frames that enclose empty space that is meant to be pregnant with unseen meaning. Readers are meant to read into these empty frames rather than skip over them because they lack visible content. These empty frames, taken out of context of the narrative, would hold no meaning or code for the reader; they only gain importance through their location at a pivotal and life altering moment for a main character. The choice to enclose a visual element inside a frame lends importance to an element that might otherwise fade into the background of a larger image. Groensteen gave the example from *Blues* (Montellier, 1979), where the author created a frame that contained an empty coat hanger hanging on a nail. If the coat hanger were in the background of a larger image, it would not carry special importance or meaning in the story. On its own, the coat hanger is an everyday household object. However, contained in its own frame, this object gains importance and centrality to the narrative; the reader must take time to "read" the image of the empty coat hanger and make sense of how it fits into the larger story.

Groensteen (2007) used and critiqued the analysis of Peeters (1994) as part of his larger construction of a system to organize graphic texts. Peeters created a way to understand the layout, shape, and position of panels on a page by its use: for conventional, decorative, rhetorical, or productive effect. The conventional page layout is a standard series of panels that remains unchanged by graphic or textual considerations. The work of Delisle's (2010) *Burma Chronicles* is an example of the conventional page, with each page containing the same number, size, and organization of panels. Decorative page layouts place aesthetic considerations above all others in the layout, placement, and shape of panels on a page. The rhetorical page layout is determined by the needs of the narrative flow; panels are placed and used primarily to move the story forward. Finally, productive page layouts drive, change, and move the story rather than reflect elements of the story. Groensteen renamed and reframed the "conventional page" as the "regular" one; the panel elements of the page remain constant as the visual elements within the panels change. The constancy and predictability of the page layout make the content of each panel more impactful: "it is evident that the differential value of every shrug or frown of the eyebrow is accentuated when no element is changed" (Groensteen, 2007, p. 97). If the consistency of the regular page layout can increase the attention and importance of the panels' contents, then widely ranging layouts could distract from the importance of what occurs in individual panels. Also, when the layout is regular and predictable, the effect of even minor changes to the order causes a stir. This layout structure "possesses the ultimate virtue of handling the possibility of sudden and spectacular ruptures from the initially given norm"

(Groensteen, 2007, p. 97). For example, in Delisle's (2007) *Pyongyang*, the author uses a mostly regular page layout of three rows of four panels each. At the beginning of each section, the flow of the regular panels is broken by a full-page panel that draws the reader's attention to the importance of that rare, large panel. Thompson's (2011) *Habibi* is a visually stunning example of rhetorical and decorative page layouts. The position, size, and relationship of the panels on the pages change in ways that often seem to be superfluous to the narrative but are a showcase for the artistic talent and creativity of Thompson. The variety adds to the visual impression of the text, but one could argue that the vast variety of visual elements takes away from the impact of the narrative elements of the story. Groensteen (2007) argued that the regular layout, though mostly associated with the traditional comic strip and "sketchily drawn satirical comics," can also be used by underground and innovative authors.

Groensteen (2007) devoted separate consideration to the word balloon (also referred to as the speech bubble) in the panel as a way to manage space in the hyperframe and direct the reader's gaze. There is a distinction between the word balloon, which generally contains speech or thought from one of the characters in the narrative, and the caption, which refers to narrative description from the author/narrator. The written words, whether part of the word balloon or caption, are elements that unite with images to constitute the frame. A comic can have frames with no text but (according to Groensteen) not text without frames. Generally, the text in a frame exists in the space that is empty of drawing. Within the frame, the relationship between image and text can be discussed in terms of depth, forms, area, and position. The differing illusion of depth of the image/text in a panel is a result of the flat plane of the "text zone" set within the three-dimensional perspective of the "image zone" (p. 69). "It is legitimate to assert that the cohabitation of the drawing and the balloon generates a tension, since the three-dimensional space constructed by the cartoonist is contradicted by the presence within it of this piece that is added, a stranger to the representative illusion" (p. 69). From this perspective of the frame's construction, the image is the primary and first part of the panel, with text added in a space empty of image. As I analyze the form and content of select graphic narratives, I will be noting several examples that contradict this hierarchy and split between the image and text within a panel (especially Thompson's *Habibi*, 2011). The empty nature of this space is reinforced by the color of the word balloon, which generally is the same color as the paper and gutter (most often white). However, this "emptiness" represents an opaque object laid on top of the drawing plane rather than a hole that cuts away from the drawing. Whether the balloon is added to an already-complete drawing or if it is part of the initial layout for the panel, it accomplishes an "effect of concealment" in the frame, taking and covering up space that otherwise would be part of the drawing. The bubble is also a form relating to and affecting the shape of adjacent forms in the frame. The shape and size of the bubble will necessarily change the shape and size of the space used for drawing in the boundaries of each frame. Generally, these balloons can be right-angled, elliptical, or irregular in form. The right-angled balloon conforms to the shape of words that are arranged in traditional lines and rows, using space economically and leaving little space around the words. Elliptical balloons, if surrounding traditional straight rows of text, leave space around words. Often, authors who use abundant or lengthy text choose to use right-angled text balloons because they are "relatively discreet. They carefully provide the drawing with a homogeneous area and a regular form. The text hangs over the image, but does not overrun it" (p. 73). If the text is (almost) always confined to a box in the upper portion of each panel, it is predictable and does not cause the reader to take special notice of the text element.

Representing Self/Other

Carefully constructed graphic narratives can be a particularly useful way to generate discussion about difference. They appeal to students and can bring abstract concepts into the classroom. Direct lived experience is the most straightforward way to interact with the world, but we are all limited in our direct experience through geography, resources, and time. All other information about the world and other people must be represented, literally re-presented to us through the filter of someone's perspective and lens. The closest form of representation to lived experience is the representation of self. Stories told and images created about the self give the author's or artist's perspective on his or her own life and experience. When the representation is filtered through the lens of someone else, the fidelity to the original experience is less certain. The farther the author or artist (or filmmaker or reporter) is from the lived experience, the greater the possibility of misrepresentation. I theorize three layers of representation that move from least to most likely to end in misrepresentation: representation of self, representation of imagined self, and representation of self-and-other (Bailey Jones, 2011). The second layer, the representation of imagined self, occurs when the people creating the representation see the subject as part of their imagined community, as similar in fundamental ways to themselves. This representation looks to present the lived experience in ways that focus on the connection between producer and produced, that see the subject as an extended self in some way. The final layer of representation involves creating images or text about a person who is not part of any imagined community. This layer focuses on the differences between the producer and the produced, and it reinforces the opposition of "us" (those part of my imagined community and most like me) and "them" (those excluded from the imagined community due to a perceived difference). This layer is most likely to result in misrepresentation, because it is produced by those who have little in common with or knowledge of the experience of the other. In some extreme cases, the intention of the representation may be to create misinformation about the other to unify the community. Important examples of representation of self-and-other are the images created during colonial rule that were used to solidify colonial power by presenting the "natives" as fundamentally different and less "civilized" than Europeans.

Transnational Feminist Theory

Examining the roles that gender and sexuality play in the representations of difference in graphic narratives necessitates a discussion on fundamental ideas of the history of feminist theory, its relationship to postcolonial theory, and transnational feminisms that have evolved globally. The most visible work in the feminist era of the 1960s and 1970s (in the United States, a time period referred to the second wave of feminism) was created and publicized by middle and upper class White women trying to increase opportunities to work outside the home and bring about reproductive choice. Even as the movement and theoretical framework that informed the mainstream feminist movement was shaped, several counter, marginalized voices were calling for a more diverse understanding of what it means to be a women. Though it seems obvious today, it was a radical thought that the experiences of and issues facing women vary widely depending on class, race, sexuality, nationality, ethnicity, and so forth. African American feminists and womanists such as Audre Lorde (1984), bell hooks (1984), and Alice Walker (1983) wrote about how their own experiences and voices were excluded from White feminist critique. Lesbian feminists were often purposely excluded from mainstream, liberal feminist events that focused on the concerns of straight women. These diverse voices led to a much more complex conversation about the way that context, social location, and the intersection of identities impact gendered practices and perspectives. Gayatri Spivak (1994) was one of the first scholars who merged the postcolonial critiques of Western imperialist power and privilege with a concern with gender:

> It also needed to be emphasized, many argued, that while women in North America and Western Europe deal with discrimination, sexism, and violence on a daily basis, outside those borders many women are concerned with issues that are often less pressing in first-world nations, such as sanctioned rape, the right to vote, to educate, reform of unequal property laws, sexual trafficking, forced sterilizations, multi-national exploitation of labor, and so on. (Reilly, 2007, p. 30)

Several recent issues of local gendered experience illustrate the fact that Western mainstream feminist responses to issues of global complexity remain problematic. Some Western feminists have framed the practice of veiling in Islam and in the Christian Middle East as inherently oppressive and the central issue of concern. Muslim feminists and grassroots organizations working for women in many predominantly Muslim countries choose to focus on other areas that are considered most vital, such as access to education, rights to property in the case of divorce, and the right to vote.

Feminist Theory and Visual Representations

Transnational and postcolonial feminist theories provide frames to analyze and interpret visual representations of difference, whether or not they deal directly with gender. Feminist visual theory is a frame that organizes the visual representation of difference in gender and sexuality. The comics that are analyzed in the following chapters have representations of gendered as well as racial and ethnic difference. Intersectionality, a key precept of contemporary feminist theory, provides a framework for understanding the way that various forms of marginalization or oppression intersect and impact lived experience. In the image/text world of comics, the representation of difference can challenge stereotypical representations of difference or it can reinforce stereotypes and assumptions. Are women in the text central to the narrative structure in ways that are not purely as sexual or romantic partners for the men? Are they mainly rewarded and valued for their appearance? Are female characters presented in ways that reinforce the virgin/whore dichotomy? Are they either pure and good or sexualized and evil? In texts that present representations of women outside the West, are women expected to conform to Western standards of dress and behavior in order to succeed? Are men presented as the hero, supervisor, or primary actor in the narrative?

"The gap between object and intelligent perception of the object is, of course, one of the prevailing problems of making art at any time in an alienated society" (Lippard, 1995, p. 39). In examining the representations of gender, power, and difference in graphic narratives, it is important to note the extent to which experience is homogenized and normalized through a Western lens. Do the representations simply reproduce Western experience with different cultural trappings? Is the narrative rooted in the local issues and concerns or does it rely on assumptions and stereotypes of those who look different or live differently from the author? Feminist theory that critiques dominant modes of thinking and representing women, gender, and sexuality offers ways to examine visual expressions that confront and question patriarchal and colonial modes of representing the other. "When names and labels prove insubstantial or damaging, they can of course be exposed as falsely engendered and socially constructed by those who experience them; they can be discarded and discredited" (Lippard, 2000, p. 55). The naming of groups of people, land masses, and locations in the form of claiming territory is a legacy of patriarchal colonialism; explorers believed that things previously used as part of daily life for "natives" were discovered for the first time when seen by White men. Feminist theorists question the use and misuse of women's bodies as metaphor for nation, land, and object.

At the heart of feminist theory applied to the visual realm is a questioning of dominant modes of representation and a re-representation that questions the center/margin dichotomy. "Postcolonial politics, a vital part of postmodern visual culture, are an integral part of the questioning of modernity advanced by feminism over the last four decades" (Pajaczkowska, 2001, p. 1). Shohat (1998) worked to articulate a feminist multicultural visual theory that constructs multiple centers:

Given these complexities, an anti-essentialist multicultural feminist project is obliged to formulate identities as situated in geographical space and "riding" historical moment, to work through a politics whereby the decentering of identities, and the celebration of hybridities does not also mean that it is no longer possible to draw boundaries between privilege and disenfranchisement. (p. 6)

All of the graphic narratives that are examined in this text engage with hybrid identities through various uses of visual codes, some from modernist, colonialist tropes that reinforce false binaries. Most, however, use these visual codes to question traditional binaries and to represent the complexities of lived experience. Visual forms must confront the traditional, patriarchal visual codes in order to challenge them. Butler (1990) articulated the following in her seminal work in queer and feminist theory, *Gender Trouble:*

> *Representation* serves as the operative term within a political process that seeks to extend visibility and legitimacy to women as political subjects; on the other hand, representation is the normative function of a language which is said either to reveal or distort what is assumed to be true about the category of women. (p. 2)

The process of representation articulates the marginalized experience of women, but it also creates new norms that may flatten or essentialize the experience of the other. Butler names the standard cultural understanding of gender as a "matrix of intelligibility" that regulates behavior and performance of gender norms. A standard, solid box can stand in for the "matrix"; the outside edge is the border of what "acceptable" behavior is, and beyond the border, you are punished or policed. A boy is crying, yet we are told that "boys don't cry." Does that mean this person is not a boy or that the truism is disproven? It means that to be a boy in the matrix, he must stop crying.

Feminist Comics Theory

Chute (2010) wrote in her seminal work of feminist comics theory, *Graphic Women: Life Narrative and Contemporary Comics,* that she is "interested in bringing the medium of comics—its conventions, its violation of its conventions, *what it does differently*—to the forefront of conversations about the political, aesthetic, and ethical work of narrative" (p. 3). For Chute, and the growing number of comics scholars, the worlds of the image/text created in comics create uniquely situated opportunities for expression and reception. One of the fundamental differences between typed books and comics is that the writing within each text is produced and reproduced differently. The typed book contains words that are produced and crafted by the author but visually formed by a computer with a (generally) standard font. The words are unique to the author but they are not physically drawn or formed by the author's hand. Comics are unique in that the letters, words, and thoughts are hand-written by the author; the author mentally forms the words as in other books, but the author's hand also physically forms the words. This creates a personal connection to the author's hand and body on the page of graphic narratives. The fonts in graphic narratives are unique to the author's hand, rather than widely available on word processing software.

This bodily presence of the author lends the medium of graphic narrative to autobiography, to memory and recollection. Memories often appear as disconnected images and thoughts that we must piece together through acts of interpretation. Chute (2010) wrote primarily about comics of traumatic memory and how women authors use the medium to visualize and materialize memory and representation. "The complex visualizing it [comics] undertakes suggests that we need to rethink the dominant tropes of unspeakability, invisibility, and inaudibility that have tended to characterize trauma theory as well as our current censorship-driven culture in general" (p. 3). Many graphic narratives create visual and textual records of memory, trauma, and encounter that are striking for the presence of the author's hand and also for the willingness to represent subjects that are difficult and sometimes painful to imagine. It is a multimodal and multimedia form of representing self and other over space and through time. "Graphic narrative establishes what I here, writing about Marjane Satrapi, term an expanded *idiom of witness,* a manner of testifying that sets a visual language in motion with and against the verbal in order to embody individual and collective experience, to put contingent selves and histories into form" (p. 3). Feminist comics theory specifically analyzes the representation of women, gender diversity, and sexuality drawn and written against the grain of the patriarchal, masculine comic trope of the manly superhero. The graphic novels written by women that Chute analyzed are all deeply personal and critical of the normative positions of heterosexuality and masculinity in society and in the pages of comics.

Multicultural and Postcolonial Comics Theory

Postcolonial theorists work to make visible and problematize the legacy of colonial modes of power and privilege. Important figures such as Homi Bhabha (1994), Edward Said (1979, 1993), Gayatri Spivak (1994), and

Frantz Fanon (1967) offered critiques of European imperialism from various perspectives. The common threads of these theorists' work are a de-centering of European perspectives, a rethinking of historical, artistic, and scholarly works created about the so-called third world (also problematically referred to as the developing world, the colonized world, the global south), and a privileging of marginalized voices and perspectives. Some more recent theorists worked across geographies and disciplines, creating feminist postcolonial theory and border theory, ways to theorize the meeting and negotiation among cultures, people, and ways of thinking. The visual and textual representation forms of the graphic narrative can be used to disrupt and challenge traditional and stereotypical representations of groups of people and of difference. Of course, they can also be used to reproduce and reinforce these very same problematic representations. There is nothing inherently liberating or repressive in the medium of graphic narratives; each work must be analyzed for its own effect. The work of postcolonial and multicultural readings of the narratives is to identify how and where difference is represented and what visual and textual codes are being used to create meaning.

Multicultural Pedagogy

The work of educators interested in critical visual literacy and engaging students with complex ideas about difference that challenge stereotypes and intolerance is challenging. Many forms of pedagogy propagated under the banner of multicultural education introduce benign forms of surface difference and then move on to other areas of curriculum. Many attempts to address demands for greater multiculturalism result in a sort of cultural fair approach, showcasing the food, "costumes," dance, and cultural and religious customs from various "exotic" lands. This approach generally steers clear of potentially troubling or controversial discussions of poverty, class, or imperialism. The curriculum rarely moves into challenging students to question their own place in the global hierarchies of power and privilege or to understand the use of military and political power in contributing to understandings of difference. Most American students learn about colonialism through the lens of settler colonies in North America and how they evolved into the United States through the hard work and perseverance of the colonists, along with courage in waging war against the British. Information about other forms of global colonialism is generally left to discussions of resources and how Europe gained access to valuable natural resources and economic gain through their colonies in Africa, Asia, and South America.

How can critical multicultural education be more effective at disrupting stereotypes and encouraging critical questioning of assumptions? One model I propose is a grounded universal system: we begin examining differences through a universal lens that included homogenized assumptions about others based solely on how it relates (generally unfavorably) to our own experience. The first step in disrupting the universal is to showcase the "everydayness" of others' experience. The final step is to revisit the universal, with a new understanding of the complexity of lived realities, including the political, historical context and a willingness to accept uncertainty. A grounded universal education does not simply introduce students to benign forms of difference as a matter of groups of people believing and living in different ways. It introduces difference through individual experience and narrative, providing an opportunity for students to create personal connections to the story of someone whose experience may be quite different from their own. This personal connection and the possible creation of empathy for the humanity of the Other is a crucial step in disrupting stereotype. Once the universalized assumptions of the Other nameless person are punctured (or as an ongoing part of the process), students need to be given access to historical and political context to situate the individual story. The nature and depth of this context is quite important, and it must include critical information about the legacy of colonialism and global imperialism, the imbalance of power and privilege in the so-called developed and developing worlds, and the often-obscured alliances created through self-interest. Many of the texts analyzed in this book include individual stories with political and historical context; *Persepolis, Palestine, Zahra's Paradise*, and *The Photographer* are examples of graphic narratives that provide compelling individual stories of those whose lives may be quite different from the reader. In *Persepolis* (Satrapi, 2004), for example, readers are deeply involved in the story of a spunky and thoughtful young girl in Tehran. We get to know Marjane as an individual trying to navigate through the complexities of a cultural and political reality that is quite different from that of Western readers. The text simultaneously gives insight into the distant and recent history of Iran and the complex and problematic role of the United States in the overthrowing of democratically elected Mohammad Mosaddeq. While not providing a complete picture of the history and politics, Satrapi provides a perspective that could lead to critical questions and to more in-depth research. Therefore, these texts offer powerful opportunities to engage students in the process of the grounded universal. There is also great educational value for students to be able to identify stereotypical assumptions and codes in texts, images, and media. It is important for critical multicultural educators to use texts that present problematic and stereotypical representations of different groups of people to provide skills of critical analysis. Students need to develop an understanding of grounded universal difference while receiving specific instruction on the loaded visual codes and words used to create the homogenized assumptions of the universal.

Postcolonial and Feminist Visual Codes

Using precepts from postcolonial and feminist theorists, I created a list of visual codes that I use to evaluate and analyze the graphic narratives in this text: Colonial Gaze, Postcolonial/Anticolonial Gaze, Violent Difference, Patriarchal Gaze, Covered/Uncovered Bodies, and Marking the Other. The Colonial Gaze is a visual code where someone with power and privilege is looking at and representing a person or a group of people with less power and privilege. Traditionally, this means that a Westerner is viewing people from the "third world" and representing them as inferior in terms of level of culture, civilization, development, and humanity. The Colonial Gaze results in an image that reinforces ideas of a hierarchy of humanity with Western Europe/United States as the pinnacle of human development and all others falling on lower rungs of the hierarchy. The Colonial Gaze can either result in negative images that belittle those who are "inferior" or images that celebrate and romanticize the "purity" and "innocence" of those who are less developed. Historically, Western artists have both demonized and romant- icized the colonized other. Paul Gauguin's images of romanticized Poly- nesian women are sensual and alluring, but their visual difference, their bare breasts and bronzed skin, set them apart from European women and place them on a lower rung of rational humanity.

The Postcolonial/Anticolonial Gaze is in many ways the opposite of the Colonial Gaze, originating with those who (traditionally) have less power and privilege on the global stage looking at and representing those with greater levels of power and privilege. Though similar in constituents, the Anticolonial Gaze implies a more direct challenge to authority and to historical representations that reinforced colonial structures. The Postcolonial

Gaze relates directly to postcolonial theory and literature; it can be a challenge to colonial structure directly or it may be a subtler reimagining of the global regime of representation through decentering the West and highlighting the valid experience of those in the (traditional) margins. Though in many ways more difficult to locate, a very good example of using the Anticolonial Gaze is the film *The Battle of Algiers,* from director Pontecorvo (1966). The film presents scenes from the French colonial occupying forces and the Algerian resistance, both from an Anticolonial perspective that was critical of French colonial power, tactics, and moral authority.

The visual code of Violent Difference involves the representation of violence as being the by-product of a cultural, religious, or ethnic difference. The effects of this kind of violent imagery are not that a small part of any population is capable of violent acts in the service of some cause but that some entire populations are more prone to violence and less capable of moral, ethical, and rational thought. An example of this Violent Difference is the coding of Arabs in Disney's *Aladdin* as thieving, violent, and distrustful. Other examples of this trope are the tragic murder of unarmed Black teenager Trayvon Martin in Florida by neighborhood watchman George Zimmerman. The race and gender of Trayvon Martin played into the code of Violent Difference, where young Black men are coded as inherently dangerous and suspect. Martin was walking after dark and wearing a hoodie when he was killed because he was "threatening." The hoodie became a form of Postcolonial Code after his murder, when celebrities, star athletes, and others took selfies in hoodies and posted them to social media in anger about the murder and acquittal of Zimmerman due to the Stand Your Ground law in Florida.

The Patriarchal Gaze is the visual trope that has received the most theoretical attention as a key analytical tool of feminist film and visual culture theorists for decades. Feminist film theorist Laura Mulvey (1989) first addressed the Patriarchal Gaze (also referred to as the male gaze) in her seminal piece, "Visual Pleasure and Narrative Cinema." She used tools of psychoanalysis such as scopophilia, the pleasure of looking at the nude or sexual bodies, to describe and give meaning to the way that film constructs the (male) filmmaker and (male) viewer as gaining voyeuristic pleasure from watching the (female) object on screen. "In a world ordered by sexual imbalance, pleasure in looking has been split between the active/male and passive/female. The determining male gaze projects its fantasy onto the female figure" (p. 19). The displaying of the female body as an object for male pleasure is neither new nor exclusive to film; the tradition of male artists painting female nudes in various positions and states for the pleasure of primarily male audiences is longstanding. In 1998, the feminist art collective, The Guerrilla Girls, created a billboard reading, "Do women have to be naked to get into the Met. Museum? Less than 5% of the artists in the Modern Art sections are women, but 85% of the nudes are female." This piece points to the historical male gaze in the art world that extends to film, television, the Internet, and to some graphic narratives. The Patriarchal Gaze is present in graphic narratives when the male author draws female bodies as objects for the reader's pleasure. It objectifies women characters and uses their bodies to move the narrative along. In an (in)famous quote from feminist theorist Catherine MacKinnon (1989), "Sexual objectification is the primary process of the subjection of women. It unites act with word, construction with reality. Man fucks woman; subject verb object" (p. 124). The male gaze is sexualized power and includes the idea of the power to be all seeing and to have others available for your viewing and pleasure.

Related to the Patriarchal Gaze in its connection to gendered power and visual codes, the Covering/Uncovering of Bodies is almost always applicable to women's bodies:

> To the west, "the veil" like Islam itself, is both sensual and puritanical, is contradictory, is to be feared. It is also concrete, and is to do with women, and since cultural battles are so often fought through the bodies of women, it is seized upon by politicians, columnists, feminists . . . . (Soueif, 2003, p. 110)

Historically, and in nearly every culture around the globe, the covering or uncovering of women's bodies carries particular importance and meaning. In the United States, girls and women are pressured to be both sexy and sexually pure at once, stuck in the virgin/whore dichotomy. Mainstream media present barely covered women's bodies, famously featured in the annual *Sports Illustrated* swimsuit issue in which barely covered models are shown in various poses on beaches, and the Victoria's Secret runway show that runs on primetime television around the holidays. Simultaneously, some women are publically vilified for how they dress if it is deemed overly provocative. Women's bodies are centered as dangerously provocative when available for men's lustful gaze and in need of covering in public spaces.

Women's bodies are centered in most cultures as a site of political and religious struggle, a battleground for laws, ordinances, and dress codes that are based on the idea of the Patriarchal Gaze, the idea that men are insatiable sexual animals and women's bodies must be regulated to control men's sexual desires. For many in the West, the covering of women's bodies is similarly centered as the ultimate signifier of oppression:

> The familiar and much analysed Orientalist gaze through which the veil is viewed as an object of mystique, exoticism and eroticism and the veiled woman as an object of fantasy, excitement and desire is now replaced by the xenophobic, more specifically Islamophobic, gaze through which the veil, or headscarf, is seen as a highly visible sign of despised difference. (Donnell, 2003, p. 122)

Of interest to critical visual literacy is not simply the centering of the covering or uncovering of women's bodies but the meaning given to the bodies and the coverings. The assumptions of purity, shamefulness, freedom, or oppression are seen as inherent to the sartorial choices of women, making analysis of this code of great importance. The graphic narratives analyzed in this book include women's bodies centered as sites of narrative importance. Here the codes of covering and uncovering must be examined in the context of author and reader and the gaze involved. Is the author drawing his or her own body or the bodies of others? What is the intention of including the bodies, and how does it relate to the treatment of the characters?

Finally, Marking the Other includes visual tropes of all kinds that are used to mark one person or group of people as fundamentally different from others. All of the texts included in this book represent differences of one or more type, and the authors of these texts made conscious decisions about how to draw the differences to make them intelligible to the reader. Marking the other can be done through reliance on visually different features, stereotypes of difference, or communication through other metaphorical forms. The representations of racial, ethnic, religious, gender, and sexual differences need to be examined for the intention of the author and the effect of these representations. One of the fundamental questions of this book is whether these representations, through the marking the other function to reinforce or challenge assumptions and stereotypes. These visual codes of difference (the Colonial Gaze, Postcolonial/Anticolonial Gaze, Violent Difference, Patriarchal Gaze, Covered/Uncovered Bodies, and Marking the Other) present a unique way to analyze graphic narratives. By framing the analysis in terms of not just textual and visual literacy but also in terms of these codes gives educators a new way to teach critical literacy skills that honor rather than flatten the complexity and messiness of representing difference.

CHAPTER TWO

Situating the Discourse: Orientalism and Islamophobia

To situate the analysis of the representation of difference in graphic narratives, we need to understand the historical context. My particular interest in the Western representation of Muslims and/or Arabs in the media and popular culture post-9/11 necessitates going into some depth about the colonial creation and distribution of Orientalism as a form of cultural control. The systematic control and the historical evolution of Orientalism facilitated and provided fertile ground for the rise of Islamophobia in the post-September 11th era.

The creation of the Orient and Occident as divergent, unequal geographical and cultural spheres dates historically to before the Crusades, when European Christians went east to fight Muslims and drive them out of the Holy Land of Jerusalem. Called to fight by Pope Urban in 1095, western European leaders fought under the banner of the Pope and Christianity, wearing the cross as a sign of their religious identity. The Crusades finally ended after the fall of Crusader capital Acre in 1290. The Crusades, as with most historical periods, are hotly contested territory for historians. There are those historians, most famously Steve Runciman (1951–1954), author of *A History of the Crusades, Vol. I–III*, who present the Crusades as the unprovoked attack and aggression of the Catholic Church and western Europe on generally peaceful Muslim civilization to the east. Other historians, like Thomas F. Madden (2014) in his reissued volume, *The Concise History of the Crusades,* present the Crusades as a moral and righteous defense against warring and invading Muslim armies. If scholars disagree about the intent and context of the Crusades, their views are even further afield in drawing historical conclusions from the period. Amin Maalouf (1984), author of *The Crusades through Arab Eyes,* wrote, "At the time of the Crusades, the Arab world, from Spain to Iraq, was still the intellectual and material repository of the planet's most advanced civilization. Afterwards, the centre of world history shifted decisively to the West" (p. 261). According to Maalouf, despite military victory, the Muslim world was set back on its heels and remained a spectator to the sweep of modernity that became indelibly Western. "And there can be no doubt that the schism between these two worlds dates from the Crusades, deeply felt by the Arabs, even today, as an act of rape" (p. 266). Maalouf presents the Crusades as a deep and festering historical wound for Muslims that informs much of the contemporary conflict with the West. While Madden (2014) positioned the result of the Crusades as a victory for Islam, "The crusades contributed nothing to the decline of the Muslim world. Indeed, they are evidence of the decline of the Christian West, which was forced to mount these desperate expeditions to defend against ever-expanding Muslim empires" (p. 204). Madden's interpretation of the historical record is quite different from that of Runciman and Maalouf. All of these writers agree that the Crusades were vitally important historical periods and the first real encounter of weight between the Christian West and Muslim East. Though the meaning of the legacy may be contested, the importance of the legacy in contemporary political rhetoric cannot be denied.

The legacy of the Crusades and the varying interpretations of their meaning were called to the foreground of the global stage in the wake of 9/11. Both George W. Bush and Osama bin Laden used the term *crusade* to describe Western action in the Muslim world. Bush (2001) said, "This is a new kind of—a new kind of evil...This crusade, this war on terrorism is going to take a while" (para. 14). Bin Laden (2001) took hold of Bush's use of "crusade" and made specific rhetorical links between the historical Crusades and the U.S.-led war in Afghanistan in fall 2001. "Bush left no room for doubts or the opinions of journalists, but he openly and clearly said that this war is a crusader war" (para. 33). The use of crusade as a way to refer to current global conflict necessarily renews fears of a Christian West versus a Muslim East:

> President Bush's reference to a "crusade" against terrorism, which passed almost unnoticed by Americans, rang alarm bells in Europe. It raised fears that the terrorist attacks could spark a "clash of civilizations" between Christians and Muslims, sowing fresh winds of hatred and mistrust. (Ford, 2001, para. 2)

When Bush invoked the word "crusade" to refer to American response to the terrorist attacks, he played into the rhetorical strategy of al-Qaeda that proposes the West is engaged in an ongoing crusade against Muslims globally and there must be jihad against the crusaders.

The legacy of the Crusades in contemporary political debate is inextricably linked to the history of colonialism, postcolonialism, and the Cold War. In these historical eras (all of which do not have a definitive end date), the complex and fraught struggle for global supremacy and power forced encounters of the West and East. During the height of European colonial control, colonial powers Spain, France, and England gained political and military control of the so-called Muslim world. The British administration in Egypt and the French control of Algeria were two of the pivotal colonial contexts on which particular attention is focused here. In these contexts, the supposedly superior culture and moral values of the Europeans were enforced and entrenched through tight control, violence, and degradation of native cultural practices.

Colonialism and the Veil

During the height of European imperial reach, European powers were working variously to establish the superiority of Western culture, religion, and intelligence while simultaneously degrading the culture, religion, and mental capacity of the "native" populations. In European colonies located in predominantly Muslim countries, women covering their head, and sometimes face, were the native cultural practices at the center of colonial critique. Male colonial administrators spouted rhetoric of concern over women's rights and the liberation of women through uncovering them:

> One noteworthy fact about the unveiling movement is how it originated not in precolonial Middle Eastern notions of the meaning of the veil, notions rooted in Islamic, Christian, and Jewish local meanings, but rather in Western nineteenth-century ideas about the veil's meaning. (Ahmed, 2011, p. 44)

However, the same administrators were generally not supportive of women's rights in the colonial center; their interest in women was pragmatic rather than a matter of principle. To construct the native culture as inferior, the administrators professed a belief that the liberation of women was central to cultural superiority and advancement.

In Egypt, Lord Cromer was a major figure in the popularization of the idea that the British were inherently superior to the Egyptians in many ways. Of particular interest for my work are Cromer's (1908) writings on the veil and the interest of British rule in dismantling and discrediting the practice of veiling as a matter of women's rights and position. In his own native land, Lord Cromer was not in favor of women's rights outside the home and in the political arena. "Cromer, it should be made clear, was most emphatically not a supporter of the movement for women's rights—in fact, he was its formidable opponent, serving for a time as the president of the Society Opposed to Women's Suffrage" (Ahmed, 2011, p. 31). Though he argued for unveiling Egyptian women to improve their societal position, it was in fact a way of critiquing native cultural practices to assert European superiority and enhance British control over Egypt. Many Egyptian women were concerned with their rights to obtain an education, inherit property, and take care of their families, but Cromer focused solely on the veil as the source of women's oppression. The veil was the most visible sign of difference and of Egyptian cultural practice that Cromer targeted as "primitive" and oppressive to women. Cromer (1908) wrote in detail about the seclusion of women from public life and its deleterious effect on society at large in his tome, *Modern Egypt*. "It will be sufficient to say that seclusion, by confining the sphere of woman's interest to a very limited horizon, cramps the intellect and withers the mental development of one-half of the population in Moslem countries" (p. 580). According to Cromer, this seclusion of women that stunts their intellectual growth and impedes them in their sole roles as wives and mothers also produces a "deteriorating effect on the male population" (p. 580). The book lays out myriad arguments for why the native Egyptians are less civilized, educated, advanced, and moral than the British colonizers, therefore supporting the British authority to rule. The treatment of women is but one of these fundamental flaws that Cromer details, masking his distaste for women's suffrage and advancement.

In Algeria, the French colonial administration was similarly involved in degrading the practice of veiling as a form of savagery that led to native inferiority. French authorities reversed many Algerian laws and practices, including revoking a statute based in Muslim law that allowed for the inheritance of property by women. They also restricted access to education for girls. Simultaneously, the French administration made public displays of their desire to uncover and unveil the women of Algeria. The French believed, according to Fanon (1959/2003), "if we want to destroy the structure of Algerian society, its capacity for resistance, we must first of all conquer the women, we must go and find them behind the veil where they hide themselves" (p. 38). The veil served as a visual barrier to French control and the unveiling of women in Algeria was a more targeted offensive against resistance. For both the French and the Algerians, the veil became a potent symbol of Algerian resistance and the forced removal of veils became a French weapon of control. In one infamous example of this, in 1958 the French army gathered 100 women in a public square in front of an audience of Algerian men and unveiled them while chanting patriotic French slogans. During the Algerian resistance, women would use their dress and the prejudice of French troops to resist colonial occupation and provide arms and material assistance to the resistance. At the start of the armed resistance to the French colonial power, Algerian women would wear body-covering veils that allowed them to hide contraband weapons underneath their covering in order to pass through French checkpoints. Once the French authorities caught onto the tactics of these women and began searching beneath veils, the women changed resistance tactics and dressed in Western clothing. French soldiers assumed that women dressed in Western clothes were aligned politically and ideologically with the French occupation and let them pass through checkpoints. Though dressed like French women, the Algerian women were using the assumptions and connotations of gendered dress to transport aid to the resistance fighters. It was the assumption that the way a women was dressed indicated her political and cultural affiliation; this blind spot of cultural chauvinism and colonial Eurocentrism contributed to the downfall of the colonial administration.

Western European and American interest in the veil and controlling women's dress resurfaced after the attacks of 9/11 and in the midst of increasing immigration of Muslims to Europe. In the most publicized example of centering the veiling and unveiling of women, the French government instituted a ban on the veil (and other religious symbols) in public schools in 2004. This original ban excluded universities, though there is a stalled effort to expand the ban on veils or headscarves by the French government. The moves in France restrict the religious expression of Muslim women under the name of easing religious intolerance and tensions. In April 2011, the French moved beyond the walls of public schools to impose a ban on the wearing of face-covering veils in public spaces. The Belgian government followed the French and banned wearing burqas or niqabs in public in July of 2011. Although there is no national law in Germany, several states ban teachers in public schools from wearing any form of head covering. Several predominately Muslim countries (Turkey, Tunisia, and until recently, Syria) ban burqas and niqabs in schools and government buildings. All of these laws place women's bodies and how they are covered or uncovered at the center of policy and debate over religious expression, freedom, and tolerance of difference.

Clash of Civilizations

The work of dividing the world and creating hierarchies from these divisions began during the Crusades and the colonial era, but it was solidified for the contemporary context by such texts as *The Clash of Civilizations and the Remaking of the World Order* (Huntington, 1996) that presented simplified descriptions of complex and varied groups of people as naturally different and incompatible. In this book (which was called upon in the wake of 9/11 to make sense of the terrorist attacks), Huntington (1996) predicted that with an end to the Cold War, the new world order will be decided by clashing between fundamentally different and divergent civilizations, which he labeled Western, Latin American, Confucian, Japanese, Islamic, Hindu, and Slavic-Orthodox. Rejecting the binary separation of the world into Western and non-Western due to the complexity and diversity of those encapsulated under the banner of non-Western, Huntington appealed to many looking for an organized analysis of causes and trends in global conflict. He also rejected that the world is becoming one big group of globalized humanity, "the assumption that the end of the Cold War meant the end of significant conflict in global politics and the emergence of one relatively harmonious world" (p. 31). After 9/11, the discourse of civilizations that are fundamentally different and at odds with one another became an explanation for the extremist Islamists and their violent attacks. The idea that the terrorism was a result of difference in civilization magnifies and naturalizes differences and applies them to large groups of people. If 9/11 was a result of the "clash of civilizations," then there is no hope for bridging the divides or viewing Muslims as part of our own civilization.

Postcolonialism and Orientalism

Representations of Muslims and Arabs by those in the West in the post-9/11 era must be contextualized in the history of Western colonialism and imperialism. Though this history of imbalanced relationships of power is often lost in the contemporary era of the endless War on Terror, we must attempt to educate about the full complexity of international relationships. A key force in this imbalanced history of representation is Orientalism, a specific form of colonial regulation most often associated with the work of cultural studies scholar Edward Said. Said (1979) defined Orientalism as the following:

> A *distribution* of geopolitical awareness into aesthetic, scholarly, economic, sociological historical, and philological texts; it is an *elaboration* not only of a basic geographical distinction (the world is made of up of two unequal halves, Orient and Occident) but also of a whole series of "interests" which, by such means as scholarly discovery, philological reconstruction, psychological analysis, landscape and sociological description, it not only creates but also maintains. (p. 12)

Western representations of the Arab and Muslim worlds (usually conflated) both in the mass media and in educational materials highlight either the connections of Islam, extremism, and terrorism or focus on a bland religious and cultural tolerance. "For decades in America there has been a cultural war against the Arabs and Islam: appalling racist caricatures of Arabs and Muslims suggest that they are all either terrorists or sheikhs, and that the region is a large, arid slum, fit only for profit or war" (Said, 1993, p. 301). Tolerance is an important step away from intolerance and ignorance, but it does not include critical awareness of difference and the political and social power that affects the position of the Other. In writing of Said's critique, Clifford (1988) posited that his work is most effective in the "critical analysis of Orientalist 'authority'—the paternalist privileges unhesitatingly assumed by Western writers who 'speak for' a mute Orient or reconstitute its decayed or dismembered 'truth,' who lament the passing of its authenticity, and who know more than its mere natives ever can" (p. 258). The discourse of Orientalism started in the colonial era with European scholars and artists who studied and presented the "truth" about a whole section of the world to fellow Westerners. Due to the weight of the academic and artistic standing of the Orientalists, combined with racist conceptions of the less advanced, less intelligent Oriental, their work functioned as true. Interest in Said's work and discussions of neo-Orientalism surfaced in the post-9/11 era, as many in the West struggled to define and describe a part of the world that previously held little interest.

Indeed, Orientalism was a grand and misguided project of representation of the Other. It begs the question: Is it possible to represent the Other in ways that are authentic, true, and respectful? Clifford (1988) discussed the content of this fundamental question in *The Predicament of Culture: Twentieth-Century Ethnography, Literature, and Art,* based on his work in critical ethnography and anthropology. Anthropologists have been at forefront of arguments about how possible it is to truly "know" and truthfully represent the Other. As global travel has become increasingly affordable and fast (to those with money and privilege), and the Internet creates instantaneous communication across the globe, representations of people and cultures become greater in quantity, if not in quality. "It is more than ever crucial for different peoples to form complex concrete images of one another, as well of the relationships of knowledge and power that connect them" (p. 23).

Eugenics and the "Science" of Visual Racism

The imagining and imaging of racism begins with creating types, groups of people that look fundamentally distinct from the self. While those within the group are recognized for their full and individual humanity, those from other groups are lumped together and dehumanized:

> In the cosmology of typecasting, the mental picture of evil assumes a vague shape. Within the socially reinforced familiarity of their own group, people readily acknowledge the importance of their individuality and their individual thoughts and actions. Within the constructions of the "foreign" or the "strange," however, images are indistinct. (Ewen & Ewen, 2006, p. 496)

The characteristics of the Other move from distinct, individual features, to symbols that are vague and applied broadly. These symbols form the basis for visual semiology, the analysis of visual codes. These codes are symbols that visually separate the self from the Other and are repeated in the media, popular culture, and in the imagination. Many examples of how visual symbols of difference were used and created can be traced to colonialism and the racist pseudoscience of eugenics. Those with power used racism (both covert and overt forms) to create distrust of and superiority over the colonized populations across Africa, Asia, and South America. Eugenics represented a legitimating of racist visual codes by crafting a "science" around how to visually spot, code, and assign meaning to difference. Racial categories, and the visual codes that carry racial meaning, are constructions of hierarchical power; those with power created lesser groups of people and made the distinction into a firm category of difference to ease the exploitation of others. What was/is considered White in one context may look and be quite different than its construction elsewhere:

> There so-called blacks were not only the most important exploited group, since the principal part of the economy rested on their labor; they were, above all, the most important colonized race, since Indians were not part of that colonial society. Why the dominant group calls itself "white" is a story related to racial classification. (Quijano, 2000, p. 534)

Visual codes of difference were cemented and infused with hierarchies of power and privilege during colonialism and eugenics. Whiteness, labeled as "Caucasian," was constructed as the ideal visual form, with the attendant skin tone and presumed facial features.

An important forerunner in the "science" of eugenics was the "science" of craniotomy, the analysis of skulls from various locations around the globe and the assignment of value and characteristics to "races" of people based on these skulls. Much of the socially constructed and maintained racial categories that we have today can be traced to the work of two men: German Johann Friedrich Blumenbach and American Samuel George Morton. Blumenbach (1865), a collector of skulls and professor of medicine, originally published *Treatise on the Natural Variety of Mankind* in 1795. In this text, he laid out a classification and ordering system for human difference based on the visual characteristics of his human skull collection. He decided on the skull in his collection that was the most "perfect" (clearly a subjective determination based on aesthetics of one man), and since this skull belonged to a woman from the Caucus mountain region, he created a racial category of Caucasian and decided it was the most perfect of all human types. Blumenbach went on to create the following groups of humanity: Caucasian, Mongolian, Ethiopian, American, and Malay. He wrote in his tome that the Caucasian represented the most perfect form of humanity (assigning it to Northern Europeans like himself) and the others as lesser, degenerating forms of humanity. These varieties were all related to one another, devolving from the Caucasian. "Despite its aura of certitude, classification is never a neutral act. Naming is a form of exercising power, and the ways that things are named often reflect the outlook of the namer" (Ewen & Ewen, 2006, p. 61). Although racial categories have shifted and evolved, the racist hierarchy established by Blumenbach has remained stubbornly relevant.

Morton, a physician from Philadelphia, also collected human skulls and used visual examination of these skulls to group humanity and assign value and worth. Morton extended Blumenbach's work in even more overtly racist and "scientific" ways. Rather than promote the idea that all of humanity is related and degenerates from a perfect, Caucasian ancestor, Morton stated that humanity was broken into distinct and separate races that evolved separately and distinctly. His skulls were not ranked simply on visual aesthetic quality but on visual measurements that lent an air of objective science to the racism inherent in the work. He took the measurements of facial angle and brain size (which he supposedly determined through measuring the size of the cranial cavity) and used these to make value judgments on the intelligence, superiority or inferiority, and level of "civilization" of the racial categories he used. "Beneath the allegedly objective surface of Morton's cold numerical measurements, however, laid a visceral revulsion, a palpable hatred of those he related to the lower orders" (Ewen & Ewen, 2006, p. 115). The classifications from Morton as a physician served as medical and scientific "truth" and were important sources of fundamental principles of eugenics.

Eugenics was/is the idea that there are "good" and "bad" genes that can account for all sorts of traits (deafness, criminality, poverty, intelligence, etc.) and that controlled human reproduction could breed a superior race of humans. Some genes were identified as "defective" by eugenicists who believed that the eradication of such genes and traits would benefit society. Francis Galton (1883/2001) was the man who created the term *eugenics* and the racist and classist basis for the pseudoscience in his text, *Inquiries into Human Faculty and its Development*. This was the "application of scientific knowledge to stem the tide of racial deterioration and bring about the perfection of the bloodline" (Ewen & Ewen, 2006, p. 269). Eugenics used imperialist and racist ideas of the time, those that provided the supposedly moral arguments for spreading civilization to the "savages" through colonialism, and then utilized measurements, statistics, and faulty scientific understandings of genetics to lend weight and truth to the racism. "Mainline eugenicists (those eugenicists who were explicitly preoccupied with issues of race), believed that some individuals and entire groups of people (such as Southern Europeans, Jews, Africans, and Latinos) were more predisposed to the 'defective genes'" (Stoskopf, 1999, para. 5). This work clearly drew on Blumenbach and Morton, with the Northern European/Caucasian race reinforced through "science" as superior to all other human groups. This was not a limited or radical movement; eugenics was very popular in the United States in the early 20th century and had many powerful adherents. The movement succeeded politically in working with 30 state legislatures to pass bills legalizing the involuntary sterilization of those deemed "unfit" to reproduce. The eugenicists also succeeded in selling the ideas as "science" to teachers and administrators in schools around the country. "A recent analysis of 41 high school biology textbooks used through the 1940s revealed that nearly 90% of them had sections on eugenics" (Stoskopf, 1999, para. 8). In education, the eugenics movement is closely tied to the Intelligence Quotient (IQ) movement in the 1920s that led to the mass testing and tracking of American students into college preparatory, general education, and remedial classes. Lewis Terman, who popularized the IQ test in the United States, was also a eugenicist who believed and wrote that some racial and ethnic groups were genetically less intelligent than others (Leslie, 2000, para. 8).

The overtly racist ideas of intelligence and breeding that were propagated in the late 1800s and early 1900s fell out of favor after they were picked up and taken to their horrifying and genocidal extreme by Adolf Hitler in Nazi Germany. The IQ test is still used, although not generally to track students into remedial coursework, but the achievement gap between White and minority students persists. The unnamed work of eugenics still gets popular attention; in 1994, Charles Murray and Richard Herrnstein published *The Bell Curve,* which presented testing and employment data in misleading ways that suggested a correlation between race and intelligence. Though dismissed by most scholars as unscientific and even racist, the book was a best seller and widely read. Scientists have worked with ideas of race, which have become much more complex since this movement was discredited, revealing racial categories as true social constructions rather than scientific fact. The legacy of scientific racism legitimated racial categories and the assignment of value to visual characteristics of difference.

Maalouf (1996) wrote of identity formation and its connection to the visual, especially within and across difference: "Identity is in the first place a matter of symbols, even of appearances" (p. 120). There are visual cues, appearances, that connect people in some way whether it be skin color, dress, accessories, hair, and so forth. These similarities that can draw people together are then turned into the differences in visual form that drive people apart. The visual is one form of connection that drives a Manichaean divide, "for people directly involved in conflicts arising out of identity, for those who have suffered and been afraid, nothing else exists except 'them' and 'us,' the insult and the atonement" (p. 33). The work of critical visual literacy is to teach the visual codes of identity, of difference, and of the other. If we can understand how these codes were constructed historically and in contemporary media outlets, we can educate to think beyond codes and the assumptions they can carry.

Globalization: Tentative Definitions

Globalization is a complex and shifting term that has been used to define the flow of global capital, the movement of people through travel, migration, exile, and diaspora, and the increasingly global networks of information and media. There are at least five forms of defined globalization: industrial, referring to the rise of transnational corporations; financial, the movement and investment of financial resources; political, the increased global awareness and action of political actors; informational, the flow of communication through telephone, television, Internet, and so forth; and cultural, the creation of hybrid cross-cultural practices ("Globalization," 2007). Many have decried the death of the nation-state, as borders seem to be blurring under the pressure of all aforementioned forms of the global flow. The effects of globalization are as complex as the varying definitions of the term. Transnational corporations (mostly based in the United States) seem to be obvious beneficiaries, growing in size and wealth as international treaties remove barriers and regulations that slow international trade. The overworked and underpaid global workers who ensure the functioning of transnational corporations are an often-invisible effect of this financial form of globalization. As financial resources flow more easily due to trade agreements and deregulation, the global rich (often referred to as the first world) are getting richer at the expense of the global poor (third and fourth worlds).

With intensifying globalization of political alliances and organizations, the certainty of national sovereignty and rigidity of borders is increasingly under interrogation, as movement and flow of capital and information blur traditional boundaries. For many nation-states, the fall of Soviet communism and the end of the Cold War has led to a more dynamic, less stable world order. The United States has defined itself for the past 60 or so years primarily against the negative identity of our enemy. For many years in the 20th century, we had the Soviet Union and communism as the darkness to compare to the shining light of our capitalist democracy. In popular culture, the "bad guy" was easy to predict and understand; he had a thick Russian accent and was intent on disrupting or destroying the "American Way." There was an unspoken comfort in having an enemy that was so clearly defined, a communist "them" to rally our nationalist sentiment around. With the unraveling of the Soviet Union and the fall of the Berlin Wall in the late 1980s and early 1990s, the Iron door that we had been pushing and leaning against collapsed. We were left hanging in midair, no longer able to define our national identity by pointing to a stable, geographically contained enemy.

After several years in the 1990s of lacking an outside force against which to define an enemy, the attempted bombing of the World Trade Center and the bombings of U.S. Embassies in Africa created a new foe. In the years since September 11th, global terrorist networks have replaced the Soviet Union as the force we need to defend our freedom against. Globalization is not only associated with the movement of capital and people; it is now tinged with the nebulous fear of terrorism in the United States. The fear has been directly linked to organizations like al-Qaeda and Hezbollah, which in turn have represented Islamic extremists, which in many minds are equated simply with Islam. Media outlets have exacerbated this connection of terror and Islam through the labeling of those in Islamist groups as "terrorist" and those acting in state-sponsored terror as "soldiers," even when the acts committed are similar. A Palestinian suicide bomber is clearly identified as a terrorist, while an Israeli air raid that levels a village is not an act of terror. Both acts kill civilians with brutal force, but the difference in state and nonstate actors signals the difference in terminology. The U.S. foreign policy increases the connection between terror and Islam in its strategy toward diplomacy and war. We engaged in unilateral war with Iraq for "regime change" at even the slightest hint of nuclear weapons (evidence of which has been proven to be fabricated), and we adopt a hard-line hawkish stance toward the nuclear aspirations of Iran. However, when North Korea develops and tests nuclear warheads, we urge sanctions and multilateral talks. While the situations may have more to do with strategic oil reserves than religion, many view our foreign policy as anti-Islamic.

Anderson's Imagined Communities

In *Imagined Communities,* Benedict Anderson (1991) wrote of the imagined national community that involves the creation of far-reaching commonalities between diverse groups of people. I extend the term *imagined community* to any felt common bond that is not based on the face-to-face meeting of people. Religious affiliations, ethnic ties, global humanity, along with nationalism, are all examples of imagined communities. Most human affinities beyond family relations are based on constructed similarities. These community ties overlap and overlay, though there usually exists a hierarchy of attachment. I consider myself to be part of many communities at once, but I would privilege immediate family and global human identity over national, religious, and regional communities. The privileging of certain ties depends on the real or perceived threat to that imagined community. When the U.S. offensives were launched successively in Afghanistan and Iraq, many felt that it was Islam that was the real target of the violence. Thus, the imagined Muslim community gained strength and global support. Though this community is not united by specific geographical or language commonalities, the differences of country, region, language, and particular sect can be set aside for allegiance to the greater religious community.

One of the legacies of European colonialism is a definition of nation and nationalism as exclusive to certain people who belong to common racial, ethnic, or language groups. The Indians educated by the British, administered by the British, could never *be* British. A system of native education put in place in the British colony of India was meant to educate the culturally specific identity out of the Indians without conveying British citizenship. "But the important thing is that we see a long-range policy, consciously formulated and pursued, to turn 'idolaters,' not so much into Christians, as into people culturally English, despite their irremediable colour and blood" (Anderson, 1991, p. 91). For example, to be "French," ultimately means to be White and native to France for generations. Immigrants, especially those from previous colonial holdings of France, are always physically marked with their difference and geographically marked by their location at the actual margins of Paris.

Recent events, like the rioting of teenagers in France who are children of immigrants of Northern Africa, reveal the result of this idea of national identity. Growing tension and poverty in the mostly immigrant communities of certain Parisian suburbs erupted in riots after two teenage boys were killed when running from French police. There are stories of French citizens with foreign-sounding names being discriminated against in the application for jobs, and the rampant poverty and unemployment in the suburbs of Paris add to racial tension. While visiting a poverty-ridden area, interior minister Nicolas Sarkozy said, "crime-ridden neighborhoods should be 'cleaned with a power hose'" and described "violent elements as 'gangrene' and 'rabble.'" ("Timeline: French riots," 2005). The issue of urban crime is often paired in Sarkozy's speeches with tough talk about curbing immigration, conflating the issues of poverty, unemployment, crime, and difference. Official policies of police conduct in the suburbs have led to a feeling of impersonal patrols, watching for trouble instead of ensuring the public good. Teenage residents of the mostly North African population of the Clichy-sous-Bois neighborhood, where the rioting began, have this to say about the police presence: "We don't want a police station here. Some cops are racist," "Riots are caused by police. They think we are all delinquents," "The cops don't respect us. They come in and smash doors. They systematically suspect blacks and Arabs," "Some cops are aggressive and use racial slurs when they check you," (Astier, 2006, para. 3). Though these youth are French citizens by birth, they are marked with difference in name and appearance; the prospect for success in education and career is bleak.

Nationalist right-wing politicians in France have used the rioting as an excuse to tighten immigration laws and curtail civil liberties in the poor suburbs:

> Governments impotent to strike at the roots of the existential insecurity and anxiety of their subjects are only too eager and happy to oblige. A united front against the "immigrants," that fullest and most tangible embodiment of "otherness," promises to come as near as conceivable to patching the diffuse assortment of fearful and disoriented individuals together into something vaguely reminiscent of a "national community." (Bauman, 2000, p. 109)

Like the backlash against immigration to the United States from Mexico, the fears and uncertainty of difference lead to increased legal regulation that promises to improve the lives of those in France by increasing policing and removing those considered to be outsiders. Fear of changing social and economic circumstances is used to locate scapegoats in immigrant and urban areas; national identity is used as a weapon to separate and conflate the "pollution" of those who are different from the pure national identity and the societal ills that call for difficult change and self-examination.

In *Fences and Windows: Dispatches from the Front Lines of the Globalization Debate,* Klein (2002) collected essays and speeches about the complex and messy idea of globalization and how it has variously been deployed to excuse Western military offenses, promote multinational corporations, and create spaces for resistance. I am particularly interested in her section entitled "Capitalizing on Terror" that moves through a critique of Western media coverage, trade deals, consumerism, and rebranding of America in the post-9/11 era. In her critique of Western media coverage, she highlighted the "Brutal Calculus of Suffering," where the blood and lives of some people are more important and tragic than others. The loss of a single American life at home or overseas could create headlines (depending on issues of age, class, race, and geography, of course), while hundreds of Afghan, Iraqi, or Syrian lives are background noise or to be expected. A one-time editor made this math clear, telling Klein of 114 dead in Afghanistan: "Don't worry. Those people kill each other all the time" (p. 164). This works on the level of exclusive xenophobia, where the more different and farther away one is from the in-group, the less value their lives and experience hold. It also works on the legacy of colonialism, imperialism, and the transnational slave trade that were predicated on the inherent worth of some lives and the dehumanizing, devalued nature of those human beings they colonized and enslaved.

Group and Belonging

The movement inward that is one result of the global expansions and openness needs to be understood through political and historical lenses, but those are not sufficient. There are distinctly psychological elements in the in-grouping and xenophobia that are found in global terrorism and the responses. In the current global situation of increased communication and travel, the seemingly heightened desire to identify with a group of people like oneself that leads to nationalism and acts of violence must be explored through psychological frameworks. This intense need to belong to a group of people that share common geography, language, religion, or ethnicity is explored in Vamik Volkan's (1997) *Bloodlines: From Ethnic Pride to Ethnic Terrorism*. Volkan described identity in theoretical terms that help frame the relationship between individual identity and connection to one's group. The metaphor of the "ethnic tent" (p. 27) is useful in theorizing the rise of terrorism and violent nationalism. The tent represents the second layer of identity, larger and encompassing more members than personal identity (represented in the metaphor by clothing). "While the tent pole (the leader) holds the tent erect, the canvas itself, in its own right, is a protector of the group" (p. 28). When the group is threatened by imagined or real conflict with an outside force, group identity (in the form of the tent) becomes more vital than individual identity. Threats, described as tears in the ethnic tent, can be caused by actual physical aggression by those outside the tent or can be revived remnants of a shared traumatic event from the group's past. Fear of violence or humiliation to the group causes members to rally around the leader, who in turn often uses the group's fear to consolidate power and influence. This past event that is real and current in the group's imagination is named the "chosen trauma" (p. 36) that results from a historical tragedy that has not been properly mourned. The event comes to stand in for all the current wrongs and failings of the group, a repository of humiliation that feeds feelings of group inadequacy. "If historical circumstances do not allow a new generation to reverse feelings of past powerlessness, the mental representation of the shared calamity still bonds members of the group together" (p. 47). Members of our government invoke the terrorist acts of September 11th as a point of group solidarity around trauma, reminding and reviving feelings of group powerlessness and humiliation. The feeling of vulnerability is reinforced every time the "terrorist threat level" represented by a color-coded diagram is raised from yellow to orange or from orange to red (the very vagueness of the color-coded warnings increases the level of fear, specifically of those who "look Muslim"). If the mourning process from the attacks were completed, the trauma would no longer be able to be used as rationale for continued violence and retribution.

These concepts of the ethnic tent and chosen trauma can also be applied to imagined communities of Muslims who feel powerless and marginalized by the West, first by the physical oppression of colonialism, and then by the increased Western global hegemony. For those countries that are on the receiving end of this hegemony, change often is presented in Western terms and through a Western lens. Cultural traditions and customs are threatened, or perceived to be under threat, from many of the economic and social trends of globalization. For those not part of the dominant culture in the West, "modernization has constantly meant the abandoning of part of themselves... it has never been adopted without a certain bitterness, without a feeling of humiliation and defection" (Maalouf, 1996, p. 72). Transnational networks of terrorists rely on the humiliation of chosen trauma to recruit and retain members. Western symbols of wealth and indulgence, like fast food outlets and Hollywood movies, are daily reminders to many that globalization and modernization are being sponsored and defined by Western economic power. The continued U.S. offensives in Afghanistan and Iraq serve to reinforce the historical traumas and the argument that the violence is intended as an attack on Islam.

Identity Formation in the Context of Globalization

The official imagined communities of the nation-state and of religious groups seem to be moving further toward binary definitions of good/evil, us/them, and those who are inside/outside of the community. Those who function between and within official communities but who retain ties to multiple, other, smaller communities seem to display an alternate path to identity formation. Appiah (1998) wrote of the relationship of identity formation to community:

> It is social life that endows us with the full richness of resources available for self-creation, for even when we are constructing new and counternormative identities, it is the old and the normative that provide the language and the background. (p. 98)

It is within existing social structures that we define how we think of ourselves and whether we are constituted in relation or opposition to the social order. Those who are forced to live on the margins of society have to create strategies for connection and survival that are defined *against* the dominant culture of exclusion. Others who choose to live at the margins, or are able to move between margin and center, are able to form counternormative identities that are oppositional to the dominant, unitary definition of self in relation to the group. Three theoretical frameworks for this form of inclusive identity are diaspora discourse, the transcitizen, and the rooted cosmopolitan.

CHAPTER THREE

Visualizing Difference, Decoding Representation

The contemporary field of visual culture and visual literacy relies on the vast array of technology, mobile devices, and the Internet. The formations of identity, connections that create imaginary communities of affiliation, are processes that do not happen in a vacuum. Many scholars label a relatively new form of identity, the cosmopolitan, more at home in the global community than any local one. This idea of a certain identity does not have a single mooring but rather a sense of home that moves across borders. Another, but distinct, relation to the idea of the cosmopolitan is the idea of border theory. Border theory focuses on the literal and figural space that exists near and at the border of countries and cultures. These border sites are places of interaction and exchange that create new forms of identity. Visual images travel instantly around the globe and are shared on social media sites, news sites, and in other uncontrollable and unpredictable means. Many of the images of difference encountered on social media sites such as Facebook are from global travel of friends and associates. The images help shape and frame our understandings of what other lands and people look like and how they relate to our own lives. Critical anthropologist James Clifford (1997) wrote of many forms of travel and how the movement of people and the representation of those travels form key sites of identity construction and understanding of the other. "If we rethink culture and its science, anthropology, in terms of travel, then the organic, naturalizing bias of the term 'culture'—seen as a rooted body that grows, lives, dies, and so on—is questioned" (p. 25). Travel, especially when used in the context of "tourism," carries connotations of wealth, status, mobility, free time, along with assumptions about class, race, and gender. Clifford worked in his text, *Routes,* to reinvent the term to describe any kind of physical or mental movement and encounter with difference. In this work, "the goal is not to *replace* the cultural figure 'native' with the intercultural figure 'traveler'. Rather, the task is to focus on concrete mediations of the two, in specific cases of historical tension and relationship" (p. 24). In this era of increasingly omnipresent technology and information, the idea of identity construction and how it connects to how groups of people relate and represent each other is vital. Complexity and history, especially related to the horrors and oppression of colonialism, fascism, and dictatorial regimes, are difficult to communicate on a website or in a Twitter feed. The ability to sit with contradiction, uncertainty, and ambiguity is one form of education that has thus far not been added to content standards or standardized tests.

The graphic artists who create narratives of negotiating cultural codes are border writers who use a combination of image, text, and experience to create and translate meaning. For example, Satrapi (2003, 2004) negotiates the cultural codes of her childhood homeland in Iran with the very different values and codes of her adopted home of Europe. She translates her experience through the psychological border areas of these lands. Hicks's (1991) conception of the border writer is someone who is the product of two sets of referential codes: "the reader of border writing may experience the deterritorialization of signification; to read a border text is to cross over into another set of referential codes" (p. xxvi). Border artists create images/ experiences that draw on the visual semiotic codes of multiple cultures. Border space exists not just at the physical, legal border between two nation-states; it is a space that exists metaphorically and culturally wherever there is an overlap or negotiation of cultural codes. Satrapi (2003, 2004, 2006), Bashi (2009), and Yang (2008a) are border writers; their graphic narratives exist in the border space between their countries of origin and their adopted countries. Their work involves the visual negotiation of these cultural codes. The work cannot be viewed as a product of any pure, distinct culture or regime of representation. It is both rooted in the distinct geography of their homelands and uprooted in the crossing of cultural borders and the physical travel between lands. "When one leaves one's country (deterritorialization), everyday life changed. The objects that continually remind one of the past are gone. Now, the place of origin is a mental representation in memory" (Hicks, 1991, p. xxxi). This "place of origin" that exists in the memory of the border crosser is detached, fragmented, and reconfigured in relation to the place of displacement. Cultural codes are both reified and deconstructed in one's memory; the fragments of origin are reassembled with fragmented cultural codes of the new location.

Border Theories of Representation

Shohat and Stam (1994) lay out the "Tropes of Empire" in their text, *Unthinking Eurocentrism: Multiculturalism and the Media*. The tropes include the animalization and infantilization of the native. As part of the trope of animalization, colonial regimes constructed the natives as animals, lacking control and less than human. The infantilization trope creates Western men as the most central and rational human adults, while the colonized are like infants: emotional, irrational, and incapable of complex and advanced thought. These tropes were global in reach, yet adjusted to the local context. "They associate Latin America, and especially Latin American women, with verbal epithets evoking tropical heat, violence, passion, and spice" (Shohat & Stam, 1994, p. 138). The more that the tropes of empire constructed the native population as emotional and close to nature, the easier it was to flatten their humanity into stereotype. "It can project Africa as hypermasculine, grossly corporeal, and incapable of abstraction, while projecting Asia as dreamy, feminine, and overly abstract" (p. 139). The work of constructing colonial power included dehumanizing the people in the colony to make ruling over them appear inevitable and for their own good.

In postcolonial theory, the traditional centers of Western Europe and the United States are questioned, and monolithic accounts of truth, knowledge, and beauty are deconstructed. However, some cultural producers and scholars in the West have taken up the call of globalization and multiculturalism in ways that reinscribe the power and privilege differentials of colonialism. If the cultural and educational producers in the West present difference as unproblematic window dressing, then the realities and complexity of global inequalities and colonial legacies are erased. Gomez-Pena (2001) said the following:

The depoliticized World Beat and New Age movements, and the Third World
adventures of David Byrne and Paul Simon seem to be telling us that there is a
gentle way out of our race, class, and nationality; that we can all be friends within
safe and neutral space of poly-ethnic music, weekend meditation centers, and
"primitive" memorabilia. (p. 10)

Gomez-Pena called this kind of surface cultural sampling the transculture
and opposed it to neonationalism, the retrenchment of singular, xenophobic
definitions of the nation and its imagined community. In the transculture,
those with time and resources from various parts of the globe interact and
celebrate multiculturalism as an accomplishment. Neither the transculture
nor the neonational calls for separatism truly reflect the experience and
struggle of those working for justice. He proposed working within the
postcolonial frame of the hybrid to muddy the cultural waters. "Hybrid
culture is community-based yet experimental, radical but not static or
dogmatic. It fuses 'low' and 'high' art, primitive and high tech, the
problematic notions of self and other" (p. 12). Though few of the narratives
analyzed in this text could be called outwardly radical, they represent
important sources fusing the high and low art and representing hybrid lives
and cultural experiences. While the graphic narratives are not outwardly
radical, the presentation of voices and lives of those traditionally
marginalized is a subtle form of radicalism. The memoirs are written by
border crossers, living in multiple cultures and making sense of their
experience through writing of their transition and translation between
cultures.

According to Gomez-Pena (2001), the works of the border writings, for
example Satrapi (2003, 2004, 2006) and Bashi (2009), are intended to
complicate easy dichotomies and bring attention to inequalities of privilege
and power in the messy border zone. "I make art about the misunder-
standings that take place in the border zone. But for me, the border is no
longer a fixed geopolitical site. I carry the border with me, and I find new
border wherever I go" (Gomez-Pena, 2001, p. 5). The borders we often think
of are those between nation-states, but border zones occur when any
identities, ideologies, cultures, languages, or beliefs mingle, clash, or meet.
Gomez-Pena collaborated with feminist artist and art critic Coco Fusco in the
early to mid-1990s. Together, they created art performances that created
radically different border spaces that disrupted assumptions and expectations.
One of their practices at disruption was to segregate the audience, giving

preferential treatment in admission and seating to audience members who were bilingual, ethnic minorities, or immigrants. Those who identified as monolingual Anglo-Americans were marginalized and treated as "other." "The idea was to create a fictional center which we would occupy for the duration of the performance, thereby forcing monolingual/monocultural Americans to feel like outsiders and 'minorities' in their own country" (p. 95). For the brief time of the artistic performances, these audience members experienced a total reversal in their usual cultural and social status; traditional sources of unearned and often-unacknowledged privilege functioned as liabilities while traditional liabilities functioned as sources of power.

Another of Gomez-Pena and Fusco's collaborative artistic performances is a powerful example of radical reexamination of global networks and relationships of power. In the piece entitled "The Guatinaui World Tour," also known as "Couple in the Cage" from 1992–1993, the artists parodied the exhibition of human beings as exotic objects of curiosity that were popular in World's Fairs and National History Museums of the late 19th and early 20th centuries. The artists created a fictional "exotic" people, language, country, and culture from the fantastical land of Guatinaui. They embarked on a world tour, exhibiting the piece in natural history museums and art galleries. The piece centered on the artists' bodies, dressed in parodies of native garb, existing, talking, interacting from behind the bars of a large cage. The artistic performance was a hybridized parody of cultural "authenticity" that was/is fetishized in the West and included Fusco wearing a bikini top, grass skirt, and Converse sneakers while being led out of the cage on a leash to use the bathroom. "Besides performing 'authentic rituals,' we would write on a laptop computer, watch home videos of our native land, and listen to Latin American rock music on a boom box" (Gomez-Pena, 2001, p. 9). Despite what was intended to be a clear mockery and parody of barbaric practices of human exhibition, Gomez-Pena wrote that over 40% of audience members in every location believed that is was a real and truthful exhibition, and yet no one tried to intervene (p. 9). The truly amazing number of audience members who believed the authenticity of this exhibition despite so many cues to the fiction belies the authority many give to museums as keepers and arbiters of truth. Since this performance was set up in open spaces of a museum with visitors passing by and through, those who believed the performance to be true may never be disabused of their misinterpretation. Without critical analysis of the piece, what messages do they take away? They may go home and tell friends and family about the exotic humans from Guatenaui and how strange and different they are. Assumptions and dichotomies about first/third world, us/them, primitive/advanced are reinforced if there is not specific guidance in how to read the performance or text.

Postcolonialism, Race, and Education

Postcolonial theory, though relatively well supported and entrenched in at least the margins of the academy, is little explored in the realm of K-12 education. Most attempts to revise curriculum conform to a traditional, modern conception of identity and global relationships of power and privilege. Current curriculum is steeped in a romanticized view of settler colonialism and Eurocentric ideas about difference. Meaningful revision of curriculum should engage with the complexity and often difficult to understand language and theory of postcolonialism. Thus far, only a small group of scholars of education have engaged in how to reimagine K-12 education through postcolonial pedagogy (Dimitriadis & McCarthy, 2001; McCarthy, 1998). Much of the scholarship on postcolonial education refers to the postcolonial as a geographical distinction rather than an ideological or theoretical one. The geographical postcolonial refers to the now independent nations that were colonized by another nation; the theoretical postcolonial refers, however, to an analytic perspective that de-centers the West or those with power and privilege. It examines both the aftereffects of colonialism and the newly formed identities and positions in the postcolonial era. While the form and content of education taking place in former colonial spaces are vitally important, my interest is in rethinking American educational practice and content in postcolonial terms. In the text, *Reading and Teaching the Postcolonial: From Baldwin to Basquiat and Beyond,* Dimitriadis and McCarthy (2001) began to reimagine a curriculum that asks K-12 students (mostly at the high school level) to engage with postcolonial literature and art to bring the postcolonial into the classroom. They contended that bringing literature and art that asks students to view identity, race, and power in complex, relational, and new ways is an important first step in postcolonial pedagogy. "By *postcolonial art,* we mean artistic work engaged in the radical reassessment of center-periphery relations, produced in the crucible of colonization and in its aftermath of independence and postindependence movements and struggle" (p. 3). The authors argued for the use of textual and visual works of art as a first step into the use of curriculum to address the changes of globalization and question stereotypical representations of difference.

In their call to engage the postcolonial in curricular reform, Dimitriadis and McCarthy (2001) focused on the need to address "ressentiment," which they defined as, "the process of defining one's identity through the negation of the other" (p. 110). The other is defined as, "that which is not me," with firm boundaries constructed between self and other. The authors described three discourses of ressentiment: the discourse of origins, discourse of nation, and discourse of popular memory and popular history. The discourse of origins relates to the Eurocentric and Afrocentric debate over curricular reform as two related ways to envision the way we teach the world through certainty and exclusion. These approaches reify a specific geographic location as the point of origin of culture and humanity. In an attempt to break down the center/periphery hierarchy of colonialism, postcolonialism cannot leave the dichotomy intact while merely changing the order to periphery/center. Dimitriadis and McCarthy are not looking to re-center but rather to de-center, where stable, universal truth is replaced with tentative, contextual truths. "The dreaded line of difference is drawn around glittering objects of cultural heritage and secured with the knot of ideological closure" (p. 111). These lines are drawn to demarcate the imagined communities (Anderson, 1991), the affiliations and ties that we create to tie ourselves off from those around us, to decide whom to include and whom to exclude from our inter-actions and relations. These are also the lines of xenophobia, where the imagined difference of the other is converted to apprehension and fear of difference.

The discourse of nation works in concert with the certainty of origins, creating the glorious nation-state as the primary actor on the global stage and repository and negotiator of all difference. The discourse of popular memory and history brings the focus to the relationship between the official school and unofficial media curriculums of history. Historical dramas based very loosely on fact traditionally focus on the White male hero as the central actor, generally a benevolent figure treating the natives fairly. High budget Hollywood movies become part of the historical discourse, and over time, dramatic elements and casting choices begin to function as true. Disney's *Pocahontas* (Pentecost et al., 1995) replaces the historical figure of Pocahontas, becoming the developed young woman who fell in love with the dashing John Smith. The historical girl was merely 12 at the time, and John Smith was much older and not good looking. This historically based fantasy includes, at least, some sense of the greed and lack of understanding of native ways from the British. The song "Savages" portrays the British under-Governor Ratcliffe as racist and violent and begs the larger question of who was more "civilized" in this historical confrontation. The lyrics of the original version were changed from, "Their whole disgusting race is like a curse!" to "Here's what you get when the races are diverse!" and "Dirty redskin devils" to" Dirty shrieking devils" (Pocahontas trivia, n.d., para. 13). The original lyrics were harshly racist and offensive, but the purpose of the song was to highlight rather than sugarcoat the racism that was a historical reality. Some of the commentary online about this song seems to conflate the representation of racism with acts of racism: "The lyrics of the song "Savages" are extremely offensive. They lack cultural sensitivity and are incredibly detrimental to Native Americans" (Nunez, 2010, para. 10). These lyrics are offensive, but they attempt to show the historical realities of racism and colonialism; whether this nuance is lost on the young audience of Disney's version is another important question to consider.

In his text, *The Uses of Culture: Education and the Limits of Ethnic Affiliation,* McCarthy (1998) presented the concept of postcolonial texts and education from a different, more complex and nuanced perspective. McCarthy, who was born in Barbados and moved to the United States, writes from his experience of moving from the periphery to the center. He argues that many postcolonial theorists oversimplify the margin/center dichotomy and that they speak for, or in place of, those who live in the so-called margin. "The postcolonial theorist therefore appoints her/himself as a stand-in or proxy for the oppressed third world; a third world of the imaginary—a world that is unstratified and uniformly underdeveloped" (p. 5). This model for postcolonial theory assumes that scholars, educated in the first world, must speak for rather than engage with those from the third world. In looking at race and education through a uniquely situated postcolonial and postmodern lens, McCarthy's text asks educators to give up the certainty of racial lines and classifications in favor of a liminal space with its attendant complexity and fluidity. "I refuse the manichean model of racial identity formation, I challenge the glib opposition of West to the non-West and the curricular project of content addition that now guides the thinking of many of the proponents of identity politics and multicultural reformist frameworks" (p.

14). The heft of contemporary social studies textbooks is a very good example of this multicultural addition of content. To make sure that various groups are represented in global and American history, sections, pages, or sidebars are added to the traditional historical narrative. Rather than rewriting or rethinking more traditional perspectives, the curricular revisions to these books seek to maintain the status quo, steer clear of controversy, and cover all the bases. Generally, these textbooks break out groups of people by race or geography and create the sense that racial, ethnic, and national groups are clearly defined with rigid boundaries. For my work in analysis of the curricular potential of graphic narratives for visual literacy, McCarthy's call to question a multicultural curriculum that reifies rather than challenges the nature of identity and affiliation is vital. Indeed, most of the graphic narratives that I choose to analyze (especially those that are first-person memoirs) foreground the struggle to navigate the shifting, complex nature of identity and where to fit. Authors like Satrapi (2003) and Bashi (2009) use the medium of the graphic memoir to chart the course of their physical and psychological movement among worlds, cultures, and identifications. *Qahera* (Mohamed, 2013; see Figure 3.1) offers a different view of a veiled woman, using her identity and clothing as a source of power.

Willinsky (1998) wrote of the colonial exhibitions and the use of human "types" to educate the Europeans about variety and difference. The production of an "educational spectacle" (p. 58) is a part of the imperial past, but I argue, very much a part of graphic narratives written about difference. Each narrative teaches the reader something about the characters in the narrative, the author's hand and voice, and about the interaction of reader and text.

Figure 3.1. From "On Sexual Harassment" in *Qahera* (Mohamed, 2013).

When the narrative clearly engages with difference as one of its primary themes, the educational lessons on difference must be the source of analysis. I argue that the presentation of the vaguely constructed Arab/Middle Eastern Wanatolia in Thompson's (2011) *Habibi* is an educational spectacle that provides lessons on the development, or lack thereof, of the people in the story, the treatment of women, the values and morals of this semifictional location.

How do we learn to see other people, those who live far away from us and are outside of our imagined community? How is difference represented to us in school, literature, and the media in ways that make us feel as if we understand or can organize difference? Recently celebrating 125 years of publication, *National Geographic* continues to be one important source of information for Americans about cultural and ethnic differences. Though many, including me, have been critical of the Eurocentric and imperialist undertones of the coverage of the world, the magazine historically offered and continues to offer a window to view the world that may have been the only one available outside of Hollywood movies like *Tarzan* or *Lawrence of Arabia*. The magazine increased curiosity about the world and broadened the imagined community of humanity to those previously imagined as fictional and without humanity. The representations of difference found in the magazine opened up a world to its readers, but the world was presented through a distinctively Western lens. I propose that the graphic interventions into this cultural legacy of *National Geographic* and other Western sources about difference can effectively challenge this Western lens.

Visual Semiology and Myth

To choose and interpret the visual images that construct the dominant visual discourse and those that subvert it, I am relying heavily on the critical visual methodologies that are presented in Gillian Rose's *Visual Methodologies*, written in 2001. She wrote of three criteria for a critical approach to choosing, viewing, and analyzing images: taking "images seriously," "thinking about the social conditions and effects of visual objects," and "considering your own way of looking at images" (pp. 15–16). These criteria foreground the cultural contexts of image and audience, while not ignoring the content of images within greater social critique. I examine historical and current Western images of Muslim women through two of Rose's metho-dological lenses: visual semiology that examines the cultural meaning embedded in visual signs and visual discourse analysis that looks at the combined cultural meanings and discourse produced through the repetition and institutional force of the images.

The field of semiology that was first introduced to the field of linguistics by Ferdinand de Saussure (1972) is a useful methodological tool when applied to the visual. In a visual representation of Muslim women in Western media, very specific meanings are embedded in location of the image, the angle of the figure, the level of covering or uncovering of the body, and the woman's eyes in relation to the photographer. These loaded signs construct a cultural code, "a set of conventionalized ways of making meaning that are specific to particular groups of people" (Rose, 2001, p. 88). The visual signifier of a covered face creates very different signified meanings based on geographical and cultural context. Roland Barthes's (1972) concept of cultural myth is made up of visual signs that are embedded with this cultural meaning and presented in a way that combines individual signs to change or reinforce meaning. "Semiology has taught us that myth has the task of giving an historical intention a natural justification, and making contingency appear eternal" (Barthes, 1972, p. 142). Myth functions to turn socially and historically created classifications and difference into biological, natural fact. The myth of the victimized, oppressed Muslim woman colors any interpretation of an image of a veiled woman. Automatic assumptions about the woman are made, agency is denied, and ideas about the openness and freedom of the West are reinforced. The force of cultural myth and the regime of representation are related to an imbalance of power in discourse as theorized by Michel Foucault (1972). "Each society has its regime of truth, its 'general politics' of truth: that is, the types of discourse which it accepts and makes function as true" (p. 73). Orientalism matches this description of a regime of representation exactly. Representations of Muslims during the colonial period created layers of "knowledge," images that were created from European fantasy but functioned as proof.

In my analysis of graphic narratives, I use more traditional qualitative methods of textual analysis and theoretical research methods from feminist and postcolonial perspectives. To capture the unique image/text content of the graphic narratives, I employ and transform the visual methodologies of Rose (2001). Two of her visual methodologies are used throughout this text as a way to make sense and meaning from the various and diverse representations of difference in graphic narratives. The first, visual content analysis, is useful for examining very specific codes that authors use to represent difference in a text, while the second, visual discourse analysis, is a tool to examine the context and construction of representations of difference.

The method of visual content analysis is used in reading the frequency and nature of representations in *Habibi* (Thompson, 2011) and other graphic narratives. In examining the field of visual representations of difference, I use methods of visual discourse analysis, contending that the body of visual representations of a group of people, Muslim women for example, by a certain group of people, Western mass media outlets for example, can be examined as a discourse.

Discourse as a site of analysis originated with Foucault (1972). "It refers to groups of statements which structure the way a thing is thought, and the way we act on the basis of that thinking. In other words, discourse is a particular knowledge about the world which shapes how the world is understood" (p. 142). Discourse is produced through the combined effect of many forms of texts and representations, which makes discourse analysis a meaningful vehicle for analysis of image and text in graphic narratives. Rose (2001) wrote of the term "intertextuality" as a way to describe the relationship of various written and visual texts that make up a discourse. Discourse analysis is at the level of the sociocultural representation; the sediment of representations accumulate over time as we are exposed to images and headlines on traditional print media and on the Internet and to endless repetition on the 24-hour cable news networks. One line or image can gain the status that Rose described as an "icon" through quick and widespread repetition.

How was the objectivity/subjectivity of the Muslim woman created through political and cultural visual discourse? Methodological tools of visual discourse analysis, which were developed by Stuart Hall (1997) in *Representation: Cultural Representations and Signifying Practices,* Nicholas Mirzoeff (1999) in *An Introduction to Visual Culture,* and by Rose (2001) in *Visual Methodologies,* inform my analysis of the current regimes of representation of Muslim women in the West:

> Discourse analysis can also be used to explore how images construct specific views
> of the world, in which case . . . visuality is viewed as the topic of research, and the
> discourse analyst is interested in how images construct accounts of the social world.
> (Rose, 2001, p. 140)

The visual Orientalism of the colonial era was highly eroticized, with European and some American male artists creating lavish, richly colored, and textured images of women. Favorite subjects of the Orientalist painters were interior spaces populated by women in various states of uncovering, scenes that were the product of the artists' imagination. Men, especially Western, unrelated men, were not allowed in such private spaces. So these were fantasies of the Western imagination, sexual fantasies of women bathing, lying down, touching, and desiring attention. These paintings were very popular in Europe and were displayed in galleries and museums as exotic proof of the sensual other. Three of the favorite Orientalist scenes were the harem, the hammam, and the odalisque. The hammam scenes are large baths, with the ultimate sexual fantasy of nude women standing, sitting, and bathing. The harem scenes show the chamber women who were sensuously lazing on pillows in the harem waiting for the sexual encounter with the sultan. In *Habibi*, the graphic tome by Craig Thompson (2011), I analyze these Orientalist codes of the veil, the hammam, and the harem. He reproduced the visual discourse of Orientalism for a contemporary audience. Malek Alloula's (1986) *The Colonial Harem* provides an example of one form of Western historical representation of Muslim women in Algeria. Alloula theorized the meaning of the covered women's bodies in relation to the gaze of the French photographer. The Algerian women were veiled, unavailable to the penetrating gaze of the colonizer, refusing to submit. "The photographer will respond to this quiet and almost natural challenge by means of a double violation: he will unveil the veiled and give figural representation to the forbidden" (p. 14). What visual signs were coded in the earliest representations of these women and how have the meanings of visual signs been altered by their relationship to other signs and forms of representation? The visual codes of different levels of covering or uncovering of women's bodies, and the visual location of the image as public or private space, are important to my analysis. The veil is the most often represented sign of difference that I trace through historical and contemporary images. I study multiple visual and textual sources that represent the veil to create a genealogy of the Western discursive production of the Muslim woman. The works of Satrapi (2003, 2004) and Mohamed (2013) present images of Muslim women that challenge the Orientalist discourse through strong, intelligent, and powerful women wearing the veil as part of their religious and cultural identities.

Visual Culture

The field of visual culture is a relatively new one that is defined by Mirzoeff (1999) as, "concerned with visual events in which information, meaning or pleasure is sought by the consumer in an interface with visual technology" (p. 3). Since Mirzoeff defined visual culture in 1999, the visual nature of representation and experience has expanded. All content viewed on the Internet is mediated through the visual; websites are built on the combined meaning of images and text. With the expansion of the visual event, the need to educate on how to read, analyze, and interpret visual events increases.

> The visual, in our view, never comes "pure," it is always "contaminated" by the work of other senses (hearing, touch, smell), touched by other texts and discourses, and imbricated in a whole series of apparatuses—the museum, the academy, the art world, the publishing industry, even the nation state—which govern the production, dissemination, and legitimation of artistic productions. (Shohat & Stam, 1998, p. 45)

The visual, thus, carries with it the weight of past and current represent-ations. Visual representations are particularly fraught, carrying a history of racist and/or sexist imagery used in the service of domination. Imperial representations of difference are particularly important to my analysis of graphic narratives because they were created by those in the colonial center of those on the margins and were used to establish and maintain a hierarchy of worth and value. Shohat and Stam (1998) called for a polycentric visual culture that relocates the traditional center of cultural production and examines the relationships and connection between and among visual events and cultural production.

Mirzoeff (2011) has, in recent work, shifted the discourse from "visual culture" to the field of "visuality," as a particular Western invention and weapon deployed in the surveillance and regulation of the other. Carlyle coined the term in 1840 to describe the "dominant view of Hero over History" (p. 125). Visuality is a term that encompasses much more than seeing; in fact, Mirzoeff traced the inception of visuality to the time in war when battlefields expanded beyond the visual field of one general. How could the general map and visualize the entire battle and war? The combined descriptions and representations of multiple informants produced visualized battlefields that no one person could compile. This particular construction of visuality is a tool of authority, particularly imperial authority over the "native," and required the construction of a countervisuality or "the claim for the right to look" (p. 24). The "right to look" for Mirzoeff requires a mutual subjectivity, an acknowledgment that the viewer and those viewed are aware of their relationship and consent to the looking. This is the opposite of visuality, where authority is used to enforce visual availability.

I contend that the scope of visuality, and thus countervisuality, must also include the right to be unavailable to other's view and the right to control one's image. In colonial Algeria, the right to not be seen was a powerful tool, and both women and men used traditional hijab to cover their bodies and faces from view of French colonial forces. The ability to hide, be unseen, is a powerful force for resistance to power and oppression; to exercise power, one must always have the potential to (over)see. Mirzoeff (2011) wrote of the plantation overseers as the ultimate arbiters and regulators of power in slavery. One of the major roles of the overseer was to watch for rebellion, any threat to the imposed order of the plantation power structure. The realm of potential rebellion, the area in need of oversight, has expanded. The role of authority, as "overseer," has shifted to imperial authority visualizing the native from the bow of a gunship, to the global system of surveillance through satellites today. With the cellular nature of the global terror networks, the threat could come from anywhere; the battlefield for the never-ending "War on Terror" can be anywhere, either at a physical location or online. With the potential location of threat expanding, the visuality of the surveillance state has expanded in relation. The visuality includes visual representations (images) but also textual information that gives a bigger picture of movement, activity, and relationships that may lead to threat. Methods of imagining and imaging threat have been the subject of recent whistleblower Edward Snowden and his releasing of information about the massive amounts of Internet and cell phone data collected on American citizens by the National Security Agency (NSA). Though the phone records and Internet search data are not images, they are a form of government visuality asserting the authority of the state over the likeness (information and relationships) of its people. The surveillance of threat is not limited to the threat of a terrorist attack; visuality in the colonial sense also works to construct the other (native) as less human and fully available for scrutiny. The objectification of the other through visibility and imagery is akin to Said's (1979) critique of Orientalism as a Western academic and artistic construction of a fanciful colonial space.

Mirzoeff (2011) analyzed shocking visual imagery of prisoner abuse in the Iraq War in the infamous Abu Ghraib prison. The images of prisoners tortured, mocked, and abused in multiple ways as "official" protocol in the United States military offensive and occupation of Iraq caused an uproar of disgust when they were publicized, but the outrage was fleeting and did not lead to sanction. As Mirzoeff (2011) wrote, "no military figure above the level of the prison itself was subsequently disciplined: indeed everyone in the chain of command leading to the Abu Ghraib scandal was promoted" (p. xiv). While visual cultural theorists like Mirzoeff, Shohat, and many others contend that the visual is of unprecedented centrality to the Internet age, this very centrality of the image may lead to its lack of sustained effect. While the power and impact of images as a whole is growing and expanding around us, the power and impact of each individual image may in fact be diminished.

In this age of expanding visuality and imaging, where the volume of images and representations is affecting the attention given to any single image, what role does countervisuality play? The right to see and be seen can also expand through use of the Internet and social media. Control over the production and distribution of images and image/text representations is now available to anyone with a smart phone or computer and Internet access. Central authority, the visuality of the state and other nonstate organizations have trouble containing the viral spread of a meme, image, or video posted on Twitter, Instagram, YouTube, or Facebook (though some are successful at geographically specific censorship, like the limiting and blocking of sites by the Chinese government). It was the social media web that activists in Egypt used to call for mass protests against the Mubarak regime and then publicized photographs and on-the-ground narratives of the revolution.

Graphic narratives enter into this crowded field of image, text, and representation as forms that could be analyzed as supporting visuality and countervisuality. The graphic narratives that are analyzed for this text primarily fit into the trope of countervisuality, seeking to represent and visualize stories that are reciprocal and challenge the authority of official images. The collection of comic strips in *Rise* (Shahin, 2011) specifically confronts the Egyptian state (among others) about the authority of the regime. *Palestine* (Sacco, 2001) creates a countervisuality by confronting the American mainstream media representations of Israel and Palestine that dehumanize all sides, though especially the Palestinians are reduced to rock-throwing insurgents with due cause. Others, primarily *Habibi* (Thompson, 2001), offer narratives that represent the other in ways similar to that of colonial visuality. By visualizing other people in a distant and fanciful land, Thompson (2011) did not create a reciprocal look with the other. Though the author intended to challenge Islamophobia and distorted images of Muslims and Islam in the West, the effects of his representations are much more complex and may reinforce the distortions. *Habibi* brings up a conversation of whether visuality has to be intentional in order to act with authority.

Critical Visual Literacy

The field of literacy has expanded in the 21st century to include concepts of both critical literacy and multimodal literacy. One of these newly defined areas deals with the political and social context and content of literacy, while the other refers to the expanded field of texts that are included in the concept of what it means to be literate. Critical literacy centers on the relationship between the production and reception of texts with power. I understand and use power from a poststructural perspective: power is not something that one person or group holds as a possession; it is fluid and circulates depending on context. Power can be "productive and not simply a negative force of domination" (Janks, 2000, p. 175). Multimodal literacy includes multiple forms of text that depart from the traditional written word; for my purposes, the inclusion of visual imagery in this expanded notion of literacy is central. Visual literacy is an offshoot of both literacy and art education fields, gaining in attention due to the visual nature of virtual and computer-based spaces. The visual field can be experienced on multiple levels; certainly one can "read" an image in a surface way without having mastered specific skills. However, to read images for meaning, visual literacy needs to be taught and understood. Combining the work of critical and multimodal literacies, I work for a critical visual literacy that analyzes texts for the deployment of power in social and political terms to read the world through graphic narratives.

I argue for a multimodal form of reading the world that uses the particular visual representations that combine image and text in graphic narratives with the focus on the regulation of racial, ethnic, gender, sexual, age, ability and class differences of critical literacy. What role do graphic narratives play in regulating, maintaining, and challenging the status quo including stereotypical ideas about difference? The visual marking of difference has been central to representation since the earliest markings;

however, the sustained use of images to rank and order difference in the service of power and privilege began in earnest during the height of European colonialism and imperialism in the 18th and 19th centuries. In a combined effort of artists, scientists, and naturalists, Europeans set out to create ranked hierarchies and orders for all of nature, geography, and humanity. The quests to both know and to classify contributed to the colonial project by creating "scientific" justification for the subordination of natural resources and groups of humans. By ordering and classifying humans into a hierarchy of evolution and level of development, those with power in the colonial systems could justify the subjugation of people as simply preserving the natural order:

> Encountering or, more often, relying on travelers' accounts of people with varying skin tones, hair textures, facial structures, and body types, Enlightenment scientists, philosophers, and dilettantes strained to construct intricate, well-ordered systems of classification in order to situate each particular variant within its "proper place" in the natural order of things. (Ewen & Ewen, 2006, p. 59)

If some groups of people were determined to be less than fully developed, therefore less human, one could support equality of rights and treatment for all people and at the same time strip those lower on the ladder of humanity of even the most basic rights. Several pseudosciences sprang up in the late 18th, 19th, and early 20th centuries to support this classification:

> Throughout the nineteenth century and well into the twentieth, the exhibition of "primitive" types would become a mainstay of an expanding science-as-entertainment business. Group after group of "natives," some actual persons plucked from afar, some actors, would be paraded before European and American eyes, providing a visual argument on behalf of the inherent superiority of Western civilization. (Ewen & Ewen, 2006, p. 89)

I split the representational systems of colonialism into two distinct aims: the first, the painting and art of difference served to illustrate the exotic difference of colonial peoples and create fantasies to satisfy the European tastes, and the second, the use of art and photography to capture the "truth" about the natives and provide proof of eugenic ideas about superiority and inferiority of groups of people. The art and photographs were used as proof of the inferiority of non-White people, a task that began with the use of curiosity cabinets and exhibitions of living "specimens" at fairs and museums. European artists went abroad to study and visualize the native other. Images could be reproduced in ways that live exhibitions could not, and the "average" American and European citizen could view images of those from elsewhere and confirm their own privileged place in the eugenic order of things. Once the technology for photography was created, studios were set up to record the special humanity of those wealthy enough to pay for the service and the supposed inhumanity of those who were forced to sit for portraits to prove their "scientific inferiority." "Portraits of the willing and unwilling—of those who sought to be photographed and those who were photographed as objects of 'scientific' investigation—when juxtaposed with each other offered sustenance to those who believed in the truths of facial politics" (Ewen & Ewen, 2006, p. 180). The facial and other physical features in collections of photographs allowed for more careful study and categorization into racial types without having to rely on artists' renderings or the procurement of actual human beings, live or dead.

The Educational Spectacle

In conceptualizing the use of graphic narratives as a tool for critical visual literacy, it is important think about how difference is produced and received visually. There are some forms of difference that are clearly visual in nature, though still contested in terms of meaning and value of difference: skin color, facial features, height, weight, gender expression, some physical disabilities, and the wearing of visual religious symbols. Many forms of difference are invisible or can include visual and nonvisual codes. Part of the work of critical visual literacy is examining how difference of all kinds is visualized in graphic narratives. I have identified three main strategies in visualizing difference in the graphic narratives that I have examined. The first strategy, difference through juxtaposition, is to directly compare forms of visual difference in the same panel or on the same page. The second strategy, difference through amplification, is to exaggerate difference to stereotypical levels to confront preconceived notions of what visual difference means to the reader. The third strategy, difference through metaphor, is to take what is essentially an invisible form of difference and create a visual code that is used as a metaphor for the difference. Two examples of the first strategy that are highlighted here are *Persepolis* (Satrapi, 2003, 2004) and *Nylon Road* (Bashi, 2009). In these narratives, religious identity and the difference in expectations for dress of women and men in traditionally Muslim and Christian/secular cultures are visually represented primarily by the covering or lack of covering of the hair and face for women. Both of these memoirs of growing up in Iran and moving to Europe show the visual differences of dress in these two locations as a stand-in for the less visible ideas that differentiate expectations and regulations. Both also use difference in visual dress of women to showcase the different level of personal freedom of expression for women in public versus private spaces in Iran. Both texts use visual and special juxtaposition to highlight the visual differences in dress and also give the reader a sense of the meaning behind the pieces of cloth.

One very effective example of the second strategy is the narrative *American Born Chinese* (Yang, 2008a). The author represents the subtle visual racial differences of the main character but then also plays with and mocks the Western stereotype of Chinese culture through his use of the character Chin-kee (a character whose very being represents the accumulation of decades of Western slur and stereotype of Chinese and Chinese Americans). By creating such a visually jarring character, the author is forcing the reader to make meaning of visual signs of difference. Taken out of context, the images of Chin-kee (and his highly stereotyped speech patterns and dialogue) could be read as blatant reinforcing of the worst cultural and ethnic stereotypes and racism that has been directed toward Chinese Americans. However, read in the context of the narrative, the character of Chin-kee is ridiculous; while the character is discussed as an embarrassment to the main character Danny, the reader could realize the embarrassment is not from the character but from the horrifying stereotypes that he embodies.

The third strategy involves examining how authors in graphic narratives visualize difference when the difference is not inherently visual in nature. One notable work in this visualizing of difference is *Epileptic* by David B. (2006). This narrative is the nonfictional account of the author's family, especially the story of his older brother, Jean-Christophe, and his battle with epilepsy, which consumes the entire family. Other than the visual nature of seizures, epilepsy is an invisible disease and form of difference. David B. makes the disease visible to the reader by imagining it taking the form of a dragon-like monster that must be battled. The monster lives in his brother's body and invades his psyche. This monster stalks the family, especially Jean-Christophe, though in some panels the monster seems to be a normal member of the family. The disease is also visualized as an insurmountable mountain that the family must climb but also that they are dragged upon against their will.

The visualizing of difference in these graphic narratives is also influenced by the relationship of the author and the reader to the difference that is illustrated in the text. Representation can be broken into three layers that deal with this relationship (Bailey Jones, 2011). These layers are representation of self, representation of imagined self, and representation of self-and-other. The representation of self is fairly straightforward: you are telling your own story and representing your own concept of your identity and how you are different from others you perceive. The second layer, the representation of imagined self, utilizes the concept of imagined community (Anderson, 1991), that we form imaginary connections to those we do not personally know but to whom we feel connection by nationality, religion, ethnicity, gender, sexuality, or other reason. The third layer is the representation of self-and-other and means that the author or artist who is creating the representation does not identify with the characters as part of their extended community. Many of the graphic narratives that are examined in this text are autobiographical memoirs that clearly represent the first layer of representation (*Persepolis, Nylon Road, American Born Chinese, Fun Home, Epileptic, Blankets*). By representing the self, these narratives tell stories that present a version or form of reality and difference. Those that represent imagined self (*Zahra's Paradise, The Photographer*) use the imagined connections to present an understanding of experience and difference that is based on affiliation of some sort. *Habibi, Pyongyang, Palestine* are examples of cultural outsiders representing the other through image and text. These texts present the third layer, the most removed from the original source and therefore at the most risk of stereotyping, making assumptions, and creating flawed representations. Of course, stereotyping is not guaranteed in this final group, but those who choose to represent the other must be aware of their position and interrogate their presentation for how it constructs the other for the reader. The separation of these texts into various categories of strategy for visually representing difference is problematic, because most of them do not fit neatly into just one. For instance, in *Epileptic,* David B. (2006) created an autobiographical memoir of his childhood and his family. Thus, it is primarily an example of self-representation, but by drawing his brother, family, and others in his life as major characters, he also represented his imagined self. In *Nylon Road,* Bashi

(2009) used comparative visual difference to illustrate the divergent dress of women in public in Tehran and those in Zurich, but she also used exaggerated visual difference, with exposed nipples and extremely tight clothing, as a way to highlight these differences.

CHAPTER FOUR

Post-September 11th and the Visual Regime

This chapter focuses specifically on the deployment of visual representations of Muslims created by Western artists, journalists, and photographers for Western audiences. In this chapter, I analyze media coverage and images and find global connections for a rise of anti-Muslim sentiment. There has been a great deal of interest in regulating and controlling the terms of visual representation of Muslims in the West for Western audiences. "Since September 11, 2001, much of the West has been gripped by a stereotyping frenzy. In the United States, it has been particularly virulent" (Ewen & Ewen, 2006, p. 495). The visual representations focused on in this chapter were created and reproduced with the intent to be provocative and in some cases with the explicit intent of inciting Islamophobia.

There have been several important and disturbing cases of provocative Western media critiques of Islam in the post-9/11 era. The publication of political cartoons featuring the Prophet Muhammed by Danish newspaper *Jyllands-Posten* was one of the most infamous instances of Western media provoking the anger and protest of many in the so-called Muslim world. Cartoonist Kurt Westergaard drew images of clerics with their faces turning into bombs. Apparently the artist did not intend for the newspaper to show the face of the Prophet, but it titled the series, "The Faces of Muhammed." For Muslims who believe that it is a sin to create any image of the Prophet, the cartoon series was highly offensive and caused protests and calls for retraction and apology. After the initial publications of the cartoons, the offensive images were reprinted in 17 daily newspapers in Denmark and many others in European and American papers and websites. There is a Facebook group page entitled, "The Faces of Muhammed," that is a lasting record of the images for those who want to view them. In the aftermath of the publication, protests turned violent, even deadly, in some locations. In Nigeria, 100 deaths resulted from the protests that fueled simmering tensions between the country's Muslim and Christian populations. The controversy led to accusations from Western media outlets and politicians that Muslims were overly sensitive, not appreciative of free speech, and lacking the ability to accept satire.

Several high profile examples of news media representation occurred in 2011 and 2012, as the revolutions known as the Arab Spring changed into the messy formation of democratic states. *The Atlantic* ran a cover story by Jeffrey Goldberg in June 2011 with the caption, "Is This the Face of Arab Democracy? Why the new Middle East is more hopeful—and more hazardous." In the pages of the magazine, the story is entitled, "Danger: Falling Tyrants" (p. 46). This title is quite different than that on the cover. When paired with the overrepresented, stereotypically oppressed-yet-menacing fully covered Muslim woman, the question "is this the face of Arab democracy?" takes on a decidedly Orientalist tone. The image on the cover is entirely black except for a small slit showing the dark eyes of a presumably Muslim woman staring out at the reader with a sideways glance. The story that accompanies this image is more complex and focuses on the policies of the Obama administration, especially Secretary of State Hillary Clinton, in working with the realities of the post-Arab Spring. "Creating an overarching doctrine suitable for the moment is an almost impossible task, particularly during a crisis that demands from American policy makers analytical humility, doctrinal plasticity, and a tolerance for contradiction" (p. 49). This call for uncertainty is repeated in many places in the article, though the author focuses much of his discussion on whether postrevolution countries such as Tunisia and Egypt are headed toward hazardous Islamist states or hopeful beacons of democratic change. One of the bellwethers of this dichotomy used by Goldberg is the role of the hijab, whether women are allowed to wear it, have an authentic choice about whether to wear it, or if they are required to wear it in public spaces. The centrality of the covering or uncovering of women's heads has historically been used by those in power on various sides as the issue that means national and religious autonomy of the postcolonial nation state or Westernized secular modernity.

Another story that caused even more of a backlash was on the September 17, 2012, cover of *Newsweek* that declared in huge letters, "MUSLIM RAGE: How I Survived it, How we Can End it" (Hirsi Ali, 2012). The author of the article inside the magazine is a politician with connections to Dutch political Islamophobia. She connected the motives for the attacks on 9/11 and the use of child brides with the tenets of Islam, painting a grim picture of the religion and focusing on the Western critique of Islam rather than on the diversity of views and beliefs of those who practice the religion globally. She wrote that intolerance has "become the defining characteristic of Islam" and "The Muslim men and women (and yes, there are plenty of women) who support—whether actively or passively—the idea that blasphemers deserve to suffer punishment are not a fringe group. On the contrary, they represent the mainstream of contemporary Islam" (para. 8). In a powerful use of social media and satire, Muslims coopted the *Newsweek* Twitter handle #muslimrage and created a counternarrative of humor. Some of the most popular Tweets include, "Lost your kid Jihad at the airport. Can't yell for him. #MuslimRage" and "I'm having such a good hair day. No one even knows. #MuslimRage." The response on Twitter showcases the American media's obsession with extreme visions of Muslims, generally associating Islam with terror, rage, and oppression of women.

Another high profile case of Islamophobia in the Western mass media is that of the Canadian weekly magazine, *Maclean's*. In fact, the Canadian Islamic Congress filed human rights complaints against the magazine with the Canadian Human Rights Commission, claiming that the magazine published 18 offensive articles between 2005 and 2007. The most inflammatory article was published as the cover story to the October 20, 2006, issue, ominously entitled, "The Future Belongs to Islam." The cover image is quite similar in subject to the image of a single female figure veiled entirely in black from *The Atlantic*. The *Maclean's* cover features a group of figures (presumably women, though we do not see their faces), a literally faceless sea of people with one small girl facing out to the reader, glaring at the photographer from beneath her black veil that covers all but her face. The image and the text combine to create a sense of overwhelming dread, that the reader (here a part of the White, "civilized" West) is about to be overtaken by groups of Muslims. The article inside the magazine is an excerpt from Mark Steyn's *America Alone* from 2006. The article, like the book it is excerpted from, is fiercely critical of Islam and presents Islam and Muslims as overtly and inherently threatening, primitive, and motivated for world domination. The text is avowedly and proudly anti-Islam; conservative Western media figures and scholars who share this sense of impending doom have celebrated it. The argument rests on racist and ethnocentric ideas that were cemented during colonialism of the 19th and 20th centuries and the eugenics movements of the early 20th century. Steyn (2008) wrote the following:

> In a few years, as millions of Muslim teenagers are entering their voting booths, some European countries will not be living formally under sharia, but—as much as parts of Nigeria, they will have reached an accommodation with their radicalized Islamic compatriots, who like many intolerant types are expert at exploiting the "tolerance" of pluralist societies. (para. 40)

Steyn critiqued Europe and the United States of America for their "welfare states" that he claimed produces lazy, dependent populations that are ripe for conquest. He also fired against ideas of tolerance and multiculturalism, forms of acceptance of others that he felt allows the darker, different, threatening others to gain trust and then take over. Steyn used demographic data to "prove" that the populations in Europe and North America (those he considers of worth and value—the White ones) are on a steep and frightening decline. He played on racist fears of the mythical fertile immigrant population, taking the place of the rightful White inhabitants. Though this article is an unusually blatant form of the racist, ethnocentric discourse of Islamophobia, it is related to the tone of the *Newsweek* piece and other similar stories that decry the future of Islam.

The Curricular Context

Children growing up in the United States learn about their world through several types of curricula that teach lessons about people and cultures that are different and/or distant. The official curriculum of the schools includes the planned lessons, textbooks, and standards set by the federal, state, and local level. Hidden curriculum entails all of the lessons that students learn in school that are not part of the planned curriculum, including lessons from social interaction and rules and policies governing the school day. The unofficial curriculum includes popular culture, media, toys, family, and peers that shape how we see the world. Though these curricula are quite different, the lessons learned from each make up the complex worldview that children use to interpret and understand the world. I am interested in how these three layers of curricula educate American children about difference, particularly the imagined differences as constructed after the attacks of September 11, 2001. The attacks of this day created an instant focus of attention and fear on the Muslim American communities. This sharp focus on an imagined community and on Muslims globally creates both opportunities and challenges for educators interested in multiculturalism and social justice.

The official curriculum of schools ranges widely, as some states worked to address the events of September 11th and the aftermath in changing social studies standards. Other states have not made official changes to standards to address 9/11, leaving it to local districts and teachers in classrooms to determine the way forward. There are several possible explanations for the lack of official curriculum about 9/11. School curriculum and state standards are already quite full, as textbooks and standards are added while little is ever removed from the official curriculum. Another important reason for the absence is fear of controversy and very different perspectives on what kind of story should be told about the events. Should the attacks of 9/11 be included in a broader discussion about global terrorism and placed alongside the Oklahoma City bombing as examples of contemporary terrorism? Should teachers critically discuss Western actions and imperialism that played a role in the complex context preceding the attacks? Is the story of 9/11 about Islamic extremism or American bravery? Were the ensuing actions of the American government like the passage of the Patriot Act and military action in Afghanistan and Iraq reasonable and necessary responses? Many school systems that choose to discuss 9/11 avoid the thorny and possibly controversial questions in favor of a focus on patriotism and remembering the actions of firefighters on that day. It is easier to avoid dealing with complex subjects that may not have clear lessons or answers than to give them their appropriate time and energy. Discussions of the Islamophobia and discrimination faced by many Arab Americans (or those perceived to be Arab or Muslim) in the wake of 9/11 are even more rare.

The few states that have specifically approved standards related to the teaching of 9/11 take very different approaches. Generally, students are asked to learn about the concept of terrorism including 9/11 in a broader context of terror and to examine the responses of the U.S. government to the attacks. Some states ask students to simply examine the responses while others ask students to analyze the appropriateness of the so-called War on Terror. In Louisiana, approved in 2011, students will "trace the rise in domestic and foreign terrorism and analyze its effects on America's way of life" and compare "anti-Japanese-American sentiment during World War II vs. anti-Muslim sentiment after 9/11" (Robelen, 2011, sidebar). Other states have standards that more specifically tie terrorism as a broad concept to Islamic fundamentalism. Massachusetts's standards from 2003 ask students to, "Explain the rise and funding of Islamic fundamentalism in the last half of the 20th century and identify the major events and forces in the Middle East over the last several decades" (Robelen, 2011, sidebar). Washington state's standards from 2008 ask students to examine the aftermath of the events of 9/11 through a more critical lens, to "weigh the validity of the attacks on 9/11 being the sole cause of the War on Terror" and "evaluate how classroom discussions and proposed alternative resolutions have changed or solidified one's own position on the constitutionality of the Patriot Act" (Robelen, 2011, sidebar).

In their detailed study from the Center for Information and Research on Civic Learning and Engagement (CIRCLE), Stoddard and Hess (2011) reviewed the state standards on 9/11 for themes and content. They found the following themes as a result of their analysis: the impact of 9/11; international versus domestic terrorism; what terrorism means and who are terrorists; the relationship between Islam and terrorism; the role of citizens post-9/11; open questions, deliberation, and inquiry; and a comparison of 9/11 with Pearl Harbor and similar moments of national crisis (pp. 7–13). The first finding, a focus on the impact of 9/11, asks students to learn about the aftermath and impact of the attacks in place of learning about the causes and context of the international terrorist groups and acts. The standards tended to focus on international terror with a few states mentioning terrorism in conjunction with Islam. Massachusetts's standards (notably written by Stotsky, author of the Fordham Foundation publication detailed later) are the most striking example of several findings, including language that links terrorism to Islamic Fundamentalism and mentions the United States and Israel as the only victims of these attacks.

While the state standards and coverage in textbooks are uneven in tone, scope, and quality, there are many resources and supplemental curricula that are available to teachers looking to engage with complex understandings of the context, events, and aftermath of 9/11. This curriculum is highly politicized, and there are forceful voices on the political right calling any revisions to curriculum that include knowledge or tolerance of Islam and Muslims as anti-Judeo Christian propaganda (Rodriguez, Weinstein, Hanson, & Mead, 2003; Stotsky, 2004). The conservative think tank, the Thomas B. Fordham Institute, funded and published two reports specifically detailing the lack of patriotism and the anti-American slant of the post-9/11 curricular materials. "Terrorists, Despots, and Democracy: What Our Children Need to Know," was written collectively by 29 scholars, policy makers, and educators including organization president and author of the introduction, Chester Finn. Finn presented the perceived problem of the 9/11 curriculum that he believed showed a distorted and un-American view to students:

> We first detected this problem soon after September 11, 2001, as we observed the curricular and pedagogical counsel that many of the profession's myriad organizations were supplying to their members. Simply stated, it was long on multiculturalism, feelings, relativism, and tolerance but short on history, civics, and patriotism. (Finn, cited in Rodriguez et al., 2003, p. 6)

For Finn, a curriculum that asks students to consider cultural differences, their emotional response to tragedy, and tolerance is "nonsense" (p. 6). In his short piece of the publication entitled "Preserving America, Man's Greatest Hope," Hanson (cited in Rodriguez et al., 2003) wrote, "Not all cultures are equal in their moral sensibilities; few dictators, theocrats, tribal leaders, or communists welcome the introspection and self-criticism that are necessary for moral improvement" (cited in Rodriguez et al., 2003, p. 23). The message of Hanson's piece is that American values are superior to those of other nations and cultures and that to teach multicultural understanding is a form of moral relativism that allows "the great evils of the 19th and 20th centuries," like "chattel slavery, German Nazism, Japanese militarism, and Soviet communism" (p. 23) to occur. It is striking that several of the authors compare the forces behind the attacks on 9/11 to the presence and support for slavery. Some of the contributors seem hostile to the very idea of multiculturalism and argue against a focus on the very real horrors and dark periods of history in which the U.S. government was complicit. Hymowitz (cited in Rodriguez et al., 2003) wrote the following in "The Choice We Face": "Of course, children cannot grow into reverent, discerning citizens if the history they is learn is simply a parade of smallpox-infected Indians, oppressed slaves, and internment camps for Japanese-Americans" (cited in Rodriguez et al., 2003, p. 33). For many of the authors in this volume, any focus on tolerance of difference and complex discussions of oppression and justice take away from the idea of American democracy.

Stotsky's (2004) publication for the Thomas B. Fordham Institute entitled, *The Stealth Curriculum: Manipulating History Teachers,* takes to task multiculturalism and tolerance of Islam in the post-9/11 era. The publication also focuses on the ways that the Holocaust, African American history, and Native American history are presented in supplemental curriculum and professional development programs for social studies teachers. In his foreword to the text, Finn (cited in Stotsky, 2004) tellingly used the heading, "Charting a Dark Continent," to describe the "vast dark continent within our public (and private) education system" (cited in Stotsky, 2004, p. 7). He used this vestige of European colonialism, specifically the reference of darkness and lack of "civilization" of precolonialized Africa, to discuss his perspective on the danger of political correctness and multicultural history curriculum. In the foreword, Finn also made excuses for the lack of comprehensiveness or even systematic sampling in Stotsky's analysis of the curricular materials. He wrote, "We agreed from the outset, however, that this would be an exploratory review, based largely on the examples that had already made their way into her 'collection,' rather than a comprehensive study" (cited in Stotsky, 2004, p. 8). The collection includes hand-picked examples of supplemental curriculum and professional development that fit Stotsky's ideological perspective rather than a systematic review of materials available or in use. Finn and Stotsky critiqued multicultural education and the selected materials as ideologically rather than academically based, but they did not recognize their own ideological bias.

For Stotsky (2004), any curriculum that questions the inherent goodness and righteousness of America and the West is problematic and ideologically biased. She critiqued the curriculum from Facing History and Ourselves (2002) entitled *Race and Membership in American History: The Eugenics Movement.* She took issue with the linkages the materials make between the American eugenics movement and Hitler's genocide of the Jews in the Holocaust. She provided tacit defense of American eugenicists whose work supported the involuntary sterilization of Americans deemed "unfit" to reproduce. She claimed that the text "cleverly connects Hitler's use of the ideas of German scientists on racial 'eugenics' to an acknowledgement of the leadership of American scientists, educators, and policy makers in the eugenics movement that Americans appear almost directly responsible for the Final Solution" (p. 18). The author offered no explanation about why she places German eugenics in quotation marks but does not place the American version in them. It implies that American eugenics was a valid scientific movement that had no connection to racism or pseudoscience. The idea that the American eugenics movement was a shameful period of intense racism is not part of Stotsky's analysis; she argued that it is anti-American to even suggest this.

The analysis of African American history is based on two promotional guides from 1997 and 1998, respectively, and Stotsky (2004) took offense at the *Teacher's Guide* to a PBS series entitled, *Africans in America: America's Journey Through Slavery*. She critiqued the guide that "says that the Africans arriving in the English colonies in America were 'abducted from their homelands' omitting mention of indigenous African slavery, the indigenous African slave trade, and the roles played by African royal families and African slave-traders" (p. 24). She wanted curriculum on slavery in America to place at least a portion of the blame on Africans rather than on the European Americans importing, buying, and selling human beings as property. As with the eugenics argument, this critique seems to be defensive and ideologically founded in an attempt to shift as much historical blame and shame away from White Americans.

Visuality and the Arab Spring

The phenomenon known as the Arab Spring has created unique examples of Western media and public attention focused on countries and people who have been marginalized as "seeds of terror." Western images of those living in the Middle East or Arab World (both problematic categories) have historically held traces of Orientalism, without thought to the humanity and complexity of those on the ground. The revolutionary movements in Tunisia, Egypt, Libya, Yemen, Syria, and Bahrain have de-centered our (American) sense of exclusive right to the terms *freedom, democracy,* and *liberty,* and forced a reconsideration of whether these terms require redefinition. Are we the keepers of democracy or those who stand in the way of democracy if it is messy, complex, and may involve people who don't look like us? I believe that the historical legacy of Orientalism and the toxic xenophobia that has been growing in the West in the wake of 9/11 can be challenged through education that centers the struggle for liberation and courage in the face of oppression and violence that have been part of this Arab Spring. Additionally, the gendered force of this Western representation of the other can be disrupted through use of contemporary images of protest and power that alter the simple Western equation of veil = oppressed. I argue that the construction of a Islam/Middle East/Arab world (which has continually been collapsed through the connected but unique forces of Islamophobia and toxic xenophobia) is challenged through the public struggle for democracy and justice. Orientalist representations that reinforce ideas of Muslim women as voiceless and oppressed have been fundamentally disproven by media images that can't help but show images of veiled women protesting, screaming at armed guards, and leading in the revolutionary movements. The protests in Egypt have been widely publicized, and images of Egyptian women have been part of the coverage although rarely the focus of coverage. In protests in Yemen and other countries that are not on the mainstream American map because they do not attract tourism, images of the protest are rarely shown, especially images of individual protesters. Women are at the forefront of the revolutionary protests in Yemen, but this narrative of powerful women in leadership positions does not fit into the trope of the victim that has been propagated by Western images of women—who are not Western, American, and "liberated" in the way from the image of the liberation popular in the West.

The ways in which images of women yelling at security forces and taking the lead in organizing the energy of the public movement led to a breakdown of gender roles and norms in many of these cases. The majority of Western media outlets only presented gender as a central feature of these events when there were acts of violence against women, as in the case of the Western reporter who was sexually assaulted in the celebrations once Mubarak stepped down. However, there are women leading protests who are beginning to attract the attention of Western media outlets. Tawakkol Karman, a journalist and human rights advocate, has become a high profile woman in Yemen, a leading figure in the opposition protests that have rocked the government of President Saleh. The Arab Spring offers unprecedented opportunities for educators to complicate and challenge Western notions of freedom, democracy, and liberation. The imagery of protestors, especially women leading and participating in protests, can be powerful pedagogical tools in the disruption of xenophobia and misinformation that construct Islam as the enemy and Muslim women as inherently oppressed and in need of rescue from the West. These images need to be part of a reimagined critical multicultural border pedagogy (Kincheloe & Steinberg, 1997) that engages with issues of power and privilege explicitly.

Comics After 9/11

Recent popular culture and news representations are continuing to blur into what Barber (1995) referred to as the "infotainment telesector," meaning the increasing focus on the entertainment value of the "news" and the increasing "reality" of the entertainment. As channels scramble to attract viewers to 24-hour cable news stations, there is a drive to create entertaining narratives and present news from specific ideological and political positions. Fox News, though it claims the tagline "Fair and Balanced," presents local, national, and global events through a conservative lens that often focuses on a fear of difference and distrust of the government. MSNBC is a cable news network that presents events through a liberal ideological and political lens. One result of this expansion of news to 24 hours and to multiple, ideologically based channels is that Americans often listen to voices who tell them the news that aligns with their worldview. It is increasingly rare to hear disparate perspectives on issues of importance expressed and debated with respect and intelligent argument. With a dearth of nuanced interpretations of events like 9/11 on the news, authors and artists fill a void. Comics and graphic narratives provide authors with time and space to explore complex ideas through image and text. Single panel or sequence comics can capture a single idea from various, provocative perspectives, while the graphic novel gives readers complex and unfolding narratives that are not easily digestible or reducible to sound bites.

Comics of various forms and genres played important visual roles in the aftermath of the terrorist attacks of 9/11. Political cartoonists used the imagery of heroes and villains, the images of American symbols variously injured, hurt, crying, or angry and vengeful. Comics authors wrote entire graphic narratives based directly or indirectly on the attacks like Art Spiegelman's (2001) *In the Shadow of No Towers,* which is his artistic reaction to the overwhelming horror, confusion, and courage of 9/11 and a critical representation of the increased surveillance and security in the United

States after that day. The attacks of 9/11 were quite personal for Spiegelman: the World Trade Center was mere blocks from his home in New York City, and his daughter had just started high school near what became Ground Zero. The large pages of the graphic book are a complex story of Spiegelman's struggle to negotiate the real and lasting trauma of the September 11th attacks in the streets of New York City with the marketing of 9/11 as patriotic grandstanding and war mongering. Spiegelman is highly critical of President George W. Bush and the use of the tragedy in service of war against terror. One of the more striking images is a cartoon of Bush and Cheney riding a giant bald eagle. Cheney is slitting the eagle's throat as Bush says, "Let's roll!" and the eagle says, "Why do they *hate* us? **Why???**" (p. 4). The tower's burning structure frames the page, running the length of the page with the text, "Our hero is trapped reliving traumas of Sept. 11, 2001 …Unbeknownst to him, brigands suffering from war fever have hijacked those tragic events . . ." (p. 4). Events unfold on several levels throughout the book: the inner workings of Spiegelman's traumatized mind, the streets of New York City, filled with the toxic residue of the attack, and the larger geopolitical stage, where war is undertaken with relish by politicians far from combat.

The image of the burning metal structure of one tower recurs throughout the short yet hefty book. In addition to the burning shadow of the towers, the visual elements of the book veer between panels featuring painterly representations of Spiegelman's (2001) daughter Nadja in school, the author as man, mouse, and historical cartoon figures. The second full page spread of comics includes many different visual approaches and gives a sense of the fractured nature of Spiegelman's mental and artistic state in the wake of the attacks. In the first row of panels on the page, Spiegelman draws images of himself with a patriotic bald eagle, hanging from a noose around his neck. The eagle says the following in the four-panel sequence, "Everything's changed! Awk!," "Go out and shop! Awk," "Awk!," and "Be afraid!" (p. 2). The eagle represents the knee-jerk patriotism that followed the 9/11 attacks, which were far from the realities and tragedy on the ground. Even as the bald eagle spouts the patriotic platitudes, Spiegelman is driven close to madness reliving the trauma of the crashing towers. In the fourth panel of the row, Spiegelman's eyes turn into crazed red spirals and the panels turn to the side, transforming into the two towers, flaming after the attack. The next row begins with a large, painterly panel showing the author in mouse mask slumped over his desk with Osama bin Laden holding a bloody sword over one side of him and George W. Bush holding a gun on his other side. The text box under this image reads, "Equally terrorized by al-Qaeda and by his own government . . . . Our Hero looks over some ancient comics pages instead of working. He dozes off and relives his ringside seat to that day's disaster yet again, trying to figure out what he actually saw" (p. 2). The rest of the spread includes panels that veer between what appear to be pixelated photos of the two smoking towers, comic images that represent the author and his wife as the attack began, and very cartoonish figures with towers growing out of their heads. The juxtaposition of the very realistic images of the towers with the two shocked-looking characters with tower heads creates a sense of disjuncture and confusion. This disjuncture mirrors the author's own sense of chaos the day of the attacks, epitomized by the panel showing a realistic image of the billboard for the Schwarzenegger film *Collateral Damage*, about fictional acts of terror. The final row of panels on this page depicts a tragic but beautiful series of images of the crumbling, burning skeleton of the tower. The very final panel is shaped in an exclamation point with a brain in the circle. The variety of image types and the range of subject and tone between panels on each page continue throughout the text. The following page includes a panel from a 1962 comic showing the capital building under attack from alien spacecraft and an older drawing of two young children in gas masks, "NYC to kids: Don't Breathe!" (p. 3).

Many graphic artists contributed shorter pieces to two volumes of *9/11 Volume 1: Artists Respond* (2002) and *9/11 Volume 2*. The short graphic pieces vary widely in style and substance. Some are patriotic celebrations that valorize the first responders; others are more somber and poetic memorials to those who died. Still others are more metaphorical in their connection to the attacks. One of the stranger contributions is by Mark Martin and depicts happy, childlike figures laughing and dancing on a hill of daisies. A large wolf standing on a pile of explosives dons a happy figure mask and asks one to "Pull my finger" (Martin, 2002, p. 32). When one of the happy, carefree creatures pulls the wolf's finger, we see an almost blank panel that reads, "poof," and suddenly the happy creatures are in heaven with a sign for "free pie," and the wolf is in a fiery hell, holding a card that reads, "Get into heaven free" (p. 32). This single-page comic stands out for its easy dichotomy of good versus evil, total innocence versus total corruption; it also stands out for the pastel colors of the panels and the happy, frolicking figures. Most of the other contributions are more somber in visual element and in tone. Several others make the case that the days following the attacks of 9/11 were not the time to laugh, make light, or be concerned with the everydayness of life. In "Clown's Day Off" by Landridge (2002, p. 52), the panels of this single-page comic make the point that even clowns, like the main character in the panels, have to take the day off and sit in somber darkness. The final panel of the page shows the clown, a letter that was written before the news of the attacks torn into pieces at his feet while he listens to the radio in the darkness. The piece by Darnell and Barta (2002) entitled simply, "What's Important," breaks down many of the everyday obsessions, thoughts, and activities that seemed important on September 10th. Things such as "the big game," "the latest fashions," and "other people's private lives" once felt terribly important, but tragedy on the scale of the deaths on 9/11 gave instant perspective (pp. 69–70). For others in the anthology, the days following the attacks prompted questions of how the violence of the attacks would be met with violent revenge in return. The untitled piece by Laurie Ross (2002) communicates her experience trying to commute to work near the Pentagon on September 11th. The first two pages of the piece document the confusion and fear of the morning that build to a surprising ending on the third page. Ross explodes with, "Now who are we gonna bomb? That's what happens now, right? We don't live long enough to learn any lessons, much less pass them on . . . so it's the same bloody mistakes over and over again! We're doomed!" (p. 73). Though a few pieces call for vengeance, there are more that question the effect of violence in response to violence. In "An Expert Opinion," (Macan, 2002) a father is lecturing his son and the audience about the cycle of violence, that if one responds to violence with violence then there will never be peace. "And in the long run, the sole result of violence is more violence, a self-propagation of destruction!" (p. 40). The panel that directly follows this part of the lecture shows the father slapping and then kicking his son out of the frame for interrupting; the son retaliates by planting a bomb at his father's feet in the final panel. The hypocrisy of those who call for peace then act with violence. A few of the pieces in *9/11 Volume 1: Artists Respond* (2002) are openly critical of U.S. foreign policy and question the role that the Central Intelligence Agency (CIA) and politicians have played in arming the Taliban and in propagating xenophobia. In the two-page comic entitled "Which One Is Real?" (Harris & Ruth, 2002, pp. 94–95), a series of images flashes across the page, as floating pieces of burning paper above the ashes of the World Trade Center. On the pieces of paper, text narrates images of conflicting and contradictory aspects of certain figures and groups, and the reader is supposed to decide which of the contradictory questions is real. "The George W. Bush who spoke at Bob Jones University, appealing to southern racists? Or the George W. Bush who invoked benevolent Allah before Congress?" (Harris & Ruth, 2002, p. 94). The images and text go on to illustrate seemingly incompatible aspects of televangelist Jerry Falwell, the CIA, the New York Police Department, the Taliban, Oliver North, and America the nation. "America, builder of coalitions, defender of world freedom? Or America, ignorer of treaties on global warming, biological weapons, money laundering . . . arms trafficking, missile defense, tobacco control, nuclear testing, and child labor?" (p. 95). The end of the comic reveals, of course, that all of the contradictory information is real. By asking readers to accept that there is good and evil that exist in all sides, this comic stands in direct contrast to the handful in the collection that celebrate the good versus evil rhetoric. This kind of critical questioning of American policy was rare and risky in the days immediately following the 9/11 attacks. "What Is Real?" asks readers to accept ambiguity and a complex world of gray areas and the banality of evil. Is there a danger of equating the actions of George W. Bush, Falwell, and the Taliban? There are fundamental distinctions in the actions of these players on the world stage, and many would find offense at the equivalence of these actions.

In the years following the attacks, Sid Jacobson and Ernie Colón (2006) published *The 9/11 Report: A Graphic Adaptation,* a straightforward graphic retelling of the official report of the 9-11 Commission. The report was released to the public in text form, a dense 585-page report available on the 9-11 Commission's website. The authors of the original report decided to enlist graphic artists to create a comic version of the report to reach a more diverse audience of readers. The Commission Chair, Thomas H. Kean, and the Vice Chair, Lee H. Hamilton (cited in Jacobson & Colón, 2006), wrote the following in the foreword:

> It was the goal of the commission to tell the story of 9/11 in a way that the American people could read and understand. We felt strongly that one of the most important and tragic events in our nation's history needed to be accessible to all. (p. ix)

Unlike other graphic representations of 9/11 that focus on the attacks and their aftermath, the report spends the majority of its narrative looking backward into two areas: inside the terror network and the organization and planning of the attacks and inside the various government agencies and political leaders who were unable to see the attacks coming or prevent their occurrence. The story inside the minds and plots of al-Qaeda and the teams of terrorists sent to board and crash commercial airliners into key targets is disturbing and fascinating; it reads like a crime novel and moves briskly through time. The parallel story of the government agencies is frustratingly slow, with many missed opportunities and a convoluted system of intelligence and security systems that left gaping holes for terrorists to exploit. Even in graphic form, which lends the excitement of visual illustrations and the promise of action and movement, the machinations and foibles of government agencies are not very interesting. A fundamental question about this version (or any graphic adaptation for that matter) must be asked: does the image/text add a profoundly new way to understand the material and/or does it engage new audiences with the text?

This adaptation succeeds modestly on both accounts. The most interesting visual translation occurs in the first chapter, "We Have Some Planes." From page 6 through 17, the authors split each page into four columns of a timeline to represent the four planes hijacked on that day. The panels for each plane appear when an important event took place, giving the reader a vivid sense of the minute-by-minute unfolding of the attacks and their chaotic complexity. By reading this graphic timeline, important points become clear that may not have been read as easily in text, for example, the fact that due to a delay, United Airlines Flight 93 did not depart until 8:42 a.m., a full 28 minutes after air traffic controllers had lost radio contact with American Airlines Flight 11. Reading this graphic timeline adds profound new meaning to the text of the report, but other attempts to add meaning though graphic convention do not add as much. On page 36, the authors show images of the 21 flags of the nations from which Osama bin Laden had recruited terrorists. The rows of flags do not necessarily carry more weight or impact than a list of those nations. One of the most powerful sections of the report is in the recommendations section. Here, the text urges the U.S. government to "offer an example of moral leadership committed to treat people humanely, abide by the rule of law, and be generous and caring to our neighbors. The vision of the future should stress life over death: individual educational and economic opportunity" (Jacobson & Colón, 2006, p. 119). This page of recommendations focuses on nonmilitary approaches to reducing terrorism through education, humanitarianism, and diplomacy. Oddly, the image the authors of the graphic adaptation chose to accompany this text is a large drawing of two American soldiers standing with guns raised at the opening of a cave. It forms a strange juxtaposition of language that speaks to a strategy of global undertaking that focuses on peaceful engagement and understanding paired with an image of impending violence set in what looks to be a cave in Afghanistan. It is one of the few places in the book where the graphic authors took great artistic liberty with the text of the report; primarily the images are straightforward illustrations of the text and do not attempt to add or change the meaning of the report.

In terms of representing difference, the text sticks to clear visual assumptions and distinctions between Americans and Muslims. A clear example of this visual distinction is on page 117. The text is about the progress that was made in Afghanistan after the American military overthrew the Taliban but recommends that more focus be placed on diplomatic and humanitarian efforts. Visually, the page is cut in half, with an American tank and heavily armed soldiers walking toward the reader. On the bottom half of the page, a large panel is filled with angry, chanting Afghan men with guns and bullets strapped to their chests. The men range from angry, to evil, to crazy in facial expression and a large fist thrusts up in the air toward the viewer. This page clearly shows the stereotype of Afghan men and the Taliban and negates the text that calls for greater access to education and states, "the U.S. presence is overwhelmingly oriented toward military and security work" (Jacobson & Colón, 2006, p. 117).

The representations of women in the graphic adaptation are either highly professional political figures like Condoleezza Rice, whose image is nonfictional, well-known, and presented in a standard way, or highly stereotypical representations of fictional women. The nonpolitical Western women represented in the book are primarily found in the section on the actual collapse of the Twin Towers and the massive rescue operation. From pages 86 to 98, the images of injured and rescued individuals show many women, mostly in rather short skirts being rescued and often carried by firefighters (all of whom appear to be men). "The imagined women do not speak. When their faces are shown, they are terrified or defeated . . . the women are portrayed as fleeing, crying, fainting, hiding, or holding onto a man for support" (Wiederhold, 2013, p. 431). One of only two panels representing Muslim women is on page 51 and shows one woman leaning against a wall, protecting a child behind her skirt, and another covered, frightened woman carrying a young child and fleeing from men wielding machetes and automatic weapons, while the only other women are dead on the ground. The only other representation is on page 75, in the middle left panel depicting an al-Qaeda meeting in Pakistan. The woman is in the foreground and does not have any part in the meeting but is there for unclear reasons, possibly to set the scene and mark it as Muslim with the stereotypical face and head covering niqab.

Other graphic responses were less directly related to the events of 9/11 but were clearly related to the narratives of us versus them, good versus evil, American freedom versus the terrorism of Islamic extremists. Many artists used the traditional imagery of comic superheroes as symbols of American freedom and power. "The media seemed eager to turn our designated guardians of national security into action toys and superheroes . . . . The president's vows to get the 'evildoers' won him media praise *because* it sounded cartoonish" (Faludi, 2007, p. 47). On the Internet, many fans created and posted art that depicted famous American comic book heroes reacting with horror and despair in front of the wreckage of the World Trade Center towers. "At the same time, the actual superheroes—Superman and Spider-Man—were universally depicted as powerless. In the 9/11 comics, the superheroes stand in front of the smoldering mound with their arms dangling at their sides" (Faludi, 2007, p. 51). Superman and Captain America are potent symbols of American power and righteousness, and they are also heroes that are hyper masculine. DC Comics responded to the use of Superman's image in reference to 9/11 on the cover of *9/11 Volume 2*. The cover image shows firefighters, doctors, police officers, and paramedics standing proudly in the center with Superman and his super dog literally looking up to the first responders saying, "Wow." This official Superman imagery response forces the reader to question the nature of heroes and how the fantasy of the superhero may not be where true heroism lies. It is important to note that all of the many first responders, save two female doctors at the lower edges of the image, are men. This image may question fantastic images of heroic masculinity, but it reinforces the masculine identification of heroes. The overwhelming narrative that the various media outlets crafted out of the attacks was that male heroes helped rescue (primarily) female victims, even though many of the first-hand accounts tell stories of more complexity.

One of the more striking and controversial graphic publications about 9/11 is *We Shall Never Forget 9/11 Coloring Book—Graphic Coloring Novel* (2011), with ColoringBook.com listed as the author and Really Big Coloring Books listed as the editor and illustrator. This graphic coloring book is advertised by its creator: "To the American people and all others who may read this child's coloring book, We Shall Never Forget is designed to be a tool that parents can use to help teach children about the facts surrounding 9/11. This book also describes basic freedoms in America" (back cover). The images and text inside this coloring book present a very specific perspective of the events of 9/11 (and of the time before and after). The book shows a female news anchor announcing that Osama bin Laden was identified as the mastermind behind the attack and continues with, "These attacks will change the way America deals with and views the Islamic and Muslim people around the world" (p. 13). This quote equates the terrorists with all Muslims (and Islamic people, which is confusing and inaccurate). One of the more controversial pages illustrates the killing of Osama bin Laden by a member of Navy SEAL Team 6, with the Navy SEAL pointing the a gun at Osama bin Laden as he attempts to use a veiled woman as a human shield. Some of the text that accompanies this image reads, "Children, the truth is, these terrorist acts were done by freedom-hating radical Islamic Muslim extremists. These crazy people hate the American way of life because we are FREE and our society is FREE" (p. 19). The book uses very basic and American-centric concepts of good and evil to describe 9/11, and in many places it conflates Osama bin Laden with all Muslims. "When an enemy is invisible, living in caves on the other side of the earth or in the recesses of our darkest imagination, he is easily transformed into a phantom, the inchoate demon of fairy tales and childhood dreams" (Ewen & Ewen, 2006, p. 496). The customer reviews of the book are fascinating and reveal a large divide between those who believe that the story of American freedom and vengeance is a basic and righteous educational tool and those who find the book to be racist, dangerously simplistic, and inaccurate. Of the 24 reviews on Amazon.com, 13 gave the book a full five stars and glowing reviews; the other 11 gave it one star and were highly critical of its messages. There are no reviews with two, three, or four stars; the people fired up enough to write a review of the book are clearly polarized. One of the five star reviews reads as follows: "It's simple. If you are pro-America, you love it. If you're a Muslim, you hate it. I was amused by the one-star reviews, some of them obviously written by the same person. A refreshing change in content that opposes the leftist views of the public school system" (vociferous, 1/9/12). Another review reads as follows: "Teaches hatred to children. It may be directed towards muslims here, but hatred is hatred. It's our choice whether we choose to teach hate in our houses" (verychilli, 9/1/11). The second volume of this coloring book series, *We Shall Never Forget 9/11— Vol. II: The True Faces of Evil—Terror* (2012), takes the simplistic pro-America message farther and broadens the scope of the first book to include state-sponsored terrorists and terrorist trading cards. The publicity from the company's website reads as follows:

> This is Good vs. Evil. We Shall Never Forget 9/11 Vol. II Terrorist Trading Cards clearly identifies the evil that may sit next to you on an airplane, or it could be an avowed Atheist in the parking lot of your local grocer on a sunny morning. The world should look at them, make fun of them, name them—shame them, recognize who they are and rid the earth of them. (Coloringbook.com, para. 5)

This description is a straightforward call to separate the world into good versus evil, with evil extending to an "avowed Atheist" and a call to "rid the earth of them." Though the book does not call on vigilantes to violently attack Atheists in parking lots, it leads a reader toward that conclusion. The trading cards are a diverse group, including likely suspects Osama bin Laden, Saddam Hussein, and Muammar Gaddafi; the cards do include some White American terrorists like Timothy McVeigh and Jared Loughner, which broadens the narrow focus on Islamic extremism of the rest of the two books. The strangest inclusions in the terrorist trading cards are Bill Ayers and Julian Assange (founder of Wikileaks). Assange spearheaded the release of thousands of classified documents and videos from the American military and diplomatic cables. He did not plan or execute physical violence or destruction of any kind.

On the tenth anniversary of the attacks of 9/11/01, the public sentiment about what had changed, what we collectively remembered and were supposed to remember, was captured in a multitude of political cartoons that ran in newspapers and online on 9/11/11. Many of these cartoons (9/11 Political Cartoons, 2011) use the images of Uncle Sam and Lady Liberty as visual metaphors for the nation, yet these two figures represent different ideals of America. Uncle Sam is the uber-masculine idea of America as the defender of freedom, the powerful and influential actor who is willing to act with force on the world stage to protect American ideals. Lady Liberty stands for something quite different; like Uncle Sam, she stands as a reminder of the liberty and freedoms promised in the Constitution and Bill of Rights. However, she also stands for the American ideals of accepting immigrants onto our shores, being inclusive of different types and groups of people, and the sheltering of those who need assistance. The gender differences of the two mythical figures and what they represent in these 9/11 anniversary cartoons carry great meaning. In one powerful cartoon by Martin Sutovec from the *SME Daily*, Lady Liberty is shown choking on smoke from her own flame because she has been trapped under a glass dome by a paranoid Uncle Sam who is shown pointing a gun outside of the frame at some undefined threat. It is a powerful visual commentary on the price of "security" and the effect on civil liberties in the face of the amorphous and ever-present "War on Terror." Some cartoons, such as the one by Jeff Parker of *Florida Today*, show Uncle Sam as a sad, fatherly figure. In this cartoon a small girl asks Uncle Sam, "Why do we place our hand over our heart to say the pledge?" and he answers, "Well, on this day, we do it to keep our hearts from breaking" (9/11 Political Cartoons, 2011, p. 5). Uncle Sam here is more the protective father of the nation (especially for young girls, who need the most protection) than the defender of American freedom. In many of the cartoons depicting Uncle Sam, he is drawn holding his hat in his hands, as a sign of mourning but also of weakness in the face of the attack and global uncertainty. Several show a hatless Uncle Sam holding onto his hat, or a rose, or a candle. Only one of this collection show him with tears streaming down his face. One especially masculine yet mournful cartoon shows him baring his muscular chest with a ragged scar cut into his skin, "9/11." One notable exception to this mournful depiction of Uncle Sam is by Bob Englehart of the *Hartford Courant*, which focuses in tightly on Uncle Sam's iconic hat brim and eyes. His eyes are bright orange flames of fury, speaking to the rage and desire for revenge that many felt in the wake of the attacks. Lady Liberty is again shown as vulnerable and victimized in the cartoon by R. J. Matson of the *St. Louis Post-Dispatch*. Here, she is watching over a city engulfed in smoke with a giant knife stuck in her back. As opposed to the cartoons depicting Uncle Sam, many mournful but only one with visible tears, almost all of the cartoons depicting Lady Liberty show her crying.

Most of the cartoons are highly patriotic, though there are a few that are critical of American policy in the 10 years since the attacks. One cartoon by Rob Tornoe of *The Philadelphia Inquirer* shows several figures from the 10 years after the attacks that critically question American policy. A gravestone reads, "1 million plus deaths," a TSA agent is about to do a body cavity search on a naked and cowering man, a hooded figure references the torture and abuse at Abu Ghraib prison, Obama is lighting a cigarette with a flaming IOU, Uncle Sam is shown with all of his pockets turned out and empty, a New York City firefighter is denied health coverage, a diminutive George W. Bush is shown in his "Mission Accomplished" outfit holding a copy of a burning Constitution, all with a couple of drones overhead. In one panel, this cartoon effectively captures the events and policies that most Americans would rather forget, those that have had negative consequences since 9/11. The narratives of American policy as a negative global force, one that involves torture, the killing of civilians, and the erosion of civil liberties in the name of protecting freedom, are stories that make it harder to view America as an innocent victim. The reality of remembering 9/11 and the actions and policies that followed are complex and troubling on many levels. Faludi (2007) wrote of this trouble in *Terror Dream: Fear and Fantasy in Post-9/11 America*. For Faludi, the attacks were certainly important, but the reactions and media representations in the wake of the attacks are more telling and intriguing. The reaction to the attacks were not primarily based on the realities of the horrifying deaths of men, women, and children (though mostly adults) from various ethnic and religious backgrounds in New York City, Washington, DC, and the crash site in rural Pennsylvania. Much of the public media and political reaction was based on a longstanding myth of what it means to be American and to be seemingly invincible. This, according to Faludi, was a gendered process of myth reinforcement, with the hyper masculinity of the John Wayne western film held as the ideal form of American grit and protection. This gendered response to the attacks played out in images of masculine firefighters and police officers saving injured, frightened women. In reality, women and men functioned as heroic first responders and victims were both men and women. When constructing meaning from these events, the media and graphic artists crafted a highly masculine image of American patriotism and equated American manhood with a sense of safety and security in uncertain times.

In the initial days after the attacks of 9/11, there was a period of American public mourning over loss and garnering sympathy from around the globe. This was soon replaced in many media outlets by saber rattling and calls for revenge. President Bush set the tone for this call for revenge by immediately calling those behind the attacks "evildoers" and rhetorically dividing the world into good, free, Americans and evil, which included oppressive Islamic extremists. In a comic from the book, *9/11 Volume 1: Artists Respond* (2002), Moore and Gebbie respond to this rhetoric of good versus evil in their comic, "This is Information." "Dangerous now, to simplify, to trade reality's moral grey for comic-book black and white. Writing comic-book morality is embarrassingly easy. See, super-villains don't need *motives* for doing anything, killing, maiming, whatever. They're just evil" (p. 189). The image that accompanies the text depicts a villain menacingly tying Lady Liberty to railroad tracks, mirroring many post-9/11 political cartoons. "If the enemy is evil, no motive is required. History, politics, economics, all of these are irrelevant when writing super-villains" (p. 190). The comic goes on to call for learning about common humanity and a tolerance and understanding for the complexity of global history and relationships. Unlike the black and white, good and evil world of fiction and comics, in the actual world of human interaction, it does not make sense to use such Manichaean terms.

A few journalists and scholars dared to bring up the complexity of history and the international interventions by the United States that may have provided military support for the Mujahideen in their fight against the Soviet Union during the height of the Cold War. A few others dared to suggest that the United States should work globally with partners to strategically fight the Taliban, Osama bin Laden, and al-Qaeda. Author Katha Pollitt wrote in *The Nation* on October 8, 2001, in which she tells the story of a discussion she had with her daughter about whether to fly an American flag from their apartment window. By suggesting that the American flag is a symbol that stands for a complex and often bloody history, Pollitt was skewered and called all sorts of names. "She was called a bad mother, charged with, variously, 'lunacy,' 'ignorance,' 'idiocy,' 'facile insipidities,' and designated one of the 'chattering asses'" (Faludi, 2007, p. 29). Faludi (2007) contended that women who dared to speak up in the media with anything but utter, blind patriotism in the wake of 9/11 were subject to especially vile and brutal personal attacks.

Though American women who spoke out with measured or critical voices after the attacks were vilified, the Bush administration used the language of women's liberation as a justification for waging war in Afghanistan. In addition to sending American troops to topple the Taliban and find Osama bin Laden, Bush and his allies argued that the women of Afghanistan needed to be rescued from the oppression of their burqas and the restrictions of the Taliban. There was a sudden surge of attention and interest on the part of American politicians and media in the plight of Afghan women, referring to these women as "'a world of ghost women,' 'blue ghosts,' 'walking ghosts,' 'shrouded ghosts,' 'downtrodden ghosts,' and 'silent ghosts'" (Faludi, 2007, p. 40). The wives of the leaders of the United States and Great Britain, Laura Bush and Cherie Blaire, met to have a heavily promoted meeting and press conference about the plight of these women. The freedom and rights of Western women were compared favorably with the experience of women under Taliban rule, and multiple books suddenly appeared on bookshelves with burqa-clad women on the front. A small sample of titles released in the few years after the attack were *Price of Honor: Muslim Women Lift the Veil of Silence on the Islamic World* (Goodwin, 2003), *Zoya's Story: An Afghan Woman's Struggle for Freedom* (Follain & Cristofari, 2002), *Behind the Burqa: Our Life in Afghanistan and How We Escaped to Freedom* (Sulima & Hala, 2002), and more recently, *Beneath the Pale Blue Burqa: One Woman's Journey through Taliban Strongholds* (Danes, 2010). The covers of these books look like almost exact copies, one or more burqa-clad woman, unavailable for view. Other images from the time show a woman peeling away her burqa, this after the mission for rescue by the American military is supposedly accomplished. This interest in the lives and fate of Afghan women were mostly forgotten and de-prioritized after the American military began its offensive in the country. As the war progressed through time and the American military and diplomatic core were negotiating with the Taliban and others to form a new government, the voices of women were mostly excluded. It certainly seemed that the Bush administration used the rhetoric of women's liberation as a form of moral justification for attack, dropping it as soon as justification was no longer necessary. Faludi (2007) suggested that the justification of women's liberation never had feminism or the actual lives and self-determination of Afghan women at its root; the reason for the focus on removing the burqa was about maintaining American masculinity and rushing in to "save" the women from evil. Defense Secretary Donald Rumsfeld said in a National Public Radio interview from 2002, "the United States had saved Afghan women: 'Women have stopped being repressed. They can actually walk out in the street and not have their entire faces and bodies covered by burqas. They can laugh on the street'" (Faludi, 2007, p. 44). While it was true that some women had a modicum of more personal freedom in large cities, the long-term fate of women across the vast country, and their role in shaping or participating in any political process, was not part of the American agenda. It is impossible to determine the actual motives of all members of the Bush administration, but it seems as if the rhetoric about rescue and saving the women of Afghanistan reaffirmed American moral and cultural superiority to the "savage" Afghan men, and once the "saving" was supposedly accomplished, interest in real power and self-determination was lost.

This escalating cycle of fear and violence since September 11th has played out in international politics and relations that have centered on the notion of the "clash of civilizations" set forth by an influential book by Samuel Huntington (1996). The basic idea of Huntington's argument is that in post-Cold War global interactions, it will be divisions of culture and "civilization" rather than ideology or politics that will cause conflict and war. After September 11th, many scholars point to Huntington's book as prescient, that the current acts of Islamic extremists and the violent retaliation from the United States are the inevitable result of our divergent civilizations.

CHAPTER FIVE

Muslims in the American Media: *The Muslims I Know, All-American Muslim,* and Graphic Representations

All-American Muslim (Braxton, 2011) and *The Muslims I Know* (Ahmed, 2008) are two media representations of Muslim Americans that add to and disrupt the current of toxic xenophobia in the United States. Toxic xenophobia works to mark the other as fundamentally different from and outside the imagined community and trying to destroy that which the community holds most dear (Bailey Jones, 2011). I argue that the popular education Americans are receiving about difference (constructed as both inherent and toxic) is in many ways challenged by recent media interventions. The educational effectiveness and potential of these media are impacted by size of audience, scope, and backlash framed by the toxic xenophobia. The paradox of educating about difference is that efforts to change and challenge bias are often thwarted by the blinding effects of the bias. Other entries into American and global media have a stated goal of counteracting Islamophobia and the flattened images available to young people about Muslims in the media.

These works variously confront and reinscribe the tropes of the Muslim American as same, other, and toxic. The placement of Muslim Americans outside the imagined community of Americans was a collective reaction that built on a long history of Western Orientalism. The way that the ethnogenesis in the wake of 9/11 transformed into toxic xenophobia requires greater investigation. Abu El-Haj (2010) offered a framework for how toxic xenophobia is mobilized through two related yet distinct forms of nationalism. Everyday nationalism involves the everyday practices that make and remake the national project, including the curriculum taught in schools and the daily interactions that occur in the school building. America is framed in schools as the home of liberty and individual freedom, contrasted most directly with the perceived oppression and obligation of Muslim students.

The force of cultural myth and the regime of representation are related to an imbalance of power in discourse as theorized by Michel Foucault (1972). "Each society has its regime of truth, its 'general politics' of truth: that is, the types of discourse which it accepts and makes function as true" (p. 73). How was the objectivity/subjectivity of the Muslim woman created through political and cultural visual discourse? Methodological tools of visual discourse analysis inform my study of the current regimes of representation of Muslim Americans in the West. "Discourse analysis can also be used to explore how images construct specific views of the world, in which case . . . visuality is viewed as the topic of research, and the discourse analyst is interested in how images construct accounts of the social world" (Rose, 2001, p. 140). Hall's (1997) essay entitled "The Spectacle of the Other" provided a method for analyzing the repetition of media representations of difference and the other. Hall extended the semiotics of cultural texts to a system of representation, where meanings build and interact with other images and in turn are affected by the caption or text. The written and visual work together and can reinforce or alter the meaning of the overall representation. "But at the broader cultural level of how 'difference' and 'otherness' is being represented in a particular culture at any moment, we can see similar representational practices and figures being repeated, with variations, from one text or site of representation to another" (p. 232). The play of meaning, intertextuality, constructs what Hall named as a regime of representation. While meaning of visual signs may slip and change, the repetition of loaded markers of difference creates a layering and sedimentation of meaning. A "racialized regime of representation" (p. 249) is created through repetitive representation of ethnic or racial difference that serves to naturalize difference and freeze groups of people in a place of inferiority.

To capture what he sees as the difference in reception of the moving nature of the image, Mirzoeff (1999) expanded on the semiotic sign with the concept of the "visual event." "By visual event, I mean an interaction of the visual sign, the technology that enables and sustains that sign, and the viewer" (p. 15). The numerous visual events that occur every day relate and build on other events to create complex webs of visual experience and meaning. With the Internet and increasing choice of television and video options, the speed and layering of visual events are reaching new levels. I examine the racialized regime of representation that created the toxic xenophobia through the news and popular media and educational representations of Muslims and Muslim Americans since 9/11. Then, I analyze the visual and textual discourse in the show *All-American Muslim* (Braxton, 2011) and the film *The Muslims I Know* (Ahmed, 2008) to determine whether the visual and textual signs of these media reinforce and/or challenge the racialized regime of representation. In addition to analyzing the discourse of the show and film, I analyze filmmaker commentary and the news coverage of both.

Teachers need many more resources to use official forms of education to challenge the toxic xenophobia that is the result of the racialized regime of representation. When I asked a classroom of 30 future teachers to raise their hands if they felt prepared to work with Muslim students and families, not a single student did. Very few of my students know anything about Islam other than what they have heard on the news about al-Qaeda and the wars in Iraq and Afghanistan. The representations of *All-American Muslim* (Braxton, 2008) and *The Muslims I Know* (Ahmed, 2008) are important pieces of critical media education that can be used to combat xenophobia. Both media attempt to introduce viewing audiences to the "average" Muslim Americans to create different, more personal relationships to difference. The construction of the visual Orient and Oriental through colonialism's apparatus of imagination remain influential in the contemporary visual representation of difference and Islam in the West. Colonial power relied on the construction of European cultural superiority, visually imagined as clean, orderly, scientific, and rational. The native cultures of the colonies were variously visualized as dirty, savage, bloodthirsty, superstitious, sexual, and close to nature. These media rely on the power of individual experience and human empathy to counteract the centuries of constructed Orientalism. By identifying with someone who is part of a category of people constructed as fundamentally different from you, these media offer the possibility of surprising and challenging assumptions about difference. The stories offer humanity, a glimpse at the similarities of the characters to the audience and therefore an opportunity for change.

The Muslims I Know

In 2008, filmmaker and artist Mara Ahmed created a documentary film entitled *The Muslims I Know*. The film came from a perceived need to address the anti-Islam rhetoric of the mainstream American media and the ignorance about Islam and the diversity of Muslim perspectives and experience. As a Pakistani American, Ahmed focused on her local community of Muslims she knew, part of the newly constructed group of "Moderate Muslims" that were created by the American media as a result of the terrorist attacks on September 11, 2001. The film, though released seven years after 9/11, centers this day as a shift in the level of interest and representations of Muslims. "In fact before 9/11, I never thought of myself as being a Muslim first. Religion was part of my identity but something I took for granted" (Ahmed, 2009, para. 8). She took issue with the creation of "Moderate Muslims," as that automatically creates the rest of Islam as therefore extreme, violent, and prone to terror. Her son was called a "terrorist" and told to go back to Saudi Arabia by his 13-year-old classmates who had been fed on stereotypes of what it means to be a Muslim. There is a small but very well covered movement toward what some call Islamophobia, others label as anti-Islam, and I name as toxic xenophobia. Ahmed (2009) discussed her film and its intent in an interview with the public radio station WXXI, giving voice to her choices as a filmmaker. She chose to focus on a small group of Pakistani-American Muslims to provide depth rather than breadth about Muslims as a means of providing a more personal connection with audience members. "It could be a more extensive survey rather than a micro-study, but it would lack a personal touch, that sense of familiarity and comfort, like you were invited for tea at someone's home" (para. 2). By feeling personal, human connection to the Muslims in the film, those in the audience are more likely to question assumptions applied to the abstracted other.

On an important note of terminology, I generally reject the often-used term Islamophobia for two reasons: the use of Islam implies a level of understanding that is generally absent from the behavior, and the use of phobia implies a fear rather than hatred or ignorance. So, I choose to identify offensive speech and behavior as either anti-Islam or xenophobia. While both terms carry with them a piece of the problem, I have not yet discovered a more appropriate and unproblematic term to take their place. In an attempt to find more specific words to describe the phenomenon that includes the protesting of the building of mosques, the bullying of Muslim youth in schools, the move to ban Sharia law in many state legislatures, and countless other forms, I broke xenophobia into three related forms:

1. Exclusive xenophobia—you are fundamentally different from and therefore exist outside of our imagined community.

2. Possessive xenophobia—you are fundamentally different from and outside our imagined community AND you are trying to take our jobs, education, tax dollars, medical care, and so forth.

3. Toxic xenophobia—you are fundamentally different from and outside our imagined community AND you are trying to destroy that which we hold most dear, our freedom. (Bailey Jones, 2011)

While the possessive xenophobia can describe the reaction to undocumented immigrants, it does not go far enough to describe the rhetoric about perceived difference that led MSNBC morning show host Joe Scarborough to claim on September 17, 2012, that all Muslims hate Americans "because of their religion, they hate us because of their culture, and they hate us because of peer pressure" (cited in Legum, 2012, para. 2).

The media provided ample coverage of the protests over the building of an Islamic cultural center a block away from the former site of the Twin Towers (the "Ground Zero Mosque") and highlighted the protesters holding signs warning of the coming of Sharia law and the desecration of American soil by the cultural center. Unlike the TLC show, *All-American Muslim* (Braxton, 2011), Ahmed's film does not purport to describe the lives of "normal" Muslim Americans; she asks Muslim Americans to tell their individual perspectives and stories without attempting to generalize or essentialize their experience as "normal." Both the show and film express the need to tell individual stories of American Muslims as not extraordinary or extreme, highlighting the everydayness of lives. This need stems from the news media and Hollywood representations of Muslims as extreme perpetrators of terror. There is little space created in the mainstream for discussion of lived experience; it does not create sensational headlines, sound bites for politicians, or great drama or villains for action movies.

All-American Muslim

The Learning Channel (TLC) debuted a show called *All-American Muslim* in 2011 (Braxton, 2011). This reality show focused on Americans living in Dearborn, Michigan. The show switched relatively quickly between showing elements of "everyday" life and interviewing stars of the show about the realities of being Muslims and Americans. In attempts to counteract toxic xenophobia, the show purposefully showed young Muslim Americans who displayed "normal" American behavior. To the extent that consumerism, obsession with appearance, and shopping are "normal," the show succeeded. The underlying question of the show was whether attempting to show reality in this way is both educational and entertaining.

In highlighting characters that break out of the norm of family and culture, the show reinforced stereotypes about the "typical" Muslim because these are "atypical" examples. While the show got minimal attention for its merits and entertainment value, it inspired a media firestorm when an organization calling itself the Florida Family Association (FFA) wrote an open letter to companies advertising on the show:

> The Learning Channel's new show All-American Muslim is propaganda clearly designed to counter legitimate and present-day concerns about many Muslims who are advancing Islamic fundamentalism and Sharia law . . . . Many situations were profiled in the show from a Muslim tolerant perspective while avoiding the perspective that would have created Muslim conflict thereby contradicting The Learning Channel's agenda to inaccurately portray Muslims in America. Clearly this program is attempting to manipulate Americans into ignoring the threat of jihad and to influence them to believe that being concerned about the jihad threat would somehow victimize these nice people in this show. (FFA Letter, 2012)

The FFA claimed that the show was an insidious attempt to promote religious tolerance and was lulling unsuspecting American viewers into complacency about the imaginary rise of Sharia law and jihad. After the FFA sent this letter to advertisers, several corporations chose to pull ads from *All-American Muslim,* including Lowe's. The very public backlash against Lowe's and its decision to pull ads received much more attention than the show itself. The content of the show proved to be mundane enough to avoid controversy. Though the Lowe's backlash led to increased attention, the viewership was not enough to save the show from cancellation.

Reviews of the show reinforce the need for its existence. An article entitled "All-American Muslim: TV Review" (Knowles, 2011) from *The Hollywood Reporter* presents a glowing review of the show as a window into redefining what it means to be an American. The reviewer writes that, "the show follows several members of the Lebanese community as they pray, eat, get married, play football, run businesses, and generally assimilate into life in the United States while continuing to practice Islam" (para. 2). This comment reveals the underlying idea that led to the show's creation, that Muslims cannot be "real" and "natural" Americans. By asserting that the people in the show are "assimilating" into American life, Knowles reinforced the everyday prejudice that even the characters who are born in this country must assimilate to "normal" American ways to fit in.

The first episode dealt briefly with the hijab as a part of faith that is understood differently by different Muslim women. It was a surface discussion that focused on whether women who wear the hijab condition and highlight their hair. The five minutes of the first episode that deal with hijab gave a surface nod to this complex and heavily coded piece of clothing, The second episode dealt with the hijab as well, exploring in more detail the idea of hijab as an expression of your personal relationship with god, rather than a required act. One woman, Samira Fawaz, decided to wear hijab after years away from it. She abandoned the practice after September 11, 2001, due to feeling that she was physically marked as different and un-American. The show was forced to deal with the stereotypes in ways that other reality shows do not: can we present Muslim Americans without having to explain why they can be both at the same time? It is due to the overwhelming mainstream media coverage focused on how foreign and different Islam is to American values that the show's producers were compelled to take a defensive posture on the identities of its participants.

A focus of the second episode in the series was the local high school football team. Fordson High's team and coach were highlighted—a majority Muslim team that deals with taunting from other teams, calling them "camel jockeys" and "terrorists." The episode followed the families during the first days of Ramadan. This episode highlighted the tension of Muslim American teenagers working to maintain the tenets of their faith while functioning as "normal" American teens. While fasting during daylight hours for Ramadan, the team played games during hours when they could not eat or drink water. The team faced the disadvantages of hunger and thirst on the field and could not alter the times of games. The football team shifted practices from the traditional afternoon times to 10 p.m.-5 a.m. so that the Muslim players could eat and drink water during practice.

The casting choices of the producers clearly forced connections between what they felt are typical American roles and the "normal" Muslim American. The show covered several American tropes: the football coach, the police officer, the rebel, the party girl, and the feisty young parents. Additionally, the very American idea of the generational divide was an important focus and source of drama on the show. The younger generation questioned their parents on multiple traditions, some more specific to their culture and religion but nonetheless familiar to American audiences. Young adults rebelled against their parents' desire to control their lives, the disapproval of tattoos; some of the younger generation rebelled by denying the practices and faith of their parents, while others on the show rebelled by embracing more traditional aspects of Islam. The producers' choice to focus a storyline on Fouad Zaban, the head football coach, is a deliberate decision to force the connection for the audience between the all American sport of football and Muslim American's high school football is the symbol of hegemonic masculinity in this country. Another focus of attention was Mike Jaafar, a police officer in Dearborn. Jaafar gave the show an insider look into the law enforcement community, providing a unique perspective of a Muslim police officer. He spent time with the Dearborn police force on how to respectfully work the Muslim community and help bridge gaps in understanding. The show dealt with the issue of Sharia law directly, refuting the idea that there is any movement to impose Sharia law in the United States. The show filmed on the 10th anniversary of September 11, 2001, and addressed the long-term effects of the terrorist attacks and the ensuing War on Terror on the lives of the cast.

In directly comparing the content and intent of the film *The Muslims I Know* and the reality television program *All-American Muslim,* it is helpful to examine how the two productions reflect Alsultany's (2012) tropes of Muslims in American media. Alsultany described two older negative stereotypes of Muslims as the terrorist and the oppressed, silent women. She also posed two newer "positive" stereotypical representations of Muslims in the media as patriot or victim of post-9/11 hate crime. Both the negative and positive stereotypes remain harmful to the diverse Muslims in the United States and around the world because they set types and hierarchies of the "good" Muslims and "bad" Muslims. The positive tropes reflect important realities faced by Muslim Americans, especially the issue of being victims of hate crimes, racial profiling, or discrimination. The important telling of individual stories of victimization becomes an issue when Muslim American characters in the media are reduced to this one identifying factor at the expense of other human experience. In terms of the first "negative" trope, the portrayal of all Muslim men as terrorists, the cast of *All-American Muslim* overtly challenged the equation of Islam and terrorism, distinguishing Islam and extremism in the name of Islam. *The Muslims I Know* took the challenge to the trope further and confronted the very construction of terrorism and questioned the distinction between state-sponsored violence and violence from nonstate actors. The second trope of the veiled, oppressed Muslim woman is counteracted and challenged in the content of both media. Both the show and film made points to feature women and their appearance in discussions of gender roles and relationships. The Hijab is the major form of gendered negotiation in both, worn by very strong and intelligent women as a choice that expressed rather than limited their personal freedom. These media texts also placed emphasis on questioning traditional gender roles of women in the West and in Islam, illustrating the complexity of gender and breaking apart the stereotype that equates veiling with being silent. The patriotic trope was handled very differently in the two texts. *All-American Muslim* took on the pressure faced by Muslim Americans to be exceptionally patriotic to "prove" that they are Americans. The series focused one episode on the 10th anniversary of 9/11, and while some of the cast participated in patriotic services and commemorations, several cast members refused to conform to the patriotic Muslim trope. In *The Muslims I Know,* Ahmed refuted the patriotic trope by questioning the very legitimacy and actions of the American government that supported extremist and authoritarian regimes in Pakistan and Afghanistan. Finally, the trope of Muslim Americans as victims of hate crimes post-9/11 was covered in both texts, although this trope is distinct when related to real experience of discrimination rather than fictionalized and flattened accounts. *All-American Muslim* conformed to the trope by focusing on discrimination faced by women wearing hijab and football players taunted after 9/11. *The Muslims I Know* addressed this trope by telling stories of being called terrorists and being singled out for searches at the airport. Both also challenged this trope by focusing on much more than this storyline. The importance of both of these media productions is that they tell complex stories of real Muslim Americans in their own voices. This is revolutionary in a quiet but important way; post-9/11 representations of Muslims have either been flattened stories of acts of terror or oppression on the evening news or flattened stories of patriotism or victimization in fictional dramas.

"Hey! That's My Hummus!"

There are many other small-scale media interventions that attempt to create empathy and confront Islamophobia though education and human connection. "Hey! That's My Hummus!" is a student podcast hosted by Mike "Shiny" Scheinberg and Faiqa Khan (2013), bringing cross-cultural and diverse perspectives on issues of popular culture, religion (one host is Jewish, the other Muslim), and current events in the news. In one podcast, the hosts preview the reality show, *All-American Muslim*, focusing on the segments of the show where the cast members sit together on couches and discuss the overarching issues of religion, gender, and culture that are parts of their lived reality. These segments on the couches break the illusion that this is solely a "real" representation of lives. These discussions show the hand of the producers and push the agenda of the show in confronting Islamaphobia and stereotypes. The hosts discuss the title of the show, "All-American," breaking down the diversity of Muslim Americans and questioning whether the title creates a false universalizing of diverse communities. The hosts also discuss the show's focus on hijab, with Khan critiquing that focus, saying that it reflects American media obsession with outward appearance and the hijab as a sign of commitment to Islam. The podcast presents the complexities of living in a truly inclusive, multicultural America where one can talk about the controversy of Robin Thicke's hugely popular and problematic song "Blurred Lines" and the heated reaction to Boston Marathon bomber Dzhokhar Tsarnaev's *Rolling Stone* cover photo in one episode to another episode that deals with similarities and differences in religious fasting for Muslims and Jews.

Arab in America

Toufic El Rassi (2007) created *Arab in America* as a way to represent his experience of growing up and functioning in the United States of America as an Arab American. Born in Beirut, Lebanon, El Rassi experienced the changing context of his Arab identity and how the perception of this difference by his fellow American citizens shifted due to events. The first page of the graphic novel brings the reader into the morning of September 11, 2001, and an email from El Rassi's sister simply stating, "Hey man you better shave..." (p. 1). From this opening page, it is clear that the perspective on the experience of 9/11 represented in this text is quite different from that of the mass media and other mainstream American publications. The panels after the email message depict a spontaneous patriotic march in Chicago that was headed to a mosque. The intended actions of the group remain unclear because police stopped group members before reaching their target. The final panel of the page shows a woman holding an American flag with a quote, "I'm proud to be an American and I hate Arabs and I always have" (p. 1). The anti-Muslim and anti-Arab sentiments that followed the terrorist attacks are eerily familiar to El Rassi; the narrative moves quickly backward in time, to the aftermath of the terrorist attack on the Alfred P. Murrah Federal Building in Oklahoma City in 1995. Before Timothy McVeigh was apprehended and charged with the attack, the media and others rushed forward with assumptions that Muslim and Arab terrorists were involved. An older relative advises El Rassi to avoid discussing his Arab identity with anyone on that day: "Toufic, if anyone asks you today, tell them you are Greek or something, don't tell them you are Arab . . . OK?" (p. 3). El Rassi struggles with a desire to both hide and embrace his identification with his family, history, and culture. He is marked physically as different from his majority White peers in the middle and upper class neighborhood and schools by the shade of his skin, his fast and early growing facial hair, and even the music that his mother plays loudly from the family car. The basic forms of xenophobia that El Rassi experiences growing up as an Arab in America turn quickly into toxic xenophobia during the Gulf War and in the many years following 9/11.

El Rassi directly confronts Western stereotypes of Muslims and Arabs historically and in contemporary popular culture. On page 38, he connects the art of French Orientalist artists Ingres and Gerome to the mis-representations of Orientalism that created a fictional Arab culture that was highly exoticized and eroticized. El Rassi appropriates Orientalist paintings, like Thompson (2011) does in *Habibi*, but to very different effect. He does not have the technical proficiency that Thompson has in recreating the painting, and his copies are clearly reproductions included to make a larger point about the content of the originals. "The Middle East was often depicted as a land of exotic wonder, full of flying carpets, genies, and lusty harems" (p. 38). El Rassi makes a direct connection between these historical representations of Orientalism and the way that Muslims and Arabs are presented in Hollywood films as bloodthirsty savages and terrorists. Since the end of the Cold War and the immediate shift from Soviet thug to Russian ally, the American film industry lacked a recognizable enemy to portray as the "bad guy" in action films. With the first Gulf War in the early 1990s, Islamic extremists began to appear in films as the new "bad guys" that wanted to destroy the American way of life. The terrorist attacks of 9/11 cemented the new dark force in Hollywood films; taking the old Orientalist stereotypes and darkening the fantasy with fanaticism and massive acts of violence, the new villains were easily recognizable to American audiences. El Rassi points to the popular and cult success of the original *Star Wars* trilogy as an example of anti-Arab stereotypes in film that flew under the radar and are very rarely analyzed. He draws the characters of the Sand People, Jabba the Hutt, and Watto as those fitting many of the stereotypes of Arabs that were transposed into the *Star Wars* galaxy. Tatooine, the sandy desert planet, is home to all of these characters. The Sand People are desert nomads; "they are savages who roam the sparse desert planet of Tatooine and are mindlessly violent and hostile" (p. 45). These characters, portrayed as an evil force that must be overcome, do not speak a recognizable language, and roam the desert, present a negative view of people who live in the desert and move in a caravan. An even more evil presence in the *Star Wars* movies, Jabba the Hut is not related to any group of humans in size, shape, or voice; he is a creature imagined to be huge, blubbery, and gross. However, El Rassi points to several features of Jabba that could make him a negative Arab stereotype. He "lounges in his lair with his harem of slave girls. He even smokes a water pipe" (p. 45). After 9/11, the representations of Arabs and Muslims (again, conflated as the same group in much of Western media) became more blatantly focused on the extremist terrorist, intent on destroying America and its freedom.

The stereotypes build up in layers; they create residual effect for those like El Rassi who identify as both Arab and American. The popular culture representations affect how El Rassi feels about his own identity and his place in the predominantly White neighborhoods of his youth. The popular cultural misrepresentations are reinforced by a serious lack of understanding and openness to the fundamental facts of Arab people at all levels. President George W. Bush and his advisors made public speeches that assumed that all Muslims are Arab and that all Arabs are Muslim. The basic fact of the geographical makeup of the "Arab world" is an educational unit that is not included in American curriculum. El Rassi (2007) draws a map of the Arab countries from Morocco across Northern Africa to the countries of the Arabian Peninsula. "All Arabs speak the Arabic language and share Arab culture and most (but not all) are Muslim. I suppose what is most confusing for people is that one could be a Muslim (a religion) but not necessarily be an Arab (an ethnicity)" (p. 64). The distinction between Arab Iraqis and Persian Iranians is lost on Americans who receive very little education about geographical and cultural difference. In addition to the fundamental geography lesson, El Rassi provides glaring examples of top-level American officials mispronouncing Iraq as "I-rack," stating, "I just can't help thinking they can't even say the name of the country they are supposedly helping" (p. 67).

This narrative is more overtly political and pedagogical than any others that were analyzed for this book. It is successful in confronting ignorance with education and addressing stereotypes overtly; however, it is less successful at telling a coherent narrative and functioning as a graphic narrative. On some pages, the words overwhelm the images and feel as if the images are an afterthought rather than being created and read as a single image/text unit. One of the more successful aspects of the text is how El Rassi (2007) deals with illustrating his own identity crisis through his Muslim friends. One friend, Hamid, tries to cover his background as an Iranian Muslim and blend seamlessly into American culture. Two other friends, Ahmed and Laila, used the negative reactions of Americans as fuel to embrace and be proud of their cultural and religious heritage and practices. Laila, originally from Jordan, began to wear a hijab after the attacks of 9/11 as a sign of protest against American foreign policy and discrimination against Muslims in America: "Look, if they have a problem with me then they can say it to my face. I'm proud of who I am" (p. 75). The issue for El Rassi is that he does not know who he is and how to react to those around him. His mere physical presence is seen as a threat by some Americans, paranoid about anyone who might be Arab or Muslim in a public space. Projections of fear on El Rassi and other Muslim Americans were created by popular culture representations of terrorists, the very real terror experienced on 9/11, and the history of race and difference in the United States.

The subjects of representation and misrepresentation are central to the narrative of *Arab in America* (El Rassi, 2007) and speak directly to the issue of a graphic narrative like *Habibi* (Thompson, 2011). On page 112, El Rassi describes the experience of attending an opening of a photography exhibit entitled, "Images of Palestine," which included images created by a young, White college student who traveled to the Palestinian territories. The images struck El Rassi as clichéd, "mostly of destitute children standing barefoot in mud surrounded by devastation" (p. 112). The author calls these images "exploitative" because they take the realities of these people and place them out of context in a Western college gallery. Even if the intentions of the photographer were benign, the result is a reinforcing of a Palestinian other that does not speak but whose experience can only be shared by a charitable, Western observer. "It occurred to me that everything that Americans know about Arabs is almost always filtered through the eyes of a white American, no matter his/her political philosophy" (p. 112). This filtering stretches directly back to the Orientalism of colonialism, where the "realities" of other peoples' lives and cultures were created by European artists and writers. In post-9/11 America, commentators, journalists, scholars, and experts recreated an Orientalism that relied on stereotypes of Muslims and Arabs as dangerous, potential terrorists. It is this representation of a group of people by those who are outside the culture that contributes to stereotype and assumption. Throughout *Arab in America,* El Rassi details offensive encounters with White Americans in elevators, parking lots, and most disturbingly, in the classroom. Some of the encounters involve outright racist slurs, such as "camel jockey" and "towel head," while others are cases of fundamental misinformation and ignorance. All of these encounters are related to the regime of representation, built through repetitive images of Muslims and Arabs as terrorists and the consistent association of violence, guns, suicide bombings, and extremist language with these images. Living within this regime of representation, most of the people who encounter El Rassi make the easiest and most offensive connections that their brains process, Arab = terrorist. The teachers that contribute to the regime of representation are the most striking, as they are the official sources of information about the rest of the world for American students. On page 29, the author illustrates a high school teacher who had a cartoon posted prominently in his classroom; the cartoon showed a Rambo-esque American soldier cornering a stereotypical Arab sheik, who is cowering against drums of oil. On the following page, El Rassi details a teacher who makes a patriotic announcement for the outbreak of the first Gulf War. In reaction to the announcement, students started chanting, "Yeah!! We're going to shoot up some towel-heads!! U.S.A.! U.S.A.! U.S.A.! U.S.A.!!!" (p. 30). The teacher laughed with them and half-heartedly asked them to settle down. As the authority figure in the room, the teacher condoned and tacitly encouraged the kind of ethnocentric patriotism that makes El Rassi an outcast in the classroom.

Graphic Possibilities for Children

Alia's Mission: Saving the Books of Iraq (Stamaty, 2010) is one of the few graphic narratives that represents Muslims or Arabs specifically for an audience of American children. The book tells the story of the chief librarian of Basra Central Library in Basra, Iraq, in the lead-up to the American invasion to oust Saddam Hussein. The text opens with an anthropomorphized book, with legs and arms, that talks to the reader and serves as the narrator. The book opens with dispelling the idea that superheroes only come in one form, with capes and superpowers. He or she (the book is not gendered) asks the reader to imagine that real human beings can be superheroes through their special deeds and introduces Alia as the superhero main character of this story.

For the most part, the narrative steers away from overtly political content, framing the story as one of individual bravery and heroism rather than as a political act during a war of questionable motive. The one exception to this is on the first page, as the talking book introduces Iraq in 2003 as, "a troubled nation ruled by a cruel dictator, Saddam Hussein, who is hated and feared by most of his people" (Stamaty, 2010, p. 1). The author presents this stark statement as historical fact rather than a specific perspective on Iraq to the children who read the book. By referring to Iraq as "troubled," without any further details about global politics, power, and the recent history of the country and its geographical region, the author makes a broad, generalized statement that sets Iraq apart as inferior and bad. In the next panel, the book tells us, "The world is troubled too. Armies from other nations, mostly America and Britain, are planning to invade Iraq to remove Saddam from power" (Stamaty, 2010, p. 1). Disregarding the grammatical issues with this panel, the text presents the war as an invasion, showcasing it as outside powers entering a country against the will of its government. However, by going into such little detail about the stated and unstated reasons given for the invasion, the text does a disservice to the children who read the book. It assumes that children cannot understand complexity or ambiguity. The talking book tells us that the invasion was to remove a cruel dictator who was hated by his people; it presents the invasion as righteous and warranted. Though this view supports the official rationale given by the American government, it could be widely disputed as favoring one official American point of view while ignoring the dissenting voices that questioned the need and justice of the invasion.

The narrative does give some historical education about Iraq that children would not otherwise learn about in social studies class, but the history is ancient, from 1,300 to 500 years before the publication of the book. We do learn about the thriving Muslim civilization that included modern Iraq, which "led the whole world in trade, science, and culture" (Stamaty, 2010, p. 5). This piece of information that celebrates the intellectual and cultural contributions of Muslims in history is an important counterpoint to the Eurocentric curriculum of most American public schools that trace all of the important global cultural contributions from Greece, Rome, and through Europe and America. Generally, Muslims are not presented as leaders in science, literature, or the building of cities and culture. The narrative in *Alia's Mission* (Stamaty, 2010) presents positive traits for Muslims of ancient history but a more ambivalent portrait of modern-day Iraqis. Alia is clearly a hero in the midst of violence, war, and indifference from the military to books and learning. On the cover of the book, Alia is in the foreground, hiding books under her veil and shawl; in the background of the image, Iraqi soldiers are running chaotically in different directions. Alia is a center of calm in the midst of the chaos and seeming incompetence. The book focuses on this difference between the average citizens of Iraq like Alia and her neighbors versus the government officials and military. The government officials stand in the way of Alia's attempts to move the books to a safer space as the war approaches Basra. "Saddam is willing to use the library to protect his artillery . . . or force the enemy to bomb the library and look bad in the eyes of the world" (Stamaty, 2010, p. 9). If the Iraqi military is illustrated as cruel and incompetent, the British military does not receive more favorable representation. One night, Alia receives a phone call telling her that the library is on fire and the remaining books are being destroyed. As the library burns, British troops stand nearby, unwilling to help the citizens or put out the flames.

While the presentation of Iraq in the book could include more complex political analysis at a level appropriate for children, it does present the civilians in Iraq as kind, caring, and concerned about literacy and their neighbors. This portrayal of kindness and everyday heroism presents a unique perspective in the American coverage of Iraq and the war. Rather than focusing on the dictatorship of Saddam Hussein and the acts of government and military officials, this text shows the individuals on the ground trying to live their lives and function during an invasion and war. American students generally learn about the world through a series of wars and battles with very little focus on the lives of ordinary citizens. When learning "multicultural" lessons, students are introduced to the holidays, food, and basic customs of people with little focus on individual lives and experiences. The text does teach lessons of historical diversity that American students do not learn, but it also focuses on individuals that students can relate to and create feelings of empathy for. This creates fissures in universal assumptions about Iraq as a site of brutal dictatorship, war, and death. Individualized stories and experience counteract the mass media coverage of Iraq and encourage students to think more deeply about the humanity of others.

Burka Avenger

In 2013, Pakistani pop star Haroon created an animated series for children entitled *Burka Avenger,* with a female superhero, Jiya, a mild-mannered school teacher by day, and an evil-fighting superhero on the side. "The Burka Avenger is an amazing action-comedy animated TV series that follows the adventures of the Burka Avenger and three young kids in the imaginary city of Halwapur as they fight the evil Baba Bandook and his henchmen" (Burka Avenger, 2013, para. 1). The villains in the series are not named as the Taliban for political purposes, but their actions against education and women are quite similar to real battles against the Taliban. Jiya's superhero costume is called a black burqa (although it is technically a niqab due to the opening for her eyes). The billowy covering helps disguise her identity and also helps her fly through the air to fight evil. Her weapons to fight those who want to close down schools and hurt children are books and pens that she literally throws at people to stop them. One of the powerful messages of the show is about the importance of education for girls and women, an indirect reaction to the Taliban shooting of 15-year-old educational activist Malala Yousafzai in October 2012. The shooting and attempted murder of the young girl brought global attention to the struggle for girls in Pakistan to have safe access to education.

The show immediately received press attention in the United States, with much of the coverage describing controversy around the creator's choice in dressing the superhero in a burqa/niqab. The critique, which is supposedly feminist in nature, follows the mainstream American stereotype that veiling in general is always oppressive to women. The feminist critique of the veil and veiling practices has received a lot of attention due to renewed U.S. interest in Islam and Muslims since 9/11. The critique focuses on the veil as either an overtly or subtly forced piece of clothing that covers women in public to protect them from men's uncontrollable sexual desires. In this critique, veiling of all variations is inherently oppressive, even if chosen. Some feminist critics (Chesler, cited in Clark-Flory, 2009) argue that even when veiling is chosen, that choice is made within a patriarchal cultural and religious context that means it is never a "freely" chosen option. Others (Ahmed, 2011) argue that veiling is a cultural, historical, and religious practice that varies widely in intention and effect. Many Muslim women wear hijab as a symbol of their identity and freely choose to veil despite their family's wishes. The *Burka Avenger* seems to speak to this second notion of veiling, in which veiling can be empowering and a form of resistance. Haroon responded to critics: "That we are trying to subjugate women is completely incorrect. 'The Burka Avenger' is all about women's empowerment. All superheroes have disguises. The burka is simply hers. But neither Jiya nor the Burka Avenger is invisible" (Neel, 2013, para. 5).

Muslim Superheroes Trending

In addition to the *Burka Avenger,* graphic representations of Muslim men and women as superheroes have been appearing in the pages of comic books and making headline news in the United States. A major entry into this field of representation is *The 99,* a comic book series created by Dr. Naif Al-Mutawa (2006), representing the "Qu'ran's 99 Virtues of Allah" (Curry & Soffel, 2013, para. 5). The series will eventually introduce 99 superheroes split evenly between men and women and representing 99 countries. The series was created in the wake of 9/11 and in direct response to the lack of positive representations of Muslims in Western media. *The 99* creates a counternarrative to the many mainstream American comic books, television series, and movies that either ignore Muslims or show them as violent terrorists and villains. Other major comics production companies have taken note of this trend and the call for greater diversity of representation in their pages. Marvel debuted its new *Ms. Marvel* (Wilson, 2014) in February 2014 named Kamala Khan, a Pakistani American teenage girl who discovers she has superpowers. Her power is shape-shifting; she can change into other people or objects to save the day. While there are references to her religion and racial difference, Kamala stands out in her similarities to other American teenagers dealing with fitting in socially, finding one's identity, and figuring out their place in the world. "In Ms. Marvel, shape-changing seems to suggest that flexibility is a strength. Kamala is a superhero because she's both Muslim and American at once. Her power is to be many things, and to change without losing herself" (Berlatsky, 2014, para. 10). The creation of a Muslim young woman superhero by one of the most iconic American comic book publishers is a sign of the increasing interest in and openness to difference that need to be brought into the classroom.

CHAPTER SIX

From the Inside/Outside: *Persepolis, Nylon Road,* and *A Game for Swallows*

The series entitled *Persepolis* (Satrapi, 2003, 2004) is a contemporary classic in the genre of the graphic narrative, often cited as a text that provides a critical window into Iranian experience during and after the Iranian Revolution. The two books in this series tell the life story of author Marjane Satrapi, through her childhood in Tehran, Iran and her tumultuous transition to live in Europe. *Nylon Road* is a lesser-known graphic memoir by Parsua Bashi (2009), an Iranian woman who is now living in Europe. Though many details of their biographies are similar, the authors create very different graphic narratives of their experiences. Both of these texts provide a counternarrative about lives of Iranians to the ones that Americans encounter on the evening news, which focus on the regime's hatred of America and its quest to obtain nuclear weapons. *A Game for Swallows* (Abirached, 2012) is the story of the author's childhood home in Beirut, Lebanon, during the civil war that shattered homes and lives. As with the other graphic memoirs in this chapter, this text gives American readers a first-person narrative of life in countries and conflicts that are often unknown or misrepresented in the mass media.

Persepolis

Persepolis: The Story of a Childhood by Marjane Satrapi (2003) is the most celebrated graphic narrative in the West about the Middle East. The narrative series recounts the author's experience as a child in Iran before, during, and after the Islamic Revolution of 1979. Part of the positive reception of the *Persepolis* series is the position of Satrapi as a cultural insider writing a memoir of her experience. In discussing the Western reception to the series, Barzegar (2012) wrote that, "due to Satrapi's social standing and fickle religious devotions, she depicts Islamic tradition much as uninformed Westerners do: as a bizarre and extreme religion" (p. 41). Satrapi's autobiographic graphic narratives shy away from the class considerations that led to varied levels of support and responses to the revolution. In *Persepolis 2: The Story of a Return* (2004), Satrapi tells the story of her time in Austria attending school, working odd jobs, and having a boyfriend who encouraged her to deal drugs to be cool. The narrative speaks to the hypocrisy of Western freedom, that there is freedom to do anything, supposedly, but there is a lack of community and shared responsibility. The West, in this story, is not the savior for Satrapi; it is oppressive in other real ways. She wrote the following about her decision to return to Iran: "I got dressed, packed my bag, I again put on my veil, and so much for my individual and social liberties, I needed so badly to go home" (p. 91). Iran represented a lack of liberty but a place with family and the warmth of home. At the point when the narrative is written, Satrapi is back in Europe and arguably a cultural outsider to Iran. Her statement that she "immediately felt the repressive air of my country" (p. 92) on landing in Tehran leads to the question of whether this was an insightful critique of an Iranian women chaffing against a harsh regime or a Western critique of Iran that reinscribes stereotypes of Muslim barbarism and oppression?

Persepolis (2003) is a recent classic and the first graphic narrative that I ever read. The story of a young, spunky girl growing up during and after the Iranian Revolution in Tehran struck me for the details of Iranian history and political reality that I had never been exposed to. My education about Iran came from the social studies textbooks that I had in high school and the information on the evening news. This left me with a very specific, and negative, view of the government of Iran, and thus the people, since they were conflated in both of these sources. Satrapi's narrative presents the complexity of her family that loves Iran but despises the oppressive regime and the moral police that roam the streets of Tehran. One of the funniest panels of the book also nicely expresses the disjuncture between the lived reality of people and the mandates of the regime: the image shows the little girls in Satrapi's grade school class when they are given veils and told they must wear them. The girls, unaware of the rationale for this sudden requirement, repurpose the veils as part of their imaginative play. One girl puts the veil over her entire head and says, "Ooh! I'm the monster of darkness"; another says "Giddyap" as she uses the veil as reins of a classmate imagined as a horse; another uses two veils tied together for a jump rope (p. 3).

Satrapi formatted her memoir in a series of short chapters that vary in tone and scope. Some of the stories highlight the small, yet risky forms of rebellion in which Satrapi and her friends engage. She sneaks into a store to buy Western records and posters to play at loud volumes and decorate her bedroom. Other chapters are much more overtly serious in tone and content, but even these small rebellions occur against the backdrop of the oppressive regime and therefore carry serious consequences. Satrapi uses the comics language of panels and gutters in relatively straightforward ways in both the first and second installment of *Persepolis* (2003, 2004). Nearly every page has three rows of panels, neatly aligned and predictable. On select pages, panels extend beyond their row, with a few especially important panels that take up the entire page. None of Satrapi's panels bleeds outside of panel lines and none of her panels lacks a solid frame at the edge. The story flows from the top left-hand corner of the page and reads left to right and from top to bottom. The text elements are also relatively predictable; the narrative text is almost always confined in boxes at the top of panels. While the comics elements are used in standard ways, the elements of value, texture, line, and space create visual drama within each panel. The comic is drawn and presented entirely in stark black and white with no shades of gray. Backgrounds of the panels are white or black, the figures with white faces and black clothing. This contrast of face and clothing is particularly dramatic in the figures of veiled women; the face is floating in a black sea.

The story of Satrapi and her family during and after the revolution in Iran is full of complex questions about identity, nationality, religion, and position in society. Her parents were modern and secular yet fiercely proud of their Iranian heritage and cultural legacy. After the revolution, her mother demonstrated with other women against the forced wearing of the veil, while other women were demonstrating in the streets for enforced veiling. Satrapi (2003) illustrated the conflicting nature of this time and the complexity of identifications in one panel at the top of page 6. Satrapi as a child is at the center of this small panel, visually split in half. On one side, she is unveiled and surrounded by a background of gears and rulers; on the other side, she is fully veiled and surrounded by a beautiful Muslim design. The text describes the split: "I really didn't know what to think about the veil. Deep down I was very religious but as a family we were very modern and avant-garde" (p. 6). Satrapi does not at this point choose one side of this division, although she feels it is a clear division between two separate and opposing spheres. However, as the first chapter, entitled "The Veil," continues, it becomes clear that Satrapi's view of what it means to be religious does not match with the narrow definition of the leaders of the Islamic Republic. The young girl believes that she is the final prophet at the end of a long line that includes Jesus. Her view of religion is a highly personal view of connection to God. She writes her own holy book that includes rules from Zarathustra, a Persian prophet before the Arab invasion: "Behave well, speak well, act well" (p. 7). Her religious principles are based on the profound and minor injustices that she witnesses around her. It has nothing to do with the covering of hair or the enforcing of seemingly arbitrary rules.

As a child who has the clear and unfettered vision that only children possess, Satrapi (2003) feels dissatisfied with the lack of direction and vision in the revolution. A panel from the second chapter, "The Bicycle," illustrates her frustration: "The revolution is like a bicycle. When the wheels don't turn, it falls" (p. 10). The image of this revolutionary bicycle has five stationary wheels and is piled with useless people, a tangled mess of limbs and heads that are incapable of turning the wheels of the revolution and producing real, meaningful change. The narrative of *Persepolis* details a great deal of suffering, violence, death, and oppression. This horror is filtered through the lens of Satrapi the child and drawn in ways that give a stylized version of the atrocities. In panels detailing military action, battles, massacres, or other events that are painful and difficult to imagine, Satrapi used a convention of stylized repetition. One of the first examples of this visual repetition is the illustration of the burning down of the Rex Cinema in Tehran. The police are a single figure, repeated in anonymous rows in front of the flaming cinema: "The police were there. They forbade people to rescue those locked inside" (p. 14). Satrapi repeated the police in several panels, first standing in front of the cinema, then linking arms to block entrance, and then turning to beat those gathered to save the victims with clubs. This repetition leads to the faceless and senseless nature of the violence of the state. Though the panels illustrate a single, horrifying event, the repetition communicates the fact that this was not an isolated, specific use of force and repression but represented a larger and more pervasive violence. The visual repetition continues in the manner and styles that Satrapi used for the victims of violence. The dead in the cinema are drawn as screaming, burning ghosts, uniform in their pain just as the police were uniform in their brutality. One of the most haunting examples of this visual repetition is on page 40, where Satrapi illustrated the massacres under the final days of the Shah. If the leaders of the Islamic Republic inflict violence on its citizens in *Persepolis,* the Shah (installed and propped in place by the CIA) was even more brutal and less democratic in his actions. On this page are illustrated several of the author's visual and textual strategies. The chapter title, "The Party," is accompanied on a black panel with simple white fireworks, giving an expectation of a celebration of some sort. The very next panel below these fireworks shows four rows of horrified, deadly pale faces, the figures lined horizontally across the panel. "After Black Friday, there was one massacre after another. Many people were killed" (p. 40). The juxtaposition of the fireworks and these rows of dead bodies is striking. The second full panel of the chapter shows a row of ghostly white corpses repeated and without identity, pushing the Shah to the edge of the panel. The corpses in these two frames and the manner of their illustration are haunting and give the reader a sense of the scale of death and repression that led to the revolution. The simplicity of Satrapi's visual language allows the reader to look at large-scale death in a way that photographs or more detailed illustrations do not. The fact that the drawings are not graphic or gory may increase their haunting quality, especially illustrated in a text with a child narrator. When illustrating groups of people in joy, such as the panel that gives the chapter its celebratory name on page 42, Satrapi used visual elements to individualize the people rather than to create anonymity. Each of the revelers in the party after the Shah was deposed is wearing a distinctly patterned shirt. Though the wide grins and outstretched arms are similar for the people, the patterns of their shirts give each an individual identity.

The stylized representation of violence lends power and lasting impact to other panels in the book. In a chapter entitled "The Heroes," Satrapi (2003) detailed the experience and stories of two political prisoners released after the Shah fell: Siamak and Mohsen. Through Satrapi's perspective as a child, we hear about the horrifying torture that these men were subjected to in prison from guards who received training from the CIA. On the bottom of page 51, Satrapi depicts the horrifying torture of another prisoner, Ahmad, who was one of the guerillas and therefore received the most torturous treatment of all. Satrapi as a child hears of this torture, is scared and horrified, and draws the image of a faceless prison guard applying a scorching hot iron to Ahmad's back as he screams in pain. After the graphic violence of this torture, the first panel on the next page returns to the childlike stylized violence. The text reads, "In the end he was cut to pieces" (p. 52), and the image shows Ahmad's dead body with limbs and head neatly cut and removed from his trunk. It is as if Satrapi's young imagination could picture just so much violence and pain before it reverted to a less graphic representation. In this time of great violence, it is the government's execution of Anoosh, a dear family friend and supposed Russian spy, that pushes the young Satrapi out of her childhood conversations with God and her idealistic goal to be a prophet. At the end of the chapter entitled "The Sheep," she has her final conversation with God, telling him, "Shut up, you! Get out of my life!!! I never want to see you again!" (p. 70). On the following page, her young body floats in the middle of a full-page panel of black space, surrounded only by planets and stars. The pain of enduring the suffering of others and her own associated pain has caused the girl to lose a connection to the safety of the spiritual world of her own making. "And so I was lost, without any bearings . . . what could be worse?" (p. 71).

Satrapi represented difference using direct juxtaposition in some panels. Two panels on page 75 illustrate the visual difference between the fundamentalist woman and the modern woman and between the fundamentalist man and the modern man. After the Islamic Republic was established, with morality police that roamed the streets looking for infractions of dress and makeup, the outward appearance of Iranians took on life and death meaning. The West gives great attention and coverage to the requirements to veil and cover for women in Iran, but Satrapi detailed the requirements that were applied to both sexes. Women had to cover their hair, wear long-sleeved coats and pants or long skirts that covered all skin other than hands and faces. Men were expected to grow facial hair (at least a mustache but ideally a full beard) and wear short-sleeved shirts; ties were banned.

Another example of visual juxtaposition that Satrapi (2003) effectively used to convey difference in experience and belief is a series of two panels on page 102. In the top panel of this page, Satrapi drew abstracted silhouettes of Iranian soldiers, shot through with a series of sharp lines. The lines portray the real violence and death of the battlefield without showing any blood or weapons. The battlefield itself is implied in the panel, which has a stark white background broken up by contorted, falling bodies with keys around their necks. "The key to paradise was for poor people, thousands of young kids, promised a better life, exploded on the minefields with their keys around their necks" (p. 102). The death throes of these soldiers' bodies are mirrored by the contortions of the next panel, which shows Satrapi and her friends at her first real party, dancing and laughing with joy. The positions of the limbs in these panels are almost exactly the same, forcing the comparison of the very different experiences of the poor, young soldiers dying on the battlefield and the relatively carefree partying of Satrapi and her more privileged friends. The purposeful holes in Satrapi's punk rock sweater mirror the abstracted holes blown through the bodies of the soldiers.

The differences represented in *Persepolis: The Story of a Childhood* (2003) are primarily between traditional and modern Iranians, social class and ideological differences within Iran. A few examples of Western cultural references enter into the story of Satrapi's childhood in Tehran. As a seemingly universal facet of adolescence, she rebels against rules to test her boundaries and find her identity. Unlike many Western teenagers, it is not her parents' rules that Satrapi rebels against; it is the rules against Western music and popular culture along with the rules of fashion and covering of hair. Her parents aid in her rebellion; they return from a trip to Istanbul with smuggled Kim Wilde and Iron Maiden rock posters, a Michael Jackson pin, and Nike sneakers. Her mother allows her to go out by herself to buy black market tapes of Western music while wearing the Michael Jackson pin, a jean jacket, and Nikes. The clear thrill of these minor rebellions against the rules of the state is short-lived; members of the Guardians of the Revolution, women's branch, stop her on the street to question her fashion statements, particularly focusing their rage on the Michael Jackson pin, "that symbol of decadence" (p. 133). The Guardians decide to teach her a serious lesson by taking her to the Committee, where "they don't have to inform my parents. They could detain me for hours, or for days. I could be whipped. In short, anything could happen to me" (p. 134). To escape the punishment of the

Committee, Satrapi concocts a lie about a wicked stepmother who would put her in an orphanage and is released. The episode illustrates the danger of minor rebellions, the visual difference of the fully covered Guardians and the teenagers trying to push the boundaries of the rules.

In "The Dowry," the final chapter of *Persepolis* (2003), the differences between Satrapi and the strict rules and censorship of the regime come to a dramatic conclusion. The regime demands absolute obedience to authority and reserves harsh punishments for those who question or think critically. Satrapi reached a sort of breaking point from the suffering and grief of the death and destruction around her. After having seen the body of a friend buried in the rubble of her home, bombed and destroyed, she loses any sense of fear or concern over the rules and obedience to the authority of those with power. On page 143, she flouts the rules of her school by refusing to remove a bracelet after the principal reprimands her. The confrontation ends with the principal on the ground and Satrapi expelled from the school. In the next school in which she manages to get enrolled, she dares to confront her teacher over a lie that celebrates the regime: "Since the Islamic Republic was founded, we no longer have political prisoners" (p. 144). This obvious falsehood is too much for Satrapi, who has known so much repression, death, and violence of those around her. She confronts her teacher: "You say we don't have political prisoners anymore. But, we've gone from 3,000 prisoners under the Shah to 300,000 under your regime. How dare you lie to us like that?" (p. 144). This second confrontation leads to a second expulsion and the real possibility that Satrapi could be reported to the authorities and arrested for her insubordination. Enraged with worry, her mother tells the story of a young girl the family had met who was arrested. "You know it's against the law to kill a virgin . . . so a Guardian of the Revolution marries her . . . and takes her virginity before executing her" (p. 145). The images in this final chapter are generally straightforward representations of the text, though at the height of her mother's fear, we feel the fear and anger through the panel. Satrapi's mother holds her tightly by the shoulders, shaking her as her eyes appear urgent and her mouth is yelling. The emotion depicted in this panel reinforces the anger of the words. Faced with the horror of potential arrest, rape, and execution of their beloved daughter, Satrapi's parents decide to send her to school in Austria to save her life. The difference of this chapter is psychological and emotional rather than visual in nature. It is the difference between those who either agree with the regime or disagree but are silent in public and rebel more quietly, and those like Satrapi who no longer can rebel in silence while living with suffering and lies. This intellectual difference, the inability to quiet the questions and critical thinking in her head, are ultimately the most decisive and divisive for Satrapi. It separates her from her beloved grandmother, parents, and home. It is the difference that cannot be sustained in the Islamic Republic of her youth.

In *Persepolis 2: The Story of a Return* (2004), the narrative begins with Satrapi arriving in Austria to leave "a religious Iran for an open and secular Europe" (p. 1). She finds herself in a boarding house with Catholic nuns, surrounded by religion of a different variety. In the first pages of the text, she celebrates her new personal freedoms: moving throughout the city and to school without a veil, buying scented laundry detergent that was unavailable in Iran, and hanging out with male friends in public without fear of the authorities. For Satrapi, the freedoms also come with limitations; in Europe she is free to move about in public but does not have the anchoring of home and family. She experiences the dislocation of being suddenly placed in a new culture with unfamiliar customs. She is shocked to see Austrian teenagers engaged in sexual activity and discussing it openly. Upon arriving in Vienna, Satrapi lives in a Catholic boarding house, overseen by strict nuns. After breaking a rule about eating in a common area, Satrapi lashes out and yells at a nun, which results in her being kicked out of the house. After being turned out onto the streets of Vienna, Satrapi moves in with her Austrian friend Julie in her family's home. Julie proudly tells Satrapi of the 18 different men she has had sex with. "I was shocked. In my country, even if you had sex before marriage, you hid it" (p. 28). There is an obsession with surface and frivolous things like lip gloss, fashion, and parties that both excites and repels Satrapi. She cannot escape her identity as an Iranian with all of the memories of her family, home, and the life and death consequences of daily life in Tehran. When faced with news images of fiery bombings in Tehran, she attempts to run from the thoughts of home. In a large panel, Satrapi is drawn in her bed with visions of her childhood, including tender moments with her parents and beloved grandmother, tense moments of confronting the strict moral codes of the regime, and moments of sadness and loss. "I wanted to forget everything, to make my past disappear, but my unconscious caught up with me" (p. 40).

In Austria, Satrapi (2004) encounters offensive stereotypes about Iran-ians and Europeans who try to use friendship with an exotic foreigner for their own gain. On page 23, we see the confrontation that led to Satrapi's expulsion from the boarding house. One of the nuns sternly confronts her about eating pasta directly out of the cooking pot while watching the communal television. She says, "It's true what they say about Iranians. They have no education" (p. 23). Satrapi responds, "It's true what they say about you, too. You were all prostitutes before becoming nuns!" (p. 23). This incident of pride in her heritage is short-lived and she works for a time at avoiding any connection to her Iranian identity. The transition to being the sole Iranian in a sea of Austrians at the same time as transitioning from childhood to adulthood is traumatic. Satrapi illustrates her outward transition on page 35, making the awkwardness of adolescence visible to the reader. The first panel on the page is a visual metaphor of Satrapi as the Incredible Hulk, her clothes ripping to shreds as she freakishly grows to monstrous proportions. We see her physical transformation in the rest of the panels as exaggerated images of growth and development. We continue to follow her as she floats between friend groups and attempts romantic relationships and odd jobs, including a stint as a drug dealer. The time in Vienna comes to a crushing conclusion as Satrapi either loses or leaves all of these various people she had met and lives on the streets, becoming increasingly destitute and ill. "Very quickly, my savings vanished, I was broke. It's incredible how quickly you can lose your dignity. I found myself smoking butts, looking for food in trash cans" (p. 85). She was unmoored in an ultimately unfamiliar land. As a teenager, trying to find her place in her body and in a strange city, the personal freedoms of Vienna became a burden, pushing her away from her memories and sense of self. One of the most powerful images in the narrative is the transitional image; she has decided to move home with her parents in Iran after having crashed with illness and poverty on the streets. In a large panel on page 91, Satrapi dons her black veil and looks with great sadness and embarrassment at herself in the mirror. While the text reads, "...And so much for my individual and social liberties..." the look in her eyes speaks more to her feelings of failure and disappointment of her parents after they struggled to give her this opportunity to build a life in Europe.

The narrative continues as Satrapi (2004) returns to her family and to the repressive regime in Iran. The return to her parents' house is uneasy due to her embarrassment from her perceived failures in Austria. The return to Iran means the return to veiling in public, a requirement that Satrapi's mother must remind her of before she leaves the house. Visually, the veiling and modest dress in public is different from life in Austria, but the most striking difference is the visual representation of violence, death, and war that Satrapi creates to illustrate her return. The violence and pain she encountered in Austria was very different from the large-scale war and government repression of the Islamic Republic of her youth. In Austria, the pain was inflicted by individual cruelty, emotional and psychological violence of personal relationships. Thus, when she is in Austria, the panels do not contain any of the stylized repetition that was a major visual theme in the first *Persepolis*. Satrapi returns to this stylized repetition of violence once she returns to Iran approximately halfway through the second book. As she takes her first walk around the city, the propaganda murals celebrating the martyrs who died in war tower over her; the streets of the city have been renamed after the martyrs. As the walk continues, her body becomes visually surrounded and increasingly crowded by the names and then the hollow, dead bodies of the martyrs. In the largest panel on page 97, Satrapi is a tiny, shadow standing on top of a street paved over the outsized skulls of the dead. "I felt as though as I was walking through a cemetery...Surrounded by the victims of a war I had fled" (p. 97). Satrapi returns to the visual codes for devastating scenes of violence she used in the first installment of her memoir. She uses a basic human form, whether it is a skull, a running armed figure, or a blindfolded prisoner, and repeats this form multiple times in a single panel. The visual repetition combined with the basic, often faceless human forms creates a sense of unending, senseless violence. The scenes of violence invade the everyday life of Satrapi in Iran, the heaviness of death and war omnipresent in the lives of Iranian citizens. The repetitive scenes of prisoners, death, and war carry significant meaning for Satrapi after her return, representing the guilt she feels for having left Iran and lived the "easy life" in Austria away from physical violence. One of these images, a full-page panel on page 102, depicts political prisoners viewed as dangers to the regime lined up in successive rows. The back rows of prisoners are blindfolded, standing shoulder-to-shoulder, mouths starting to gape in screams of pain. As the rows continue down the page, the prisoners show greater horror on their faces and their bodies begin to crumple down, toward the ground. The large image of falling, dying prisoners is framed by the text,

"Or, they would be executed. And, well, most of them were executed" (p. 102).

The societal violence frames the personal violence and dislocation that Satrapi (2004) inflicts on herself upon her return. She is lost, sad, and deeply depressed. Surrounded by family and friends, she is alone, represented by the panel where she is shown running away from darkened figures, holding their arms out trying to embrace Satrapi as she flees their connection. Satrapi illustrates her loneliness in several frames that show her figure as completely recognizable to the reader while all others are blacked out, silhouettes against a stark white backdrop. A direct visual contrast is the strikingly simple panel on page 118, a completely black panel with a white outline of the author's body. "I was nothing. I was a westerner in Iran, an Iranian in the west. I had no identity. I didn't even know anymore why I was living" (p. 118). This sense of isolation separates Satrapi from the family that she loves but pushes away from the former friends that have drifted away. These friends remained in Tehran as she lived in Europe; she had access to all of the personal freedoms that they dreamed of having. Their expectations of her experience could never be matched. "A part of me understood them. When something is forbidden, it takes on a disproportionate importance. Much later, I learned that making themselves up and wanting to follow western ways was an act of resistance on their part" (p. 105).

The texts that Satrapi writes after her influential and popular *Persepolis* series turn the focus away from her own experience and on the narratives of her extended family group in Iran. In *Embroideries,* Satrapi (2006) tells the story of a group of women socializing and discussing love, sex, and relationships. This text is a much less traditional form of graphic narrative; there are no panels, gutters, or speech bubbles. The images and text flow together loosely, sprawling across the pages without the usual structure of the frames. The images are more loosely drawn as well; I get the sense that this text was more hastily put together, even if that is not the case. Satrapi's looser drawings and lack of frames and gutters in this story are fitting of the more intimate, less formally structured stories that are woven throughout the book. This looseness of illustrations, lack of panels separating one sequence from the next, is increased by a lack of chapters. *Embroideries* weaves the stories together without pause; they flow seamlessly from one to the next. The setting of the book is the same Tehran that Satrapi presents as a complex combination of warm interior spaces and cold, oppressive public spaces built around fear in *Persepolis*. In this text, however, the fear-inducing public sphere is closed out of the interior, intimate space of the book. The women of this text speak very freely; their men have left to spend time together and the women drink opium-laced tea and share funny, troubling, and most importantly honest stories about their private histories and lives. The political and historical context of Iran, the revolution, and the aftermath that led many to flee to Europe are absent. There are a few references to cultural and social practices that point to differences between Iran and Satrapi's second, European home. By focusing on the interpersonal dynamics of female friendship, sexuality, and gossip, Satrapi creates a more universal narrative that could take place, with minor revisions, in many different locations. Marriage, love, sex, jealousy, and the desire to connect emotionally and physically with others are themes that are cross-cultural and provide an interesting counterpoint to Satrapi's earlier work. *Persepolis* attempts to educate Western readers about Iranian history and the complexity of Iranian identity through the eyes of the author and narrator. It focuses specifically on the differences and similarities between Satrapi's Iranian and European homes and identities. The portrayal of difference is much more subtle and in the background of the series of stories related in *Embroideries*. Rather than focus on the political, religious, and cultural differences between Iran and the West, this text focuses on interpersonal relationships and romance.

The first story that Satrapi (2006) illustrates in *Embroideries* is about one of her grandmother's friends who had lost her virginity before her arranged wedding night. Panicked by the thought that her new husband would know that she was spoiled by premarital sex, she sought urgent advice. Satrapi's grandmother devised a devious plan where the woman would place a razor blade between her legs and cut herself during the first encounter with her new husband to feign virginity (pp. 17–18). Expectations of virginity in Iran are part of a thread that recurs throughout the book; the title, *Embroideries* (Satrapi, 2006), is explained halfway through the text. It is the sewing up of a woman's vagina to simulate virginity on her wedding night. This discussion leads the women to a debate about the misogynist nature of the double standard of wedding night virginity. One of the women, Parvine (an artist and aristocrat), argues that it is an outdated and cruel expectation of "asshole" men (Satrapi, 2006, p. 89), leading women to suffer to maintain the sexist expectations of virginity. She also claims that the Iranian obsession with women's virginity is one of the reasons that Iranians have not progressed as quickly as the West, where "the problem of sex is resolved, they can move on to other things" (Satrapi, 2006, p. 89). Another recurring theme is the different experiences of sexual freedom that the women had in Iran and in Europe. Two of the women share experiences of being mistresses of married men in Europe, something that would have been much more difficult if not impossible in Iran. Another part of the book (Satrapi, 2006) that discusses cultural differences between Iran and the West is the final story in this rambling tapestry, in which a neighbor named Azzi agrees to an arranged marriage with an Iranian living in Switzerland, who reputedly had great wealth and success. After a very opulent wedding night, the groom convinces Azzi to give him the gold and jewelry she was given as wedding gifts so that he can carry them to Switzerland and await her arrival. Naively, she waits to join him and in the meantime receives a letter of divorce. Part of the reason that Azzi agrees to the marriage is her fantasy of freedom and independence of the West, as she has seen on MTV. This story leads to one conclusion that her husband, and therefore the West, are more obsessed with material gain than substance.

Nylon Road

The graphic biography, *Nylon Road*, by Parsua Bashi (2009) tells the story of the author's childhood in Iran and adulthood transition from living in Iran to her contemporary time in Europe. In many ways, this book can be compared to *Persepolis*, but there are distinct differences. The narrative in *Nylon Road* does not function as a linear progression from childhood, to adolescence, to adulthood, as in Satrapi's *Persepolis* series. *Nylon Road* takes on a nonlinear presentation of Bashi's life, when her contemporary self is visited by visions of her younger selves. We meet the author at various times throughout her life, and the versions of Bashi engage in conversations and arguments on topics about identity, gender, sexuality, terrorism, violence, religion, among others. Published in 2009, the memoir engages with the hypocrisy of Islamist fundamentalists and Western democracies alike, wading into the post-9/11 world of the "clash of civilizations." Bashi argues (with her younger self) that the autocratic regime in Iran and the West benefit from the anti-Islam criticism. The criticism makes the Iranian regime appear to be upholding sacred values of Islam against the rising tide of Western aggression and sin. "By strengthening the criticism against Muslims, the right-wing conserve-atives in the West benefit too. It works like the double-sided blade for conservatives on both sides" (Bashi, 2009, p. 59). The Iranian regime uses Islam as a cover to hold power and wield absolute authority, accusing those who dissent of religious violation. Those in the west use secularism as a cover to wage wars and occupation, control the dress of women, and control immigration. Both of these positions, as presented by Bashi, are untenable uses of Islam that distort and mislead the public of nations east and west.

Bashi (2009) introduces us to the 13-year-old version of herself that was living in Tehran right after the 1979 revolution. The story of Iran postrevolution describes a time when people were searching for a group where they fit, amongst competing ideological stances. The Islamic fundamentalists who ended up taking control of the government were not the sole force in Iran at the time. Bashi brings this lesser known time to the fore by sharing the story of her strict adherence to Marxist ideology. She read Marx and Lenin and tried to convert her entire family, including the family dog, to follow her lead as a good comrade. After the ideological sorting was ended when the hardline Islamist regime of Khomeini took hold and imprisoned, tortured, and executed those who showed opposition, Bashi went underground with her Marxism and eventually outgrew it. Her contemporary self thinks of this Marxism as one form of fashionable phase. On a fascinating spread on page 110, Bashi illustrates how the same naked young girl can be transformed either into a nameless consumer, a nameless religious zealot, or a nameless comrade in a few quite different stages. The comparison of these three different identities that all erase the individual power and voice of the girl shows visually how very different ideologies can function in similarly de-humanizing ways. For all three, it is about fitting a mold that is made for you by others. The critique of Western consumerism runs throughout the memoir, comparing the oppressive nature of consumption over exposure and the uncovering of bodies to the enforced covering, morality police, and other oppressive structures in Iran. On the subsequent page, Bashi describes for her younger self that while the suffering of the three girls is not comparable, they all suffer in these strictly defined roles. The consumer girl suffers from "lack of self confidence" and "the pain of uniformity," resulting in empty head and pockets; the religious zealot suffers from "oddness, following the rules, feeling guilty all the time," resulting in empty head and heart, and the comrade suffers from "no-childhood, risk, being dumped by our leaders when the shit hit the fan," which results in empty heart and no freedom (p. 111).

Nylon Road (Bashi, 2009) involves the use of several visual codes that take mainstream representations of difference and appropriates them to tell a complex story of evolving identity. The most obvious of the visual codes used to represent Muslim women as a monolithic category in the West is the veil in its various forms. Western media often equates the covering of skin, hair, and face with the oppression of liberty, freedom, and individual rights of women; the more of a woman that is covered, the greater her level of supposed oppression. Bashi's (2009) drawings work with the text to show the many ways she evolved throughout her life, her physical appearance often mirroring the interior changes in her beliefs, values, and identity. Bashi's various stages and outfits play with and challenge this equation of covering skin with oppression and lack of voice. For Bashi, the covering level of her various selves does give the reader insight into her beliefs, values, and identity. However, at the ages when she draws herself wearing a headscarf, she has the most powerful opinions and forceful ways of expressing her ideas. Rather than the oppressed, voiceless Muslim woman of the stereotype, Bashi's voice is the most strident and forceful when she is the most covered.

The contemporary Bashi (2009), the one who is the narrator for the book, is wearing a long-sleeved, buttoned-down shirt, long pants, and looks comfortable yet modest. She is trying to form a meaningful life after relocating from her home in Iran to Zurich, Switzerland. While trying to craft a new life and identity, as an Iranian in Switzerland, Bashi begins to meet her old selves and have discussions with them about how their worldviews are different and have evolved. Bashi plays with space/time by collapsing many years of time into the same physical space. The first former self we meet is the 6-year-old Bashi, relaxed and comfortable in shorts, t-shirt, and sandals. She has a bandage on a scraped knee, a lizard she collected in a plastic bag, and a handful of wild flowers. There is a freedom and carefree feeling in this child's appearance. Clearly, her focus is on playing and exploring her physical and natural world. We are not given much other information about this young girl before we are transported through time and meet the 16-year-old Bashi a few pages later. This version of the author is living in the Islamic Republic of Iran in 1982, in the midst of the bloodshed of the Iran-Iraq War. This Bashi is covered in dark hijab, long-sleeved coat, and pants, the required dress of women in postrevolution Iran. She is living at a time where the consequences of daily life are literally life and death. The news was filled with the Iranian "martyrs" killed in the bloody war, and the Cultural Revolutionary Council was busily enforcing mandatory prayer in schools and enforcing a strict interpretation of Muslim morals on the streets of Tehran. The carefree dress of youth has been replaced by the required covering of the regime, and the beliefs and views have changed as well. This version of Bashi expresses a seriousness of idea and purpose that reflect the violence and tension of her surroundings. Next, we meet 18-year-old Bashi, dressed in a more private and relaxed manner. She wears a t-shirt, ponytail, and relaxed pants. This version of Bashi is in the narrative to tell about all of the friends and relatives who were fleeing Iran in the mid-1980s. Weary of the ongoing violence of war and the increasingly harsh dictates from the regime, many educated and upper class Iranians began to send their children to school in Europe. Though much more casually dressed in this age, Bashi remains committed to Iran and serving her country. Despite pleas from her parents for her to emigrate, she stays in Tehran for many years.

The story continues when Bashi (2009) introduces us to the mid-20s version of herself. She spent this time in Tehran, trying to negotiate her love of her country, desire to be creative and artistic, and the regulation of her identity and behavior in public. The regulation of public behavior on the streets of Tehran in the 1980s is illustrated by a powerful story of Bashi and a male classmate sent on an errand by their professor to get paper at a local art store. A Pasdar (Revolutionary Police Officer) stopped the pair for walking together in public, despite the fact that they were not touching or holding hands. They were separated and interrogated, each telling a different story to avoid punishment. On page 42, Bashi illustrates the primary types of Iranians who were stopped by the Pasdar (revolutionary police) or the Basidj (moral guard) on the streets of Tehran: dealers of music cassettes or alcohol, monarchists, bad hijabs, writers and intellectuals, political activists, boys and girls together, journalists, and artists. Each of these figures illustrates how belief systems and values affect outward appearance and thus make one subject to scrutiny. This is the age where Bashi enters into an intense relationship with a man from her workplace, an all-consuming and quick courtship that involved Bashi listening to the man (who remains unnamed in the text) pontificate. Due to the strict regulation of all premarital and extramarital relationships between men and women, the couple marries quickly. This marriage led to a daughter, the victim of a loveless marriage and horrifying divorce. Because of the regime dictates that gave women very little rights to custody, Bashi lost her daughter to a man she never truly loved.

The next past-Bashi (2009) that we meet is the 36-year-old woman who is the closest to the author in age and identity. She wears a loose headscarf, long tunic, and appears confident and strong. "She lived alone in Tehran and ran her own graphic design studio, she had to work hard to make a living, but was active, successful, and independent. Therefore, very proud...almost arrogant" (p. 76). One of the more interesting exchanges that these two versions of the same person have is when they examine books marketed to the West about Iran or other parts of the Arab or Muslim world. The book covers display the ignorance of culturally specific dress and ways of life and speak to the confusion over the diversity and depth of cultural and religious difference in this supposedly monolithic group. We then move forward in space but backward in time to meet the 21-year old Bashi, fully covered in dark gray hijab and coat. She is disgusted with the luxury and choice that those in Switzerland take for granted. The inequity of the material position of the wartime Iran and peacetime Switzerland could not be further apart: rationing of basic food and hygiene staples in the former and the liberal use of truffle oil to season abundant food in the latter. Traveling even further back into Bashi's psyche and history, we meet the 13-year-old version toward the end of the narrative. This version is very literally playing with identity and choosing which of many political and cultural groups that emerged in postrevolutionary Iran to join. Bashi ultimately joined the Marxist Leninists and embraced this new identification with the zealousness of a true convert.

Nudity, or the lack of covering, plays an interesting and quite loaded role in this narrative. On page 34, Bashi (2009) illustrates a nude, shivering version of her body. This nudity, the lack of covering here, illustrates the author's lack of knowledge of German and her inability to communicate effectively in her adopted country of Switzerland. Lack of covering is equated with lack of knowledge, lack of comfort, and lack of community. Two other instances of nudity are connected to the evolution of Bashi's identity in interesting ways. On page 73, she illustrates the suffering and pain she endured after the loss of her daughter as a literal cloak of pain. In the final panel on this page, Bashi is nude, shedding the cloak of pain and flushing the pain down the toilet. Here, the lack of covering represents a releasing of emotional burden and a rebirth of sorts on the other side of grief and pain. Is nudity then a form of freedom from burdensome emotional baggage or a form of cold overexposure to new and different experiences? The next example of nudity in the book shows that it can represent both a liberating removal of the old and a frightening lack of community and comfort. On page 93, Bashi explains the different approaches Iranians took in leaving their homeland for Europe. The idea of leaving the routine and comforts of home is illustrated as leaving covering cocoons and emerging nude to leave home and go somewhere new. These people are nude and exposed but bravely moving on to new lands. There are other illustrations in the book that show a lack of covering, though these are of women in Switzerland who are expressing their European personal liberty through the lack of covering their bodies. Their barely covered breasts are a focus of Bashi's, with exaggerated cleavage, large, round cartoonish breasts, with nipples peeking out; this type of woman is presented throughout the book. The various versions of Bashi all look down on this overly revealed woman, though with various degrees of outrage and disapproving fascination.

The overall effect of Bashi's (2009) memoir is one of searching for herself through the representation of multiple selves. She combines the self-representation and the representation of self-as-other, though the other is actually the author at various ages. She directly visually compares the dress and covering of her own body and head throughout her various stages of identity development. The question that she does not answer in the book is which version of herself is the "real" and most accurate self. We assume that she feels most comfortable with the contemporary self who is telling the narrative, but each one brings out a piece of Bashi that she identifies with closely.

A Game for Swallows

A Game for Swallows: To Die, To Leave, To Return, a graphic narrative by Zeina Abirached (2012), tells the story of the author's childhood in war-torn Beirut. The book is often compared to *Persepolis* (Satrapi, 2003), and the two share many elements of image and text. Both are stories of the author's childhood in zones of conflict in the Middle East and describe both the terrors of being surrounded by violence and death and the small pleasures of childhood spent with beloved family and close friends. Visually, the heavy graphic lines of Abirached are clearly inspired by Satrapi, with richly detailed patterns of stark black and white. *A Game of Swallows* is visually stunning, and the organization of panels and pages gives the reader a distinct sense of the loss and dislocation due to the violence in Beirut in the 1980s. Though the story is a bit uneven, the visual elements are powerfully rendered. The series of large, unbounded panels on pages 9–13 are one of the most powerfully evocative opening sequences of any graphic narrative that I have read. The full-page panel on page 9 shows East Beirut in 1984, buildings typical of any global city gathered at the bottom of the panel with beautifully chaotic antennas on the roofs. Clouds gather above the buildings and the rest of the panel is stark blackness. The only signs of violence and war are the sandbags and oil drums lined up in front of the buildings, though in this initial image, these are not easily read as the detritus of war. As the reader turns the page, the violence seeps in slowly. Subtle, but clearly readable, bullet holes penetrate the barrel on the top panel of page 10. The bottom panel on page 10 shows an empty city street, which at first appears to be unremarkable; then the reader notices the ominously gathering black drums at the end of the street. At the top of page 11, we see the rooftop garden with beautifully designed windows and take a second look to discover that the design on the roof is barbed wire. The scenes beautifully depict the surreal nature of daily life in a warzone; life must continue despite the threat and reality of bursts of gunfire. The streets are devoid of people, begging the question of how and where people in Beirut lived in 1984.

One of the most powerful ways that Abirached illustrates the realities of her childhood is through the use of various maps. The division and use of space in map form carry great meaning in the text. Over the course of the next series of pages, we learn how Abirached's family attempts to carve out a sense of security in an insecure place. The narrative centers on a short but perilous walk that Abirached's parents take to visit her grandmother, a seemingly straightforward journey of a few city blocks that crosses over the path of a known sniper. On pages 16–17, the author illustrates two maps of her parents' walk. The first map shows physical objects and landmarks, including her home, her grandparents' home, and the containers along the route. The second map follows the same physical space but details the use of the space rather than the physical objects within it. She draws the circuitous route of her parents' journey marked with "run," "wait," "climb," "bend over," and other actions that are necessary to survive the walk. The first map is more about nouns and the second about verbs, but both are part of the psychological map of the conflict zone, a scary and messy map of life in

Beirut. The next illustration of the physical and psychological geography of Beirut is a spread from pages 25–29. This series of maps shows beautifully graphic arteries of streets crossing, moving, and running through the imagined city landscape with a simple oval "here" at the top right-hand corner. The arteries of the map are abstract enough to resemble human veins that connect parts of the body as roads connect a city. The next page is the same map, except there is a large white square in the middle, with arteries/ streets entering into the white void and then disappearing into nothingness. The absence of drawing and text in this white void carries emotional and psychological weight. This emptiness is pregnant with mean-ing, a void in a bustling city, forbidden to Abirached and her family. It is a piece of a map that both exists and fails to exist at once. The following spread contains small, disconnected squares of the same map with additional text. Each square is labeled, "snipers, oil drums, containers, barbed wire, sandbags, carve out a new geography" (pp. 28–29). Abirached creates another powerful map that illustrates the contracting space of the warzone reality on pages 34 and 36. This map is more of a floor plan of the small apartment she shared with her parents and little brother. The map on page 34 spreads over four panels, illustrating the layout of the rooms in the apartment as open white rectangles of various sizes. The third panel is labeled for each space with its use, and the fourth panel contains crisscrossing arrows to show the movement of the family between the spaces. On page 36, the map of the apartment space begins to gradually change from open, white spaces to black voids. On each of eight panels, one of the rooms turns black, meaning that the space became unusable due to the constant threat of violence breaking into the apartment through the front windows that overlooked a barricade. The shrinking apartment culminates in a single, small square of white that represents the foyer where the family ended up sleeping, eating, and living together. The use of maps in the book is a powerful visual tool to show the weight and meaning of space that most of us take for granted. When every space is potentially deadly and each journey is a struggle to survive, mapping of space is a vital activity. Abirached's mapping of her childhood home and city structures the narrative around the physical, psychological, and emotional meaning of space.

Though the narrative is set in a city torn apart by religious difference, the representations of racial, ethnic, gender, and religious difference are not a major subject of the text (Abirached, 2012). The one place where religion is

overtly mentioned is on the very first map, which sets the official geopolitical context for the story. This large map of the region includes an
enlarged view of Beirut, cut down the middle by the demarcation line. The
city was divided between Muslim West Beirut and Christian East Beirut.
Abirached tells us that her family lived in East Beirut, so we assume that her
family is Christian. The tapestry that hangs in the foyer is the one other
element of the story that points to religion and its importance in the text. The
tapestry, which is in the background of many panels throughout the narrative,
belonged to Abirached's grandfather and showed Moses and the Hebrews
fleeing Egypt. In the tapestry, a serpent is the largest and most important
visual element. In the Biblical story of Moses, God turns Moses's shepherd-
ing staff into a serpent that displays the power of God. The serpent is a
powerful symbol in Christianity and creates a visual code for the power of
religion and Christianity in East Beirut and the conflict. This serpent takes on
additional meaning at the end of the text when Abirached's apartment is
bombed and the family has to flee and leave the space for good. On page 167
(Abirached, 2012), the text reads, "A shell had landed in my bedroom," and
the image is of the serpent from the tapestry on its own, floating in clouds of
smoke. On the next page, the serpent is above the same cityscape shown on
page 9, though the buildings now have much more damage. The serpent flies
off the page and out of view. This powerful symbol of both Christianity and
Abirached's childhood memories of the foyer flies off, leaving the family
and the city behind. Even as it is represented through visual symbols,
religious difference is not a central visual element, especially in the images
of people. Unlike other graphic memoirs set in the Middle East (e.g.,
Persepolis and *Nylon Road*), religious dress and differences are not overt
subjects of the text.

CHAPTER SEVEN

Graphic Narratives from Inside the Iranian, Egyptian, and Tunisian Protests: *The Tunisian Awakening, Rise, Zahra's Paradise,* and *Qahera*

This chapter examines and analyzes the graphic narratives that have very recently been published that address experiences on the ground of the Egyptian and Tunisian revolutions, parts of the Arab Spring. The media representations of the uprisings presented partial views of the protests from the outside. The work in these graphic narratives gives Western readers more complex, grounded perspectives on the lead-up to and context for the pro-tests and revolutionary movements. *Qahera* (Mohamed, 2013) is a web comic, dealing with sexual harassment in the Egyptian protest movements along with other gendered issues of importance. *Zahra's Paradise* (Amir & Khalil, 2011) is a recent narrative detailing a fictionalized account of the contested 2009 election in Iran and the disappearance of many young protesters. All of these texts were created by authors and artists living and working in the country and culture that form the setting for the texts. They present an insider perspective for those outside of the events and those looking in from other countries and cultures.

The Tunisian Awakening

The graphic narrative, *The Tunisian Awakening,* by Hussein (2011), is a hastily self-published tome that details the recent history of the Tunisian uprising against tyrant leader Ben Ali. The book is not a personal memoir but an attempt by Hussein to capture in image and text the immediacy of the revolution that started the Arab Spring. The quality of the drawings in pen with a very artistic form of cross-hatched sketching gives the work a feeling of emotion and urgent need to express memory of events before the focus of attention fades. The quality of the printing speaks to the self-published nature of the volume; the images and text are quite faint, which belies the power of the visual images.

Hussein (2011) used his text to inform those outside of Tunisia about the realities on the ground as the revolution unfolded. Many of the most powerful images in the book unflinchingly show intense violence, pain, and death. He devoted an entire page to illustrating the immolation of Mohamed Bouazizi. The fruit vendor had finally reached the end of his hope for a better future after harassment and theft by police and burned himself alive in public in early January 2011. Many of the panels speak to the police violence against protesters, using tear gas and live ammunitions against mostly peaceful, unarmed individuals. The corruption and violence of the Ali government was the focus of much of the narrative, with Hussein showcasing the yachts, palaces, and vast wealth of Ali and his allies. He contrasted this wealth with images of Tunisians from many different sectors of society protesting and organizing in a variety of ways. He illustrated the lawyers who gathered to call for human rights and were beaten by police and the multiple protestors who were shot on the street and left to bleed on the pavement. In fact, the frenetic pace of the book captured the chaotic nature of rebellion in ways that more polished works written about the Arab Spring could not.

Rise

Rise: The Story of the Egyptian Revolution as Written Shortly Before it Began (Shahin, 2011) is not a graphic narrative but a narrative told graphically through a series of comic strips. Tarek Shahin (2011) published a series of his *Al Kahn* comic strips that were originally published in *The Daily News of Egypt* from April 2008 through April 2010. The collection of daily strips brings together a funny, poignant, and pointed examination of the hypocrisies and dramas of Egypt's government and military officials, among many other targets. It gives those outside of Egypt who are interested in the cultural and political context of the Egyptian Revolution in Tahrir Square a unique perspective on the two years before the well-televised protests.

Shahin placed the epilogue of the book at the very front, beginning with his strips that represent the protests that were part of the larger Arab Spring. In the first strip, a Western news reporter stands above the famous Tahrir Square. She tells her Western viewers, "After fighting the protesters with tear gas, live ammo and weaponized camels, the ruling regime is now offering concessions but to no avail" (p. 1). The humor of the "weaponized camels" line offers insight into the way that the author uses stereotypes and turns them on their head by showcasing their ridiculousness. The Western reporter continues in the next strip, bringing in an Egyptian expert to explain the context of the protests to her viewers. She calls Dr. Ebaa Antar the "most qualified person here to give insights into the Egyptian psyche," and the sociologist replies, "Because my writings were on Egypt?" (p. 1). The reporter finishes the strip with the line, "Because your writings were in English" (p. 1). This particular strip points to several issues with mass media coverage of the world, especially the so-called Muslim world, by Western news outlets. Western television stations (especially the major American networks) generally assume that their viewers are most interested in news that directly relates to their Western lives. Many of the major cable news networks in the United States show very little coverage of global events if they do not involve American interests. The events in Tahrir Square were clearly too important to be ignored, but the use of an expert whose writings were in English speak to the media's reliance on Western experts or those most closely aligned with Western interests.

After the brief one-page epilogue, the book moves back in time to May 3, 2008. Here we learn about the fictional *Al Khan* newspaper and the reporters, photographers, editor, and publisher who form the central core of the narrative. Nada is a smart and cynical editor who is the main female character and gives insight into gender as a strong, independent, and secular Egyptian woman. She also serves as a political counterpoint to the publisher, Omar, and is highly critical of capitalism and privatization. The strips deal with the issue of gender in contemporary Egypt through the stories of several women. Nada, the editor of *Al Khan,* represents the working, secular women of Egypt who are politically active and aware. She fights with her publisher to cover the growing incidents of sexual assaults of women on the streets of Cairo. One recurring story of the strips focuses on Nada's sister, Basma, who walks to a wedding party in a slightly revealing black dress and is assaulted. In the aftermath of the assault, several strips discuss the shame and blame experienced by women who were sexually assaulted in Egypt. Basma would rather suffer silently at home than report the assault and be interrogated about how her behavior and dress brought on the attack. The rise in assaults brings in the complex character, Aisha, who is in many ways the opposite of Nada. She is married to the conservative Muslim doctor, Anwar, and wears full niqab that covers her entire body other than her eyes. They practice a very conservative form of Islam that places the husband firmly as the all-powerful patriarch in the home. In a story beginning on June 30, 2009, Aisha is fully covered and walking in Cairo as two young men sexually harass and assault her verbally. This is a particularly shocking event given Aisha's covering; it is impossible for her assailants to claim that she was somehow to blame based on her dress. Anwar reacts to the assault: "You're a fully veiled woman!! Have the men in this country become so desperate they won't spare the pious?! I feel so violated." Aisha responds, "I'm sorry this happened to you, Anwar" (Shahin, 2011, p. 69). The humor of this situation is in Aisha's response; as protector and patriarch, many view Anwar as the injured party rather than the direct victim. In the aftermath of her attack, Nada convinced Aisha to tell her story anonymously, to be published in *Al Khan*. The reaction to the cover story was two-fold; Anwar was horrified and shamed that his wife would dare talk to reporters without his permission. He threatens to marry a second wife in retaliation. Aisha's story also gave Basma the needed courage to tell her story of assault publicly, despite the risk to her reputation. The visual representation of Aisha in the strip is fascinating and speaks to the complexity of gender issues at stake in conversations about the veil. In public and representations of photographs in the comic, Aisha is depicted fully covered by her niqab. In private scenes of Anwar and Aisha, Shahin (2011) illustrated Aisha relaxed and without her niqab. However, he pixelated her face to obscure her identity from the reader. Though the characters in the strip are purely fictional (albeit potentially based on actual people), the author made the artistic and narrative choice to obscure the fictional identity of Aisha. The portrayal of veiling and gender in the strips is complex and not easily summarized. Some female characters are veiled and others are not, and this does not necessarily indicate the level of education, work, and views of the women.

Rise (Shahin, 2011) is critical of the West in many ways, but it is also critical of the Muslim Brotherhood and those who practice a form of Islam that restricts the rights of women and religious minorities. Anwar, Aisha's husband, is a complex character, representing a piously Muslim Egyptian man. He is moral, kind to the poor, and in many ways a very good man. He provides free medical care to those who cannot afford to pay and he is generous to friends in need. However, he also believes that religious minorities in Egypt should pay higher taxes and perhaps not be given full citizenship. In several strips that critique the apparent hypocrisy of the practice of Islam by some religious leaders, Anwar goes to seek the advice of his mosque's leader. In the strip from June 10, 2008, the imam tells Anwar, "And those, Dr. Anwar, are your rights as a husband." Anwar responds, "Thank you your eminence. That was a fruitful three-hour session. What about my duties as a husband?" The next panel has no text, implying that there are no duties for the husband in marriage; all duties are for the wife. In other strips, the imam instructs Anwar to hit or spank his disobedient wife and to take on a second wife to fulfill his sexual desires. The religious consultations either confirm Anwar's prejudices or encourage him to develop new ones. The character of Anwar is neither good nor bad; he is a complex mixture of kindness, piousness, and prejudice that does not allow for easy judgments.

The treatment of the West, America in particular, is also quite critical. Strips mock American media that rely on so-called experts who have not lived in Egypt or the Arab world. The character of Dr. Ebaa Antar serves as an indictment of the Western media and of much of the scholarly writing on women and the veil that has been widely available in the West. In the strip, Dr. Antar writes a very popular book entitled, "Harem and Me," in which she describes the Arab world: "Women there are not allowed to choose who to love, when to use the bathroom or which colour shoes to buy!!" (Shahin, 2011, p. 86). She conducted her research on the condition of women in the Arab world entirely from her academic desk in the United States. Her work is very popular in the West, and the strip portrays interviews of Dr. Antar on *Fox News* and *The Oprah Winfrey Show*. She writes of the overwhelming oppression of women in Arab countries, focusing on the veil as a source of oppression. Though her character and scholarly work is entirely fictional, the ideas of innate oppression of women in Islam and discussions of the veil that lack complexity and context are very real.

Zahra's Paradise

Zahra's Paradise, by Amir and Khalil (2011), is a fictionalized account of a family, a brother searching for his lost brother, and a mother searching for her stolen son. The story is set in Iran during the massive street protests after elections in 2009. In the aftermath of an election that many viewed as corrupt, young men and women took to the streets of Tehran in protest of the regime. Many of the young protestors were arrested, beaten, and disappeared from the official records. Not based on a single real protestor, the account is intended to stand in for the experience of many rather than to convey the views of one. The central figure of the narrative is Medhi, a young man who went missing after one of the protests. He is present through his absence; the book serves as a witness for all of the missing. Medhi's brother illegally blogs throughout the story, where he chronicles the search and critiques the government. Their mother is a mournful figure, drawn with eyes that are almost always downcast, seemingly on the verge of tears.

Many of the most powerful visual panels are chaotic, swirling images. The streets filled with cars or protestors mirror chaotic images of injured, bleeding individuals in the emergency room. On page 65 (Amir & Khalil, 2011), there are protestors strewn across a large panel, running away from police and security guards who are on motorcycles and wielding clubs to beat those who take to the streets against the regime. Small panels, inset onto the larger panel of the brutality, illustrate peaceful groups of protestors and menacing, aggressive, and angry security guards (basiji). The visual juxtaposition of these two groups builds tension that explodes into violence on the bottom half of the page. A different form of visual chaos is illustrated on page 81 (Amir & Khalil, 2011), where a crush of cars, buses, and motorbikes on are a main thoroughfare, with the quotes, "Traffic doesn't move anyway—no matter **what** the price of gasoline." Rather than the violence of government brutality, this image shows the annoyances of the everyday, of a city clogged with cars and people.

In addition to the visual theme of chaos, *Zahra's Paradise* (Amir & Khalil, 2011) makes visual impact with the recurring metaphorical images of the clerics and politicians leading the country. On page 25 (Amir & Khalil, 2011), a powerful visual metaphor is a line of scarecrows with the distinctive faces of Iran's powerful clerics. On page 46 (Amir & Khalil, 2011), the men of parliament are described as "pious crows and vultures," and their faces turn into various birds with pointy beaks and small, beady eyes. On pages

168–169 (Amir & Khalil, 2011), there is a large and imposing panel that fills a two-page spread showing two clerics' heads with their mouths open. Small people are moving in different directions on conveyer belts, including into and out of the clerics' mouths. The text associated with the panel says, "Look at that: they've turned Islam into a penal colony where time is a measure of pain" (Amir & Khalil, 2011, p. 169). The "justice" system is this series of belts, moving dispirited faceless figures through a convoluted and merciless system that ends in Evin Prison with torture, pain, and dark cells or at the end of a crane, hanging limp for all to see. All justice is filtered through the clerics; all "justice" is meted out through the filter of their power.

The major form of difference illustrated in *Zahra's Paradise* (Amir & Khalil, 2011) is between the regime and the people who resist its rule. Other forms of difference are illustrated but as less fundamentally different than the distinction between the corrupt, power hungry regime and the people protesting the corruption. Gender plays an interesting and unexpected role in the narrative, describing the differences between men and women in challenging the Western stereotypes of Muslim women. Most of the women in the panels are wearing the hijab that is required of women in public spaces in Iran. So, they are visually marked, yet they are certainly not demure or voiceless. Women in this narrative make the major breakthroughs in the search for Mehdi. Two very important women use various forms of personal power to force those with institutional power to divulge information. Sepidah is a deceptively pivotal character who was initially introduced as the curvaceous sex symbol of the Internet café on page 61 (Amir & Khalil, 2011). The narrator describes her as "the Islamic Republic's worst nightmare" (Amir & Khalil, 2011, p. 60), as her figure fascinates all of the men in the café and out on the streets. However, her attitude and intelligence prove to be more influential to the narrative than her body. She uses her sexual power and her affair with one of the corrupt and abusive prison officials to gain access to computer files that prove the government was responsible for Medhi's disappearance and to prove that he was killed.

Mrs. Ardalan is another woman who drives the narrative with her use of personal relationships and power. She is a wealthy woman who lives next door to the head of the judicial council, Ayatollah Zaheer. Her family wealth was almost lost when her father, a high-ranking general under the Shah, was killed after the Islamic Revolution in 1979. His housekeeper, Bibi, was left in the giant house and managed to retain control of the house and Mercedes.

Bibi used her own position to save Mrs. Ardalan and return her to her family's house. Mrs. Ardalan uses one of her family's material possessions, a valuable and rare Qu'ran, as a high-impact bargaining chip that she maneuvers to gain official confirmation of Medhi's death and to negotiate the return of his remains. Medhi's mother plays a central yet quiet and mournful role throughout the narrative, but she gives a stormy, powerful graveside speech at the end of the book. She is the center of a full-page panel, her tongue drawn across the page, stretching to fit the strength and length of her words. Fire burns from her mouth as she starts, "Burn, my son, burn with my rage, burn through this shroud of lies, burn, burn as only you can burn, burn with all your truth, burn with all your life, burn through this death" (Amir & Khalil, 2011, p. 218). The quiet mournful mother that moved through the story in pain suddenly transforms on this page into a fiery force of nature. This burning, righteous rage transforms the basiji (police) into suddenly empathetic mourners alongside the powerful mother's grief.

Qahera

Qahera is a web comic created by Deena Mohamed (2013), an Egyptian art student. The comic is available on a Tumblr site and started as a small project, a joke with her friends. "It was my way to respond in my own way to things that were frustrating me at the time and when the idea of having superpowers was fascinating!" (Mohamed, cited in Demrdash, 2013, para. 5). The comic features a hijab-wearing Egyptian superhero named Qahera, who uses her superpowers to fight Islamophobia, street harassment and violence toward women, and stereotypes. Currently, Mohamed has created five parts in the Qahera series (three of which are available in English and Arabic versions). In the first part, "Brainstorm" (Mohamed, 2013a), the creator concisely confronts the misogyny of some Muslim men toward Muslim women and the patronizing Islamophobia of Western "feminists" who preach the rescuing of Muslim women (Figure 7.1). The artist reacts to critique of her use of the hijab:

> Qahera was created to combat the patriarchy and misogyny I am familiar with. Islamo-phobic logic often means critiquing your own society will result in others using that as an excuse to claim that you are 'oppressed' and 'backwards' and 'a victim of your own culture.' Therefore Qahera combats misogyny and Islamophobia. (Mohamed, 2014, para. 6)

Figure 7.1. Two Panels from "Brainstorm" in *Qahera* (Mohamed, 2013).

In the second part of the series, entitled "Femen," Mohamed's superhero (Figure 7.2) takes on a Western feminist organization that uses "sextremism, atheism, feminism," as an "international women's movement of brave topless female activists painted with slogans and crowned with flowers" (Femen, n.d., para. 2). In the comic, Qahera, fully covered except her eyes and armed with swords, confronts the topless protestors of Femen. Upon seeing her, one protestor shouts, "Look there! It's a Muslim woman! This is why we're here! We have to save her!" (panel 11) and later, "Please!! Let us **rescue you!!**" (Mohamed, 2013b, panel 14). The powerful, active Qahera is clearly not a victim in need of rescue. One powerful transition of image/text occurs in two panels that highlight the hypocrisy. A Femen protester says, "Oh look! You can see it in her eyes!! **'Help me!'**" (Mohamed, 2013b, panel 12). In the next panel, we see an up close drawing of Qahera's eyes that portray anger, righteous indignation, and burning fire. This is a powerful juxtaposition of the pity and misinterpretation of the protestor with the clear power and will of Qahera. The comic skillfully captures the patronizing Eurocentric tone of much (but certainly not all) Western feminist discussion of Muslim women. Read in conjunction with "Brainstorm," the "Femen" strip communicates in easy to understand language the complexity of Muslim feminism, the simultaneous critique of patriarchy and misogyny

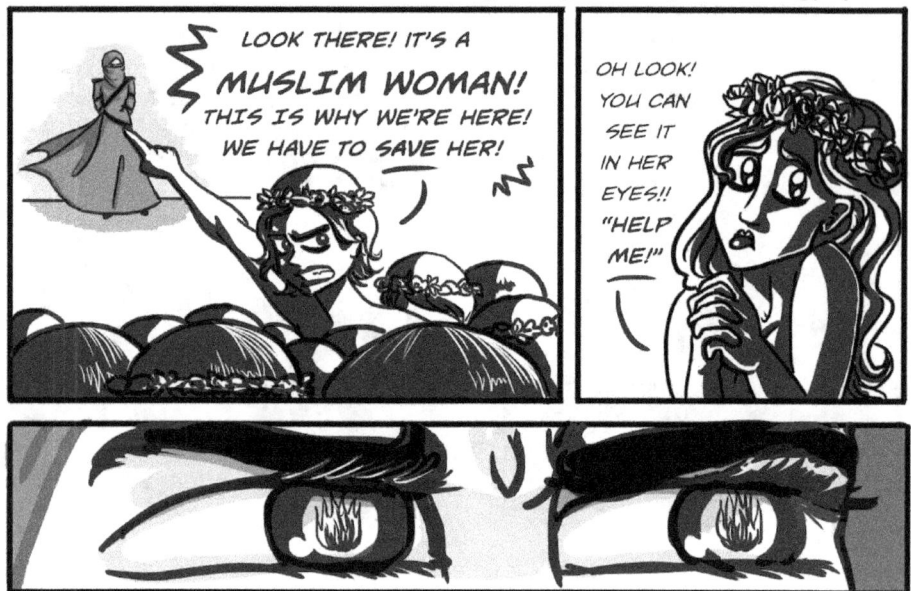

Figure 7.2. "Femen" *Qahera* (Mohamed, 2013).

within the Muslim communities, and of the Eurocentric, imperialist tone of feminist critique of veiling.

The third part, "On Sexual Harassment," and fourth part, "On Protests," take on the very serious matter of men violently sexually harassing and attacking women on the streets of Cairo. In the third part, a woman is told by a police officer that her claim of sexual harassment is pointless because of the clothing she is wearing. "But really, my dear, you must look at the way you're dressed . . . your clothes . . . they're immodest . . . inappropriate . . . and I can assure you everyone else will agree with me that had you been dressed **more modestly**, this **definitely** wouldn't have happened!" (Mohamed, 2013c, panel 13). The following panels of the comic illustrate Qahera, fully covered, and facing the same kind of harassment, showcasing the hypocritical nature of the victim blaming that places the onus for harassment onto the women rather than on the criminal behavior of the harassers. A recent story from the BBC entitled, "Egypt 'Worst for Women' out of 22 Countries in the Arab World," posted on November 12, 2013, described the findings of a survey of gender experts from member countries of the Arab League. The experts in the study drew conclusions on the poor treatment of women in Egypt based on the high rates of sexual harassment, genital mutilation, and growth in conservative Islamist groups. "A UN report in April said 99.3% of women and girls in Egypt had been subjected to sexual harassment" ("Egypt 'Worst for Women,'" 2013, para. 11). In the face of this widespread harassment, there is a culture of fear for women and girls in Egypt that needs immediate attention. By tackling the issue of harassment in her web comic, *Qahera*, Mohamed (2013) created a viral sensation that could be inexpensively produced and reproduced and shared globally through social media outlets.

Part 4 of the series, "On Protests," (Figure 7.3) is a more nuanced, psychological exploration of the sexual harassment experienced by Egyptian women in street protests. In this comic, Mohamed (2013d) used the medium of the web to both add visual interest to the panels and to add depth of meaning to the image/text. In the first panel of the comic, Qahera stands in the foreground with a mass protest in the background on the street below her perch. The focus shifts back and forth from a clarity of focus on the heads of protestors with a blurry figure in the foreground, to a sharp focus on the superhero with a blurry sea of heads. The shift in focus continues less literally in the remaining panels, with Qahera both intimately involved in confronting the street harassment of women while also watching it occur from above. Mohamed employed other interesting visual devices in this strip to question the connection and separation of bodies in time and space. The fourth panel of the comic presents the shoulders and heads of five men in a crowd with three women standing in front of them. The scene is unremarkable except for the black lines that form rectangles around each man's head, visually separating the men from each other and the women. The text in the panel adds to this separation and sense of tension: "From harassment, as they like to call it. A light word, all things considered" (Mohamed, 2013d, panel 4). The combined effects of these boxed-in heads and the text create a sense that these men are predators who are leering at these women and ready to attack. In addition to the visual blurring, this comic blurs the literary line between superhero and ordinary person, with the final panel stating, "I am a superhero because I have superpowers. They are superheroes because they do not" (Mohamed, 2013d, panel 27).

Figure 7.3. "On Protests" in *Qahera* (Mohamed, 2013).

CHAPTER EIGHT

Self-Reflexive Outsiders: *The Waiting Room, The Photographer,* and *Palestine*

The representation of self and others in a work of journalism is a different form of representation, one that makes claims to truth in ways that nonfiction and fiction do not. The works *Palestine* (Sacco, 2001) and *The Photographer: Into War-Torn Afghanistan with Doctors Without Borders* (Guilbert, 2009) are fascinating texts that can be used to examine the role of the author/artist in the representation of others. In *Palestine*, Sacco (2001) writes and draws unflinching stories of his own experience and interaction with Palestinians. While the narrative weaves through and around the lives of Palestinians, Sacco is never far from view, the stories clearly filtered through his lens. He is an obvious outsider and makes this status a central theme of the narrative. *The Waiting Room* (Glidden, 2011), *Palestine,* and *The Photographer* are graphic narratives by Western journalists who are self-reflexive in their reporting, not creating the standard objective distance expected of the craft. Sacco is especially self-conscious and creates a form of journalistic self-portrait of his time in Palestine.

These narratives are examples of Western representation that do not fall into the stereotypical representations of visual orientalism. Graphic journalism is a growing form of reporting stories that may be ignored by other forms of journalism through image/text. One of the central features of many graphic narratives is the inclusion of the author's image and voice as central narrative focus, making the author's hand and perspective apparent. The works of graphic journalism that I analyze for their portrayal of difference do not pretend to have an objective, third person stance toward the subjects of their work. These journalists are a major part of the story and the reader reads the story through their voice and eyes. It is this purposeful subjectivity that makes these texts powerful antidotes to the way that difference is often represented in mass-market journalism that pretends to be objective and removed from its subject. The obfuscation of the producer's voice, creating an omniscient unbiased façade, can make the perspective of the producer appear natural and correct instead of partial and constructed. The focus and value placed on constructed objectivity are remnants of Western intellectual and colonial traditions that naturalized the Western position at the top of an imagined hierarchy of humanity.

Illustrating Difference in Graphic Journalism

While other forms of graphic narrative tend to use more overt visual strategies to illustrate differences, works of graphic journalism tend to set up differences through establishing historical and political context as the narrative moves along, often utilizing text and maps/charts to give context. Difference between groups of people, cultures, and religions forms a backdrop to the story that the journalist is crafting. For instance, in *The Photographer* (Guilbert, 2009), we learn about the differences between the French Médecins Sans Frontières (MSF, or Doctors Without Borders) team and its Afghan and Pakistani hosts and companions through the story of the doctors' mission, work with patients, and travel through the countries to do their work. The primary story is the work of the MSF doctors and the photographer who goes along to document the work; the cultural and religious differences are present and the subject of discussion, but they serve as a backdrop to the story rather than the focus of the narrative. The works that are the focus of this chapter share a more realistic graphic style; the images and text attempt to tell the story in ways that represent the authors' and subjects' stories in straightforward visual styles. Difference, then, is a fact of the real characters in these stories rather than the focus of strategies in illustration. All of the authors in this section are Western, either from Europe or the United States, and they tell stories of groups of people in the so-called Muslim world. The stories give nuanced, detailed information about people who are often overlooked by mainstream Western media.

The Waiting Room (Glidden, 2011) is a short graphic narrative, that tells the story of refugees from the Iraqi war who have relocated to Syria.

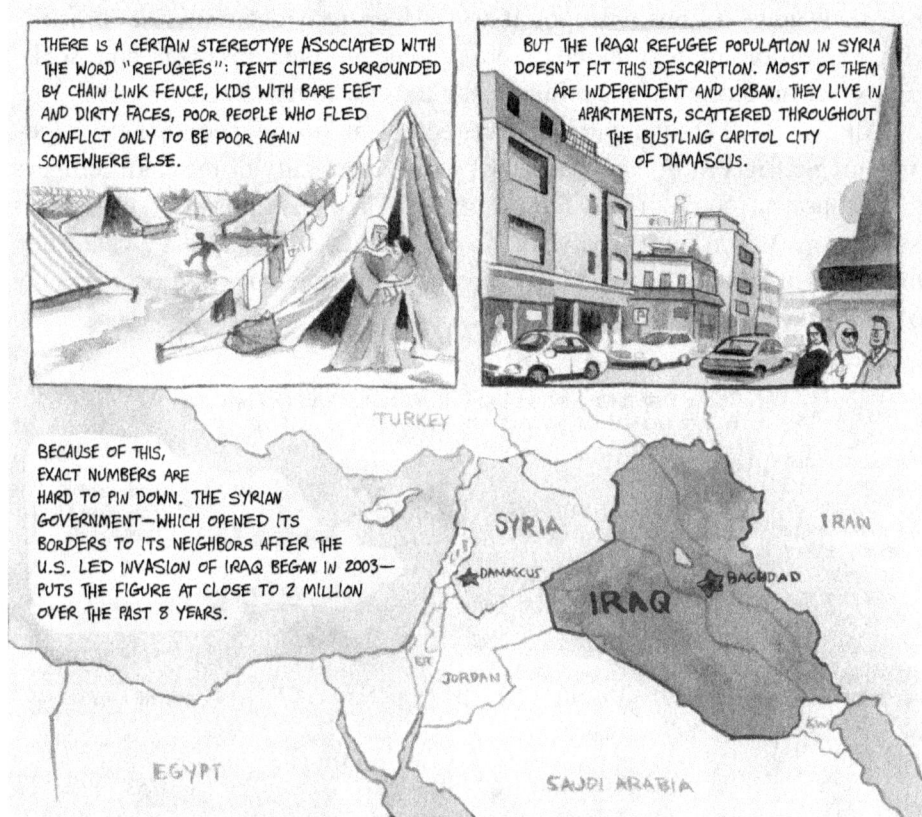

Figure 8.1 Panel from *The Waiting Room* (Glidden, 2011).

The images are painted in watercolor, giving the comic an artistic and handmade feel, as if the artist/author took a great deal of care and time to create each panel. Glidden's (2011) narrative centers on the experience of 18-year-old refugee, Maraj Ibrahim. The story starts and ends with Ibrahim, waiting for a very long time at the United Nations High Commission for Refugees (UNHCR) distribution center for food rations. She and her family had to flee their homes in Iraq during the violence following the American invasion in 2003. This is an example of the growing genre of graphic journalism, inspired by the work of journalists like Joe Sacco. Using the traditional frames, gutters, and handwritten text of comics, graphic journalism brings stories of often-marginalized voices into view. Glidden fits the role of self-reflexive outsider in this work; she is from neither Iraq nor Syria but feels empathy and a desire to let the characters tell their own stories in their own voice as much as possible. Glidden provides narrative structure with exposition in text clouds, setting the complex political and social context for the stories of the refugees and those who try to help.

Glidden (2011) illustrates the stereotypical image people have when imagining refugees on page 2 and then draws the reality of the Iraqi refugees in Damascus, Syria (see Figure 8.1). This juxtaposition challenges assumptions that refugees only live in "tent cities surrounded by chain link fence, kids with bare feet and dirty faces, poor people who fled conflict only to be poor again somewhere else" (p. 2).

Figure 8.2. Panel from *The Waiting Room* (Glidden, 2011).

The Iraqi refugees, by direct contrast, are living in urban apartments and moving throughout the city; they are part of the city but always somehow different. The refugees are not allowed to work in Syria; thus they remain entirely dependent on UNHCR food distributions and aid in order to live. On one page, Glidden illustrates a conversation with four refugees: two women, a dentist and a lawyer, and two men, an engineer and a doctor.

For many Americans who know very little of Iraq outside of mainstream news stories of the war, the introduction to these professionals, especially the professional women, is an important surprise. In the lead up to the Iraqi invasion, many American politicians and reporters conflated the position of women to that of women living under the Taliban in Afghanistan. These women are wearing hijab and are strong, educated, professional women who tell their stories to Glidden (2011). One of the strengths in the way that Glidden presents the narrative is how she does not give attention to stereotypes of Muslim women as oppressed. Some of the women in the narrative are wearing hijab, others are not, and this is not mentioned as an important or defining characteristic. The women are defined (just as the men are) by their occupation and experience rather than by their dress and appearance (see Figure 8.2). Unlike many mainstream media stories about Iraq, *The Waiting Room* does not strive to simplify a complex situation and shape the narrative into good and evil, right and wrong. Glidden presents the complex and troubling role that the United States plays in the refugee situation. Great pain and suffering resulted from actions of the United States, either directly or indirectly caused by U.S. armed forces. The American media covered some of the violence and death (skewed predictably to reporting American wounded and dead) but not those Iraqis displaced by the violence. The United States also provides the lion's share of aid and support for Iraqi refugees. It is a paradox that the same country indirectly or directly causes a great deal of harm to the Iraqi people but also provides the vast majority of aid and asylum. In addition to military and humanitarian aid, the United States takes 70% of Iraqi refugees (p. 6). Many refugees lost friends, relatives, and normal lives as a result of the U.S. action and thus are reticent to resettle there. One woman said, "I will go to any country. Anywhere but America. They have destroyed the lives of my son and my daughter" (p. 6). The formal elements of the comic frame the narrative in interesting ways. Some of the pages are relatively standard, with six equally sized panels separated by white gutters. However, some pages use one large panel with several smaller frames or scenes within the panel. Glidden uses charts and maps to help illustrate the geopolitical context of the very human stories of the narrative.

The Photographer

The Photographer (Guilbert, 2009) is a unique entry into the graphic narrative form, a combination of traditional photojournalism and the comic medium. The book is based on the photographs and experience of French photojournalist Didier Lefèvre as he travels with Doctors Without Borders into war-torn Afghanistan in 1986. Though the American audience may be more familiar with more recent American military intervention and occupation in Afghanistan, this text offers a historical glimpse into the war among the Soviet occupying forces, the Afghan government troops, and the rebellion forces of the mujahideen. The text provides an insight into the Cold War nature of the conflict, including the monetary and military support from the CIA for the mujahideen, including Osama bin Laden. The group needs the permission and favor of local tribal leaders as protection from the Wahhabi fundamentalists who "don't like to see us around here and wouldn't mind slitting our throats" (p. 43). The complexities of alliances and dangers along the journey create tension in the narrative; daily decisions about whom to trust and how to maintain safe passage are made by the group.

Visually, the mixture of photographic frames and drawn frames is interesting, though it takes awhile to get into the flow of the narrative. At first, my eyes are jolted by the visual juxtaposition of comic and photograph; the story thus feels disjointed and I wonder how to make sense of the meaning—are the photographs or the comics the "real" story? The frames of the photographs are quite similar in size to the comic cells, though the photographs are in beautiful black and white while the comics are drawn in an almost iconic style—highly simplified and spare. After 40 or so pages, the images begin to blend more seamlessly together and I realize that both function as "real" in the narrative. The comics include text and function as the internal workings of Lefèvre, while the photographs show the reader what he sees around him on the journey.

Gender relationships and roles are an undercurrent of the narrative; Juliette is the leader of the MSF group and negotiates and works among local men, the lone woman with a voice. She explains how her understanding of and respect for local tradition allow her to function in this way:

At first, I surprised all of them with my knowledge of their language. And I'd generally take advantage of that surprise to assert myself. Plus, I know their traditions. You'll never see me reach out my hand to them, stare at them, or do anything that could humiliate them. (Guilbert, 2009, p. 42)

Again, it is the primary respect for local cultural tradition that allows Juliette to lead as a Western woman and for the group to gain needed access. Lefèvre (Guilbert, 2009) focuses on Juliette's gender and how it was received as an ongoing theme in the text. He photographs Juliette brushing her hair and teeth and offers a close-up of her lovely earring as a counterpoint to the sea of bearded men. The gender of Juliette is an outlier; Afghan women are mostly secluded in the home, and if in public, they are completely covered in burqa—at least in urban areas. During one conversation later in their journey, Juliette and Lefèvre discuss gender roles and Western stereotypes of Afghanistan quite directly. Juliette returns from spending the night at a young couple's home near the village where the team is staying. She first met the couple four years earlier as newlyweds. She was surprised to learn at the time that they had married for true love (at least matching our Western ideas of love) rather than having it arranged or marrying out of material need. Now, four years later, the husband has taken on a second wife. Juliette was surprised to see such a loving marriage sullied by a second wife, but she reveals that it was the first wife's idea, the second wife serving as a useful second adult to help with daily chores. After discussing the case of this couple that confounds Western assumptions about Afghan marriages, they turn to the chadri, or burqa. Lefèvre says, "All we ever see is the same poor, helpless woman under her *chadri*" (p. 144). They discuss how the Western images of poor, oppressed, fully covered women that need to be rescued are far from the realities of most Afghan women. Juliette says that most rural women could not afford to buy chadri even if they were required to wear them, so they are not fully consumed in face-covering shrouds. Even those women who do wear chadri in urban areas often use it as a form of resistance to prevailing moral restrictions or the power of the regime. One wealthy young woman from a Westernized, aristocratic family bought a chadri for herself to disguise her identity when she snuck out to meet with her boyfriend. Others hide weapons or other help to the resistance against the Taliban under their covering. Juliette also shares insight into Afghan women that she could only find out because of her gender. As a woman, she is welcomed into the all-women interior spaces of the home and engages in many honest and engaging conversations with the women she meets. "We talk about everything, life, children, and a lot about politics. What I learn from them is crucial, especially when they are part of the entourage of the local leaders, because they have a very powerful influence on them" (p. 145). The women that Juliette meets are not the passive, voiceless women of the Western stereotype. They have a great deal of influence not just in the home but also on the political fortunes of local communities. Their voices touch Juliette the most when they are used to talk about the men who are not present: "You should hear them gossiping about the men, you'd split your sides laughing" (p. 145).

Once Lefèvre (Guilbert, 2009) enters the country and meets the MSF team, we follow his initiation into Afghan customs and traditions that he will need to navigate the dangerous journey into a war zone. The team gives him an Afghan name, "Ahmadjan," and teaches him the salutations he will need. The narrative is deeply entrenched in the geographical and cultural contexts; the minute details of the local custom and life are detailed in the first section of the book. The specificity of the setting and the attention to cultural detail set the book apart as an honest attempt by cultural outsiders to portray Afghanistan in a knowledgeable and respectful way. Lefèvre admits to his lack of understanding of the international political situation and records his experiences with a lack of cynicism and naiveté that allows the reader to go along on the journey in a unique way. An early example of this is his experience at the American Club in Peshawar, Pakistan, as the group readies to cross the border. The club is full of Westerners who flock to one of the few establishments where they can drink alcohol. Lefèvre writes, "It's obvious that the place is crawling with spies" (p. 25), but laments his lack of political sophistication. As a reader, it is this honesty and naiveté that allow me access to the narrative and the cultural experiences in a meaningful way. I learn the local customs and greetings along with the photographer. One of the more interesting and powerful visual stories is the series of photographs of the Western nurses and organizers dressed in chadri, posing in various ways and at times pulling back the face veils to reveal their identities. The images with context could be any number of Western photographs of Afghan women published after 9/11. All members of the group, men and women, buy and wear chadri to conceal their identities while being smuggled illegally across the border.

Palestine

Sacco's (2001) collection of his graphic journalism in *Palestine* was originally published in nine shorter comic books. The work follows his 1991–1992 trip to Palestine at the end of the first Intifada, the Palestinian uprising against Israeli occupation. Sacco's journalism cuts through the mainstream American media stories and political rhetoric of the Israeli-Palestinian conflict that are clearly biased toward the Israeli perspective. Most Americans have very little sense of what life inside the occupied territories is like for Palestinians; most do not even have a basic understanding of how Israel was created as a homeland for the Jews in the wake of World War II and the atrocities of the Holocaust. Sacco goes into his narrative with a story of his own history. He details his upbringing on American media stories of Palestinian terrorism, focusing on the killing of American Klinghoffer by the Palestinian Liberation Front. "Americans won't care about the problems of Palestinians when Americans get killed in these terrorist attacks. One American gets killed and it eclipses anything Palestinians have to say!" (p. 7). Although this is a story of Sacco's past, it in part inspired his trip to Palestine, to hear the individual stories, to meet the real people who were obscured behind the American obsession with the terrorist act. Sacco travels to meet people, to hear their stories, and to document these individual lives in image and text. The intimacy of his drawings and the inclusion of his own image create a densely populated and intense reading experience.

Unlike my own education about Israel and Palestine, Sacco (2001) details the historical and colonial context that enables the displacement of 700,000 Arabs living on the land that became Israel. He goes back to the early 20th century to connect British imperial power and global reach with the Zionist movement for a Jewish homeland. "And in 1917—after two millennia of Jewish Diaspora—the British dusted off the promise of the Lord. Great Powers had Big Battleships back then, Broad Pen-strokes, too, and plenty of India Ink" (p. 12). It is a complex historical context that must balance the marginalization of Jews in the global diaspora and their legitimate desire for a homeland with the unjust treatment of the Palestinian people. There is no easy way to communicate the complexity of this land and the people who all feel they have a legitimate claim to live on the same land. Sacco does not try to simplify this story; *Palestine* avoids making sweeping moral arguments or generalizations. By focusing on a variety of individual stories, Sacco punctures assumptions and universals.

The individuals, families, and communities that Sacco (2001) meets and details in *Palestine* are intense in their experience and presentation. Visually, three elements add to the intensity of the effect: the organization of panels and gutters, the use of close-up faces, and exaggerated facial features. Sacco plays with the idea of the comic panel in different ways to affect the mood and tone of the story. During several intense descriptions of violence, imprisonment, and torture, he manipulates the panels and gutters to create visual tension. In a series of pages depicting a protest that is violently broken up by Israeli soldiers, Sacco melds various perspectives, faces, and angles into large collages (pp. 54–56). Without gutters, there is no safe place for the reader's eye to rest, no relief from the chaos and violence of the protest. The full-page panels that bleed to the edge of the pages move through space and time in confusing ways. It is not entirely clear whether each page represents a single instant of protest and violent reaction or if time moves forward as the eye moves over the images. Most comics artists present people's bodies and frames from predictable angles so that the reader sees the people as if they are watching the action from a seated or standing position. Sacco plays with the position of the reader to the figures in his text; often readers see the action from a low angle as if they are children. Other times, they look down on people from above, removed from the scene. An interesting example of the changing angles and their effect on the narrative is in the short piece, "Getting the Story," that describes the different reactions of two Israeli soldiers when the American author and several Palestinian women try to get past a roadblock. In the first panel, readers are below waist-height, looking up at the scene and at the backs of the solders. At the bottom of the page, a panel shows one of the soldiers aggressively waving his gun at three veiled women. We are visually removed from the scene, but the text becomes increasingly manic: "He's got a short fuse! He's about to blow his top! His M-16's in the air! He's waving it around!" (p. 127). Once the page is turned, the angle shifts lower and closer, with the soldier frighteningly raising his gun, shaking with anger. The shifting of perspective gives the scene a chaotic, unpredictable quality that increases the level of anxiety in order to appreciate a small measure of the fear that the women may have felt.

Sacco (2001) also uses the organization of text boxes to add to the context and mood of the story. In the chapter entitled "Ramallah," he uses small, rectangular, white boxes with choppy fragments of sentences that give the short chapter an anxious, urgent feel. Sacco is tensely moving through the streets of Ramallah in a taxi as a series of explosions goes off nearby. The chaos, soldiers, roadblock, and violence of the area scare and excite the author, giving him a war story of his own. Sacco organizes the panels in a way to increase the tension, long and thin horizontal strips that move across the page with uneven separations. Back in Jerusalem, he learns that the explosions were in fact percussion grenades set off by Israeli soldiers to clear the streets of people for the mandated five o'clock curfew. In other sections, the use of text boxes and speech bubbles is more conventional, though the placement of narrative text boxes is unpredictable. Many comics authors place text boxes in a fixed location in panels, often in the top portion of panels. Sacco usually follows this convention, but his text boxes sometimes float around within and between panels. The text boxes that travel in between panels draw the reader's eye along, allowing for literal connections as the panels move through space and time. The unpredictable and evolving use of panels and text boxes lends urgency to the narrative that is matched by the stories of the many people Sacco meets in Palestine and Israel.

Sacco (2001) utilizes a wide range of comics transitions, including many panels that move from aspect-to-aspect, giving the reader several visual perspectives on a single event. On page 211, four panels show the same scene of the author watching video clips as the time approaches the imposed curfew. To heighten the tension of the curfew and the anxiety that Sacco feels about the possible consequences of walking the streets after that time, he shows four panels of the same clock, moving to a closer view of the hands in each frame. In terms of content, Sacco covers many aspects of life in Palestine and presents his perspective and conversations with different women in the chapter entitled "Women." The fact that a very short chapter is devoted to the experience of women, with a section devoted to "Hijab," displays the perspective of Sacco as a Western, male journalist. The first part of the chapter is devoted to a conversation with what he calls "the feminists," the second to those who wear hijab. He splits the Palestinian women into two groups, neither of which is presented in a particularly favorable light. "All of the feminists I met talked of the need to push their views while also resisting the occupation" (p. 136). He does not feel entirely comfortable with the feminists he meets, though he often is so self-deprecating it is difficult to figure out when he is at ease. The feminists pushed their ideas and agenda, which Sacco (like many in the West) distills down to the single issue of the veil. He concentrates the whole of women's experience down to whether they are covered. The first, large panel of the "Hijab" section shows Sacco walking in a nondescript location. Veiled women, walking away from him with their faces hidden and averted to appear without identities or expression, surround him on all sides. "You could say the hijab was more my problem than hers . . . but let's not leave it at that, the hijab is a focal point of some debate here, and it's an issue that throws the interrelationship of the intifada, Islam, and women into some relief" (p. 137). Sacco also echoes many Western scholars in his disbelief of women who say they freely choose to cover. He meets with several small groups of women in Gaza, and his focus is on whether Hamas is playing a role in forcibly veiling women in public. "One of the women seems put off by my questioning, like who am I to strut in with my Western, patronizing air?" (p. 138). The woman in question does not deny the presence of male oppression of women but is offended by Sacco's focus on the veil and claims that women's rights can be based on a strict practice of Islam. Her brief critique of Sacco's Western bias has been offered by many Muslim feminists (Mernissi, 1992; Ahmed, 2001) who lay out a form of women's rights that are based in a feminist reading of the Qu'ran rather than in the work of Western feminists.

CHAPTER NINE

Habibi: The Outsider Looking In

Craig Thompson is widely regarded as one of the most skilled artists of the medium, known for his almost obsessive attention to detail and precision in his drawing and calligraphy. He produced four major works: *Good-bye Chunky Rice* (1999), *Blankets* (2004a), *Carnet de Voyage* (2004b), and *Habibi* (2011). I follow the trajectory of his work, starting with *Blankets*. Two of the three books that I analyze are autobiographical representations of self, while the third, *Habibi*, is a sweeping fictional tale of people and places very far from Thompson's imagined community. *Habibi* is overtly referential to Orientalist painting from the late 19th century. The stunning, yet problematic, visuals are almost perfect copies of paintings of harems and hammams that titillated Europeans and created a fantastical and imaginary Orient. Though the author purposefully used Orientalism, he did so in a manner that does not cause the reader to question or critically analyze the creation, rather it is a beautiful homage to the genre that is steeped in colonialism and ethnocentrism.

Thompson's *Blankets, Carnet,* and *Habibi*

In *Blankets*, Thompson (2004a) illustrates his childhood and adolescence in Wisconsin. He draws and writes out of his memories of his mother's deep faith, the lessons about Christianity taught in Sunday school, the bullies in school who tormented him for his size, his hair, being poor, and not fitting the mold of masculinity. He also recounts with great tenderness and affection the stages of infatuation and young love with Raina. His struggles to reconcile the moral guidance and strictures of his family and church with his desire and longing for Raina form a narrative tension that carries the reader along. There are painful scenes illustrated in emotionally charged black and white, including the memory of his father shoving his younger brother, Phil, into the dreaded cubbyhole to sleep amongst the spiders because they were fighting over bed space. This memory haunts Thompson as an act of brotherly cowardice and betrayal. Its pain is relived through the narrative and comes to represent his lack of confidence in his ability to act and stand up for those who are weak (including himself). *Blankets* is a very personal representation of Thompson's strict faith, his journey through questioning this faith, and his growth into a man, independent of his parents and faith. The representation of his own lived experience reflects the author's view of the true lived experience. The characters of the book, Thompson's family and friends, high school classmates, and others, are part of his real and imagined community. The illustrations of faith in the book are real memories from the author's past and upbringing. This presentation of self and lived experience is very different from the later work, *Habibi,* and the representation of faith and groups of people far from Thompson's own experience.

Between the two major works, *Blankets* (2004a) and *Habibi* (2011), Thompson created a very interesting piece of autobiographical nonfiction entitled *Carnet de Voyage* (2004b). The book is a representation of Thompson's travels to support his first book and to research for his second major work. Beginning by landing in France, the book is a rough travelogue, capturing the external scenery of the trip but also the internal story of Thompson's emotional and visceral reaction to love, culture, travel, and so forth. While the entire book is both engaging and beautiful, the way that Thompson represents his travels in Morocco that formed the cultural and religious research for *Habibi* lacks engagement with the people of Morocco. In the pages that detail the trip through Morocco, Thompson is painfully and brutally honest about his level of discomfort and lack of trust in and with the Moroccans he encounters. He details his discomfort with the crowded city streets, the "chaos" of the medina, his fear of being taken advantage of, asked for money, and robbed of his possessions. The comfortable place that

Thompson finds in Morocco is when he travels away from Moroccans into the dessert and in drawing architecture and cats. His discomfort with difference is so honestly portrayed that it is touching. This discomfort must be reexamined in light of the reading of *Habibi* through a lens of critical visual literacy. I recognized the beautiful lines of the architecture and initial sketches of Arabic calligraphy in *Carnet de Voyage;* I also recognized the beginnings of the cultural misrepresentation in the image/text. The honest reflection on Eurocentric and sheltered American ideals in this travelogue reveals the narrow limits of Thompson's knowledge with Islam and the Arab world (which forms the nebulous setting for *Habibi*). The contrasts between Thompson's time spent in Europe and Morocco are clearly visible, most extreme in the representation of women. He is obsessed with the dress and covering of women, even though he laments the difficulty in finding access to drawing them in public. He contrasts the dress of Bedouin women in colorful layers of cloth to the Berber women dressed in face-covering black burqa, who he compared to ninjas.

The narrative in *Blankets* (2004a) represents Thompson as the ultimate insider to the narrative; autobiography is the closest form of representation to the presentation of self. When he critiques the narrow limits of his faith, the cruelty of his father's love, and the construction of midwestern masculinity, he does so from a position of cultural authority. These are his cultural, religious, and familial roots, and as a reader, I trust in the narrative and the details of the story. In the long-awaited follow-up to *Blankets,* Thompson produced *Habibi* (2011), a graphic narrative that is achingly beautiful in its imagery and extremely problematic in its cultural, religious, and chronological representations. The transition from *Blankets* to *Habibi* represents a shift from insider to outsider, from cultural authority to cultural tourist. While many of the same themes persist—the winding road toward love of self and other, the cruelty of those with power, the limits and possibilities of faith—the books are very different in their representations as culturally embedded experiences.

The narration of the graphic narrative from Thompson provides another lens to discuss the insider/outsider distinction. In addition to being a cultural and religious outsider in *Habibi* (2011), Thompson is also a gender outsider. The graphic novel uses two characters as the drivers of the story, but the primary source of perspective is Dodola, a woman we trace through her impoverished youth, sexual service against her will in a harem, explorations of her conflicted motherhood, and her tumultuous love story. The secondary narrator is Zam, whose masculinity and sexuality are questioned through his membership with a group of eunuchs to get food and survive without means. In Dodola, Thompson presents the inner thoughts and workings of a woman. Strikingly, the naked body of Dodola is presented throughout the book as a complicated object of beauty and subject of harm and desire. Dodola is sexually assaulted and raped throughout the novel, in ways that are disturbing yet strangely erotic. As a reader and viewer, I was left confused by the inclusion of so many sexual assaults; what plotline does the graphic and erotically charged imagery of Dodola trading her body for food and of sexually pleasing the sultan in order to survive serve? Her body is represented graphically in many forms, including many images of calligraphy written directly onto her form. In *Blankets* (2004a), Thompson serves as his own narrator, telling the story of his own gendered and sexual identity, including focusing on the image of his own body. The focus on sex and sexuality in *Blankets* showcases the conflicted and contested nature of the body and desire in the Christianity of his family and church. In contrasting the focus on sex and sexuality in *Habibi*, the bodies of women (including but not exclusively that of Dodola) are objects of beauty, desire, and metaphors for larger themes and ideas in the narrative. How does Thompson's gender identity relate to his conception of Dodola? How does his role as an outsider to the identification of woman, girl, and mother affect the representations of these in the text? The women and men in *Habibi* populate worlds that are defined by their access to power and their control of other people's desires and bodies.

The setting of *Habibi* (Thompson, 2011) is a semifictional one that has clear inspiration in particular geographical and historical locations. Thompson combines various elements from the Maghreb, Middle East, Southeast Asia, and Arab peninsula in a cultural and temporal mash-up. Thompson clearly understands the critique of the work and the contradictions of the setting:

> If you travel to a developing country, you see people living in incredible poverty and living very simple lifestyles similar to 100 years ago brushing up against modernity and global trade. You can see how obviously our consumerist society is feasting off of poverty in their countries and how all our waste is there. Here we just consume and produce a lot of waste and then it sort of disappears and we don't have to deal with it precisely because we are heaping it on to other people. And that's a reality .... I'm doing a fairy tale or parable version of that, but I don't feel like it's

dramatically abstracted from the world we live in. (Thompson, interviewed by Damluji, 2011, para. 20)

Thompson bristles at the idea of academic criticism of the text, stating that it is playing with self-deprecation that is inherent in comics as a medium to tell stories and that much of the analysis is overthinking and overwrought. While I respect Thompson as an artist and a thoughtful cultural critic, the work of *Habibi* was published and entered into the academic discourse of neo-Orientalism and postcolonial theory.

Habibi and the Colonial Phantasm of the Harem

Thompson's creation of the sultan's harem flows easily from the fantastical imagery of Orientalism paintings. This highly sexual imagery of nude women lounging seductively, waiting to be chosen to join the sultan in his chamber, is pure fiction from the minds of European artists and now from Thompson. "There is no phantasm, though, without sex, and in this Orientalism, a confection of the best and of the worst—mostly the worst—a central figure emerges, the very embodiment of the obsession: the harem" (Alloula, 1986, p. 317). This is an ultimate Western fantasy of a large group of sexually available "exotic" women, waiting to please the powerful, yet physically repellent, man. If this is a critical commentary on the Orientalism trope, it is impossible for the reader to see the distinction between the colonial painters and this modern-day comic fantasy.

> But, still, there's something disturbing about the way the book's not-quite-licit enjoyment of erotic imagery is ambivalently paired with a guilty reflex. The book is full of harem baths, languid odalisques, and so on, which are cool except when you realize that Thompson wants both to luxuriate in these images of caged sexuality but also comment moralistically on the fetishistic pleasure they give. (Hatfield, 2011, para. 11)

Nowhere does this fantasy feel as creepy and contradictory as in a garden orgy scene on pages 258–259 (Thompson, 2011). The repellent sultan, heavy and hairy, is shown drooling and engaging in all sorts of sexually explicit acts with the women of his harem. As a critical reader, I ask why the sexual scenes are so vivid, so over the top in their fantastical detail, why the women are drawn so sensually, their nipples featured prominently throughout the text. This is the combined effect of the Colonial Gaze and the Patriarchal

Gaze; the women are the Other, stereotypically exotic, and are represented by a White, Western, male author with more power and position.

Bodies of Women

In *Habibi* (Thompson, 2011), Dodola's naked body, highly sexualized or shown for its reproductive function, is on display with great frequency. On a page with her naked body repeated four times in different seductive poses, she says, "I'd once used my body to my advantage, but even then it didn't belong to me, possessed, instead, by the LUSTS of men" (Thompson, 2011, p. 109). Her body is the subject of other text: "People were crying out for water, but the sources had dried up and there wasn't enough to share. When the world is on its last breath, however, the masses will need something to distract them from the destruction—and my body will still be a commodity" (Thompson, 2011, p. 181). The associated image depicts Dodola's naked body, held aloft by evil, grasping hands surrounded by flames. The hands and flames are menacing, but Dodala's body remains sensual—the illustrated sensuality and sexual appeal of her body is present in scenes of being violently raped (Thompson, 2011, pp. 149–157; see also fantasized rape, p. 183), and when she is near death and limp (Thompson, 2011, p. 443). Thompson (2011) seduces the reader with sensuous images of Dodola's body, which she is forced through hunger to sell to passing caravans for sexual acts. Throughout the text, the only constant in Dodola's story is the presence and use of her body and sexuality. Her young body was the reason behind her escape from the slave market; its sexual use and abuse by others fed her and Zam in the dessert; it kept her alive and in favor in the sultan's palace. The one place in the text where Dodola's naked body is depicted as not sensual, not sexual, and even grotesque is her own imaginary of her pregnant body.

The images and text on page 63 represent one of the more overt attempts made by Thompson (2011) to "play with" the genre of Orientalism. In the large panel at the top of the page, there is a vignette in the lower right-hand corner that shows two clothed men "testing" a naked woman before purchase. One of the men has two fingers by, on, or in her mouth. This is an exact recreation of the Orientalist painting, entitled *The Slave Market* by prolific French Orientalist painter Jean-Leon Gerome. Those who are familiar with art history and the Orientalist tradition would instantly recognize this appropriation, but others would take the scene at face value.

For those familiar with the original, the message in this panel remains troubling, reproducing the sexualized racism and colonialism of the original without questioning or challenging the imagery. The slave woman is still naked, sexualized, with her potential slave master's two fingers at her lips. In the panel there are four naked or topless female slaves, while all of the men in the panel are fully covered and clothed.

The Sensualization of Rape

The most graphic (but certainly not only) rape of Dodola is the nine-page spread where an unnamed trader in a desert caravan from pages 149 to 157 (Thompson, 2011) rapes Dodola. There is a long visual history of sensual images of sexual assault and rape that Thompson (2011) continues in *Habibi*. The use of rape as a weapon of war in ancient Rome in battle with the Sabines, often dated from 750 BC, was a popular subject of artistic representation. Giambologna created a sculptural representation in 1583, and several artists created paintings of the rape, including Poussin in 1637, Rubens in 1640, David in 1799, and Picasso in 1963. However, the most clearly labeled representations of rape, the romanticized violations of the Sabine women, are not unique in art history. Famous artists, primarily men, represented naked women's bodies in various poses and scenes and often gained fame from these images. The specific representation of sexual violence, of men overpowering and abusing women's bodies, carries with it the power and control of patriarchy and the regulation of gendered orders. In a fascinating article on the gendered visual representation of rape, "From Victim to Victor: Women Turn the Representation of Rape Inside Out," G. Roger Denson (2011) wrote about the way that men and women have variously and differently represented scenes of rape in the arts. Most of the representations of rape created by men predate the feminist movements of the 1960s in the United States, when public attention to the horrors and prevalence of rape shifted and domestic violence and rape hotlines were created for the first time. The historical representations of forced sexual encounter and rape created by the men generally show helpless, yet erotically positioned, women with breast or breasts bared. The rape scenes are grand in scale and heroic in nature, with men and women depicted in forced, yet clearly sensual, positions.

The representations of rape that Denson (2011) presented from women artists date in the 20th and 21st centuries (with the notable exception of the painting *Susanna and the Elders* by Artemisia Gentileschi in 1610). These representations do not glorify or sensualize the act or prelude to rape; in fact, they nearly exclusively represent the bloody, bruised, beaten women's faces and bodies that result from the violent acts of rape and sexual abuse. Many of these representations of the violence against women created by contemporary women artists show women's bodies curled into a fetal position, a child-like position of powerlessness and shame. "Instead of the women presenting us a vividly articulated window onto rape, we are drawn into the shattered psyche of the rape victim through a kind of black hole punched through her and from which drains her life force so relentlessly, she is made blind, immobile and drawn into the deepest, darkest isolation" (para. 6) These images depict pain, both physical and emotional; the viewer is implicated in the aftermath of the violence in a way that never occurred with the heroic rape representations from male artists.

> The reality of rape's traumatic effects rings truer to sensible modern audiences than the heroic rape, even if its visualizations are harder to digest than the exalted and romanticized embellishments that artists historically used to cover over that reality, especially as a large part of the world has recognized that feminism rightfully made rape an equation of power. (para. 15)

While the heroic rape is not widely represented in contemporary art, Denson highlighted still images from contemporary video games that include violence and rape of women in the gameplay (*Rapelay,* video game, 2006, and *Hitman: Blood Money,* video game, 2006). Denson juxtaposed these stills against the historic paintings and sculptures of heroic rape to highlight the similarity of body and power positioning. These images are about the meeting of power and sex, with the focus on the strength and physical presence of the rapist. Graphic depictions of heroic rape have been relegated to the world of comic book and video game, where the taboo sexual fantasies of rape and power can be played out in a private or semiprivate sphere away from the public scrutiny of high art. Sexual fantasies of rape play out in the pages of many comics, especially in some forms of Japanese manga. In Japan, the line between exploitative and explicit sexual fantasy and the expectations for public behavior is clear and regulated. The women's representations focus on the physical presence of the victim, disempowered and left with the broken pieces of the anguish to repair.

The analysis of the historical heroic rape represented by male artists and the painful, shame inducing, bloody and horrific rape represented by contemporary women artists gives the rape of Dodola in *Habibi* (Thompson, 2011) a context and legacy. Dodola is the victim of sexual exploitation throughout the text, but the graphic scenes of her violent rape are the focus of my analysis here. Does the scene in the dessert of the nameless, sunglass-clad man raping her align more clearly with the heroic rape of the male artists or the painful, more realistic and empathetic representations of the women artists? The images of Dodola's body in the scene, with her breast bared and her back arched to heighten her sensuality for the viewer are clearly more visually similar to the women of the heroic rape scenes. Thompson (2011) represented the act of rape in a way that both sensualizes and trivializes its horrific power:

> Thompson has attempted to moralize on the atrocities committed against Dodola but also is clearly rolling around in it himself, seeming to include her debasement among her list of attractive attributes. Again this is not uncommon, in comics or anyplace else—depictions of exploitation that are themselves exploitative. (Haegele, 2011, para. 5)

In the midst of the rape, Dodola jokes about her attacker, a very unrealistic and sensationalized moment of the text. As he is attacking her, she says, "You're too ugly for us to be related" (p. 151). Throughout the horrifying rape, the presentation is light-hearted and Dodola's body is positioned sensually. We see the exterior, the act of rape that is never explicitly represented in women's artistic responses. In one panel on the bottom left of page 155, Thompson draws a panel from the perspective of the rapist. The viewer takes on the gaze of the rapist, hands reaching violently out toward Dodola's naked body. To literally take on the ultimate Patriarchal Gaze, that of a violent rapist, is disturbing. The painful aftermath that the reader witnesses is more on the side of Zam, feeling shame and despair for the violation of his object of desire. The use of Dodola's body as an object of men's fantasies continued even in Zam's pain. On page 165, Zam remembers the rape, imagining himself staring at Dodola's naked body, his hands resting on her knees, her head turned in what looks like pleasure. On page 183, Zam again dreams of the rape and this time he transforms into the rapist, holding Dodola down, her breast prominently displayed and her head bent back in either pleasure or pain. The trope of heroic rape is repeated throughout the text; whether Dodola is "willingly" trading sex for food or if she is forced into sex, her body is on display for the reader and it is almost always drawn with sensuous expression. Her head is often thrown back or to the side in pleasure/pain, as the two seem indistinguishable in the text. Many readers and critics questioned Thompson's use of rape and violation of Dodola as a major plot point. Reviewer Ellsworth (2012) wrote the following:

> He was too casually brutal. It yanks you out of the story—you start to feel like an accessory to rape. It yanked me out as a reader. Eventually I found myself asking: why is an American writing this? Why is our American, white author detailing the rape of this Arab woman? And what am I perpetuating by reading it? (para. 28)

The presentation of this sexual violence was very different from how women artists have represented the trauma of rape and is emblematic of a text written from self-and-other, someone who does not empathize with the experience of the character. The representation of sexual violence against women and transgender women continues throughout the text, including dream-like images of Dodola's figure being violated, torn apart by menacing, sexualized demons.

Sexuality and Gender

By framing *Habibi* (Thompson, 2011) as a love story and constructing Dodola as the central figure (though the narration shifts between Dodola and Zam), Thompson (2011) asks the reader to see the world of the novel through Dodola's eyes, including the scenes of her many sexual encounters. Only one of the sexual partners in the book is truly freely chosen and fully consensual, and that is Zam. The other sexual acts in the book are between Dodola and men who are not freely chosen or focused on her pleasure. The first encounter is with her much older husband to whom she was married as a child bride. The next series of sexual encounters was as a prostitute, exchanging sex for food in the dessert. It is in the period of her hunger-induced and enforced prostitution that she is violently raped. Then, she is kidnapped and taken to be part of the sultan's sexual playthings in the palace. In each of these sexual acts, Dodola has a threat of some sort hanging over her as she is forced to participate; threats of physical and emotional violence, starvation, and imprisonment are potential results of her refusal. In this fictional narrative, why does Thompson choose to create a central female character that is both sexualized and abused throughout the book?

In one trenchant review of the book, Burgas (2011) analyzed what he considered anti-male and puritanical anti-sex threads of the narrative. He highlighted the male characters; the only men with redeeming qualities are either eunuchs (Zam and Hyacinth) or insane (Noah). The men who, according to Burgas, are "whole" and sane are criminals or rapists. The claim of a puritanical nature of the book seems highly suspect, given the overtly sexualized subject matter. However, Burgas claimed that the novel is anti-sex not because it eschews sexual encounters but because the sex that is represented is so negative, traumatizing, and lacking in pleasure. The only pleasurable and sensual sexual encounter in the text is at the end of the long, traumatic roads that Dodola and Zam take that lead back to their original bond. Though we do not see the sexual acts, the reader knows that they have spiritually connected in a way that is pleasurable without physical penetration (Zam has to overcome the shame of his castration to be physically intimate with Dodola). Why is the act of loving sex possible if it in fact is impossible? The second example that Burgas offered to support the puritanical nature of Thompson's (2011) narrative is the disparity in the representation of bodies. There is a visual representation of Dodola's naked body on nearly every other page of the book, including several penetrating images of her womb. However, there are no images of grown men's fully naked bodies in the text. Thompson represents young boys' penises but not those of fully grown men. "The male body is something to be ashamed of. The female body, to a certain degree, is something to be celebrated (or, as I alluded to and as several reviewers have pointed out, fetishized)" (Burgas, 2011, para. 16). The options for how to be a man and the consequences of masculinity are limited by the men's seemingly uncontrollable biological drive for sex. "In *Habibi*, 'masculinity' is defined as the sexual element of male-ness—that's all it is, and either you tame it before you become the trollish men who populate the book, or you sever it. There is no nuance" (Burgas, 2011, para. 17). If not insane or castrated, the men in the book are insatiable sexual predators. This narrow view of masculinity has been at least part of the dominant construction of masculinity across many cultures and times. The concern over uncontrollable male sexuality was a rationale for the veiling of women in the Muslim and Christian Middle East. This was also the rationale for historical use of the chastity belt, and the contemporary victim blaming that too often occurs in the wake of rape and sexual assault.

Habibi and Race

Though not as often noted, the role of race is a theme in *Habibi* (Thompson, 2011). On first read, the novel progressively features a multiracial relationship between Zam and Dodola. Zam is a fully developed, if problematic, leading character with whom the readers feel empathy. The other two black characters given names and voices are Hyacinth and Nadidah, who are visually portrayed as so different and distinct from the rest of the characters as to lack humanity. "Thompson has cast Hyacinth as some kind of lovable hood who talks in Black American vernacular, which is stupid on its own in a Hollywood-stereotype kind of way, and also inappropriate in this context" (Haegele, 2011, para. 2). Hyacinth's first sequence in the book is a striking example of race explicitly and seemingly anachronistically presented in the text. Hyacinth finds Dodola massaging Nadidah as a way to try and equalize the slave/master relationship of the harem. Hyacinth stops this reversal of racial roles by warning of palace scandal. "You know how they feel about the role of the BLACK" (Thompson, 2011, p. 91). Hyacinth claims he knows his place in the racial hierarchy of the palace. In the following panel, Hyacinth is shown silhouetted by flames, faces of black men, and fists raised into the air in the protest gesture of the Black Power movement of the 1960s in the United States. "That is, until the moment of REVOLUTION when the black persons reclaim our ROYALTY, and no one—save you and a handful of others—will be spared our wrath" (Thompson, 2011, p. 91). It is a strange moment in a text that otherwise reinforces racial hierarchy and assumption, and because it feels out of place, it comes off as not serious. A few other racially charged scenes play out, some quite significant and some minor, like when one of the black palace eunuchs says to Zam, "HA Ha Have it your way, bro!" (Thompson, 2011, p. 388). One of the more significant scenes involving explicit reference to race is toward the beginning of the novel in the slave market where Dodola finds Zam and escapes into the dessert. A customer says, "No. This is not the variety of BLACK I am looking for," prompting the response of the slaver: "But we have several hues . . . Charcoal, Cinnamon, Shiny prune, Chestnut" (Thompson, 2011, p. 63). The joke of describing these human beings already dehumanized by their enslavement and chaining, by these ridiculous color names, is off color. The punch line of this joke is when one of the slaves (described as chestnut) looks at the reader and says, "Actually, I'm closer to walnut" (Thompson, 2011, p. 63). Making light of the slave market is offensive, especially in the context of clear Orientalist images and the legacy of colonialism brought to life on the pages. Thompson (2011) recreates the Orientalist harem and slave relationships of the women at the sultan's palace without critique. The women of the harem have lighter skin and are highly sexualized; the women serving as their slaves have very dark skin and are not given voice or agency in the novel. Nadidah does speak and has conversations with her assigned charge, Dodola. However, her entire identity in the novel involves caring for Dodola and her baby, abdicating her own will and desires to those of her master. All the characters have racial significance, especially due to the racial identity of Thompson as a White American. Dodola and all the other characters from Wanatolia who cannot be clearly distinguished as Black are generally Semitic, Arab, or Indian. Their racial difference from the author is difficult to pinpoint since the geographical context for Wanatolia seems to be a mishmash of Arab, Middle Eastern, and the Asian subcontinent. The visual codes that identify the racial/cultural stereotypes of the Colonial Gaze include the intermittent supply of camels, the chaotic street market with greedy haggling, veils, turbans, and shifty-eyed slave traders and merchants. The cast of characters in Thompson's marketplace would be just as at home in Disney's hugely problematic *Aladdin* as in the grand Orientalist paintings of the colonial era.

Habibi and Nation Time

The colonial project of mapping and imagining the other involved what McClintock (1995) referred to as the "axis of *time* . . . projected onto the axis of *space*" (p. 359). The different geographies of the globe were thought to represent different periods of human evolution, with the European in the space of most advanced, modern human. In this system of colonized space/time, a gendered notion of time is in play, with women existing somewhere outside the official nation-state and outside of the sweep of time. The representation of space/time in Thompson's (2011) *Habibi* can be read through this postcolonial critique of the global space/time hierarchy. In Wanatolia, the present is sometimes offered as the distant past, the time of *Arabian Nights,* when the sultan gathered together beautiful women for his sexual pleasure. This distant, mythical past is juxtaposed with the sudden impingement of modern construction equipment, trucks, and all of the trappings of the industrialized, generalized third world. Through the lens of the space/time hierarchy, the city represents the Wanatolia that strives toward European-style modernization with skyscraping apartment buildings and the waste and sewage that attends development. The desert and the sultan's palace represent the "traditional" and less developed space and time. The strict hierarchy of modern development as ultimate goal for humanity is disrupted in *Habibi,* due to the focus of the "modern" city on sewage, waste, filth, and starvation. Though the sultan may be evil, the palace provides food, water, and abundant cleanliness. However, as a reader, I felt that the filth of the urban present was particular to the vague Arab/Middle Eastern setting of the book. If the future/present is this corrupt and miserable, it is within a third world urban setting. Dodola certainly feels more at ease in the past/present portions of the book; her entry into the modern streets of urban Wanatolia are full of self-doubt and the pressure to appear more modern and carefree.

Anachronistic Space and Panoptical Time in *Habibi*

The setting of the book represents McClintock's (1995) concept of anachronistic space, in which "colonized people—like women and the working class in the metropolis—do not inhabit history proper but exist in a permanently anterior time within the geographic space of the modern empire as anachronistic humans, atavistic, irrational, bereft of human agency—the living embodiment of the archaic 'primitive'" (p. 30). So many elements of the image/text fit the description of anachronistic space and the humans who inhabit such a space. The imaginary society is based on the colonial vision of the "primitive" as stuck on a lower evolutionary and development level from Europe and the United States. "Linked symbolically to the land, women are relegated to a realm beyond history . . . women are figured as property belonging to men and hence as lying, by definition, outside the male contests over land, money and political power" (p. 31). Dodola is the central character in *Habibi* (Thompson, 2011), yet we come to know her experience almost exclusively through her relationships with men. Most men view her as their rightful sexual and legal property; her body and sexuality are the property and food for the men in her life. This is illustrated quite literally in the image of Dodola's naked body, floating in space and being eaten by creatures of desire and anger. Her will is not the driving force of the story but merely that which is acted upon by the will of men. The idea of panoptical time (McClintock, 1995) is that we can see all of time and development simultaneously, as in the great colonial exhibitions where one could walk through presentations of human cultures and be supposedly transported not just through space but through time, in the various levels of humanity from primitive other to developed self. The confusing and shifted time setting in *Habibi* illustrates the idea of the panoptical time almost perfectly. The reader can see the development of humanity not quite to Western standards of development but at least to the Westernized urban metropolis of Wanatolia.

Habibi and the Visual Language of Comics

Thompson's (2011) sweeping and ambitious narrative is matched and even outpaced by his visual effort and skill. The visual and tactile experience of the text is striking. It weighs in at over 650 pages, and the cover is beautifully crafted and lends the text an almost sacred air. He uses the basic elements of panels and gutters but plays with these elements, and often his drawings and patterns bleed outside of the panels and obliterate these elements altogether. Some critics find the level of detail in the graphic elements and the diversity of Thompson's use of the elements of comics to be distracting and over the top. Many other commenters and reviewers are so impressed by the commitment to artistic detail and creative virtuosity that they focus their reviews on the visual quality rather than the content of the narrative. "Thompson is acutely aware that comics are a visual medium, and that he understands and enjoys crafting pages filled not just with fine adornment, but with fluid movement" (Peagler, 2011, para. 3). "To say the work is visually stunning is an understatement. Thompson's art is simple black and white inking, yet his strokes convey a sense of live movement as if you're watching the characters move across the page" (Mann, 2011, para. 3). Many of these same reviews cite Thompson's meticulous research and presentation of Islamic pattern, design, and calligraphy as evidence of the respect he shows for Islam in the text. "Thompson isn't Muslim, and didn't necessarily grow up with an understanding or appreciation for cultures outside of his own, but his attention to detail is beyond meticulous. Every pattern and example of calligraphy, though based on existing examples of Islamic art and history, was painstakingly reproduced by Thompson's brush" (Peagler, 2011, para. 3). It is amazing that Thompson decided to devote so much time and work to calligraphy and design that was so outside of his knowledge base and comfort zone. Though he never learned to speak or write Arabic, *Habibi* (Thompson, 2011) used Arabic calligraphy as a source of visual design and also an important element in the structure and content of the narrative.

Thompson (2011) used the frames around panels and the gutters to delineate the various times, geographies, and narrative spaces that his novel travels between. When we are in the present time of the narrative, basic, thin, black frames surround the panels and the gutters are plain white. During flashback sequences that travel backward in time, the gutters are generally black. And, in the sections where Thompson uses stories from the Qu'ran and the Bible, he creates intricately patterned frames that surround the parables of the divine that give the story its moral center. Thompson follows this framing convention quite carefully; on pages that feature a mixture of religious parable panels and panels depicting the present day, the frames are split between the ornate design and the simple black (or nonexistent) frame. There are many visually interesting examples of this convention, as the novel moves from present day to parable throughout the tome. Many of these transitions are part of a story that Dodola is telling to a young Zam to calm his fears. On pages 162–163, Dodola soothes a traumatized and dehydrated Zam with water and the story of Job, whose faith led him to endure great suffering in order to be rewarded with water. A panel of Dodola's introduction curves down and into the parable midpage, and the gutter shifts abruptly into an intricate vine-like design of intertwined lines and circles. The design continues onto the top half of the adjacent page but fades away as the parable ends with a flowing speech bubble that both ends the story and transitions back to the present day. This additional detail helps tie the sweeping narrative together, giving visual cues to create some structure to an otherwise rambling and complex story.

Visually, the title pages introducing each chapter are intricately patterned Islamic designs. The glaring exception to this repeating and evolving visual design is the chapter entitled, "Orphan's Prayer," which breaks almost all of the standard graphic narrative conventions and those that Thompson used (2011) throughout this text. This penultimate chapter is broken into panels but without any imagery at all. The stark white panels contain text that moves around in the panels, and six panels have no content at all. These empty spaces are a visual break from the details and often-chaotic visual language of Thompson's *Habibi*. The chapter is quiet visually, and it is precisely this shift to white space that amplifies the tension of the narrative. At the end of the book, Zam is on the brink of suicide, standing at the literal precipice of nothingness and death. The words standing and moving in these white panels feel like the breathing of the character; this is a highly effective visual strategy.

Image/Text and Text as Image

In *Habibi* (Thompson, 2011), one of the most unique and interesting elements of the text is Thompson's focus on words and letters as artistic symbols that shift and form into other shapes. In places throughout the novel, the Arabic calligraphy becomes the image that is described in English text. Thompson plays with the relationship of image and text in graphic narratives, drawing the reader's attention to how the curves, shapes, and meaning of letters can change and drive a narrative. The complex structure of the novel is based around a nine-box grid of Arabic characters, each character expanding to form a chapter. Characters move and turn to create images, and images evolve to create words. Of the many visual conventions that Thompson (2011) created for *Habibi*, his research on the meaning of Arabic characters and his use of the visual power of language are potentially the most interesting and successful. Graphic narratives must be analyzed for the combined use and effect of image and text, a form of reading that cannot use skills of decoding solely text or imagery. I use visual literacy in a more global sense, to include the reading of images, traditional text, and the image-text relationship.

Thompson's (2011) "playing" with the genre of Orientalism is at its most referential. The full-page image of "The Baths" is an almost exact copy of the famed Orientalist paintings of baths, *The Grand Bath at Bursa* by Gerome (1883). The original painting depicts several fair skinned women, lounging in and beside the large bath, with one woman walking arm in arm with her presumed slave. The communal bath was a favorite subject in the Orientalist painting genre, offering the opportunity to imagine a fantastical world of nude women, lounging, bathing, and touching, an ideal scene of visual sensuality that the Orientalist painter could offer his European public. How should we read this image, the image that most obviously references the Orientalist fantasy? Though Thompson claimed to be "playing" with the genre, he presented us with an almost exact copy of the imagery, with no clear attempt to subvert, critique, or question the original. How would readers familiar with the paintings understand the use of the imagery in the context of *Habibi*?

The sexual appetites of the sultan are on display throughout Dodola's time in the palace. The sultan is mean, greedy, highly sexual, and physically repellent. However, his never-ending series of sexually available women highlights to the reader that when coerced by force, survival, and the opulent surroundings of the harem, these women will "willingly" serve the sultan's sexual fantasies. The scenes of "consensual" sex involving the sultan are at once visually disturbing and alluring. The large, hairy, slobbering Sultan disgusts the reader while the women are drawn as sensual, supple, and provocative. Dodola enters the sultan's bedchamber after having been imprisoned and starved for seven months. She asks, "A slave to your commands, Great Monarch, awaits your beckon. May or may she not be admitted?" (Thompson, 2011, p. 241). She is admitted to the bedchamber, and her naked body wraps around the sultan's hairy mass, sadly resigned, and yet it is oddly sensual. One of the more graphically drawn scenes is the sultan's garden party that quickly turns into an orgy (Thompson, 2011, pp. 258–259). After gathering his harem in the garden, he instructs them to drop their robes. We see multiple naked women's bodies (whose names we never learn; they are bodies used by the sultan for sex, and they remain objects rather than subjects) in various sexual positions and acts on one orgiastic cell. The sultan reaches for Dodola (referred to in the palace as Sfayi) to climax, and we see her naked body reclining in the garden, one of several women strewn across the scene.

The relationship between Dodola and Zam plays out in various contexts, beginning in the desert, in an abandoned ship. Alone, the two children forage for food and Dodola cares for younger Zam as if his mother. Once food supplies run out, the reader is taken on Dodola's search for food; she finds caravans of camels and men on trade routes through the desert and sells her body to them for food. The scenes that Thompson draws of the prostitution/rape of Dodola are graphic, violent, disturbing, and strangely erotic. Thompson uses "the repeated rape (and sometimes consensual sex by circumstance) of Dodola as an emotional tool that never feels wholly earned" (Damluji, 2011, para. 11). If, as Thompson has stated, the sexual violation of Dodola is a central element of the text, why are the forced sexual acts shown in graphic detail to the reader?

In "Can the Subaltern Draw? The Spectre of Orientalism in Craig Thompson's Habibi," Damluji (2011) lays out a balanced and thoughtful critique of the novel. The author breaks the text into three distinct sections:

the Arabic calligraphy and design throughout the book, the religious stories and historically researched parables, and finally the romance between Dodola and Zam. The first two elements of the novel were well-researched, thoughtful, and displayed high amounts of skill and care on Thompson's (2011) part. The third section, the romance of the main characters, is the problematic element that allows for the Orientalism that combines stereotypical elements from various areas of the globe, from the Arab world to the Asian subcontinent. "The late 19th-century French Orientalist paintings are very exploitative and sensationalistic. They're sexist and racist and all of those things, and yet there's a beauty to them and a charm. So, I was self-consciously proceeding with an embrace of Orientalism, the Western perception of the East" (Thompson, 2011, para. 24). Thompson (2011) admitted that the Orientalist paintings he directly references in his work are racist and sexist, but he chose to use them anyway. He claimed that the almost exact replication of these images in *Habibi* is not meant to reinforce the historical sexism and racism but rather provide commentary on these through their juxtaposition with other more authentic elements of the text. In response to the interviewers' critical questioning about his "embrace" of Orientalism, Thompson said the following:

> "Embrace" may not be the right choice of words. The book is borrowing self-consciously Orientalist tropes from French Orientalist paintings and the *Arabian Nights*. I'm aware of their sensationalism and exploitation, but wanted to juxtapose the influence of Islamic arts with this fantastical Western take. (para. 26)

Thompson wrote of his conceptual "playing" with Orientalism as a genre, as some play with Cowboys and Indians. The underlying question that is present in his concept is whether one can use a racist, colonialist genre in ways that do not reinscribe that racism. As a cultural outsider, Thompson is in the role of Western, male artist, creating highly sexualized representations of the other. Rather than playing with Orientalism, he is repeating the images, the availability of the Muslim woman's body for Western male viewing, the mythical sexualized zones of the harem and hammam. Just as with the Orientalist painters, such as Gerome, Thompson recreates a fictional space in grand, lush detail, creating a new regime of truth about other people and other women specifically. The effect of Thompson's palace harem takes its place in the "exhibitionary order of colonialism" (Mitchell, 1992/1998). As a reader, the life and body of the characters, especially Dodola, are exhibited as the exotic, sensual other. Though working in supposedly the postcolonial era, Thompson's visual and textual rendering of the imagined space of Wanatolia brings a contemporary life to the colonial visual order. Smith (1998) wrote of the "Visual Regimes of Colonialism," explaining the three-part process of visualization that colonial powers used to establish and consolidate control in a colony: calibration, obliteration, and aestheticization. *Habibi* works within the third stage of aestheticization; it creates a beautiful, exotic façade to mask the unequal power and privilege in colonial relationships. We are awed by the beauty and intricacy of the artwork and calligraphy into giving the problematic cultural representations a pass. If a work is so thoughtfully and skillfully created, it must not be purposefully or consciously biased.

It is precisely the playing with the primitive and the modern, the juxtaposition of the sultan's harem with the heavy machinery of the modern metropolis, that adds to the neo-colonial effect of the graphic narrative:

> Some of it is just fueled from my own experience going to places like Morocco or Vietnam where people's lives do feel like they're from another time centuries ago, but at the same time there's cars and televisions and all that stuff—and plenty of garbage and litter and pollution. I didn't want to make it too modern. I didn't want to have any guns or televisions in the book. So I got to pick and choose what I wanted. It's a fairy-tale world with modern things, cars, and there's plumbing and whatnot. But I'm not having people sitting around watching TV sets in the slums. Which would be closer to reality. (Thompson, 2011, para. 36)

Many comics and literary critics argue that *Habibi* is one the best graphic novels of 2011; they contend that everything that Thompson put into the novel is purposeful and ask the reader to think critically about these representations. This is part of the distinction between the intended meaning of the work from the author and the meaning as it is communicated and received. Although Thompson may have intended his tome as a playful remaking of Orientalism, his play is more of a reproduction than a reinterpretation.

Looking at the similarities between *Blankets* (Thompson, 2004a) and *Habibi* (Thompson, 2011) is instructive. Romantic relationships are at the heart of both texts. What are the lessons of each and how can these inform a critique of the cultural otherness inherent in *Habibi?* Is Thompson critiquing Orientalism through the images/text or is he reinforcing the hierarchy of cultures? Does this all depend on the reception, on the meaning-making process of the reader? If the critique, the wink of the repurposing of the Orientalist trope, relies on previous knowledge of the reader in colonialism broadly, and Orientalism more specifically, then the ultimate lessons of *Habibi* are complex at best and at least fundamentally problematic.

CHAPTER TEN

Graphic Narratives of Self and Other: *American Born Chinese*, *Pyongyang*, and *Fun Home*

This chapter expands the critical visual analysis to several texts that explore the representation of self and other outside of the geographical and cultural context of the rest of the book. Though the primary focus of this book is on the way difference is constructed and represented between the so-called Orient and Occident, the Muslim world and the West, there are many interesting examples of graphic narratives that challenge the representation of multiple forms of difference that can add to our understanding of critical visual literacy.

Fun Home

There are many graphic narratives that explore issues of identity and difference, whether racial, ethnic, cultural, gendered, and/or sexual. One of the more acclaimed graphic narratives in the recent past is *Fun Home*, by Allison Bechdel (2007). This narrative follows the troubled relationship of the author with her father. The sexuality of her father and her own sexual identity form part of the narrative and represent the larger struggle to relate to each other in ways that approach a form of honest communication. The "fun home" of the title refers to the funeral home that Bechdel's father operated, a place where she and her brothers spent quite a bit of their childhood time. Death becomes an everyday reality for the kids because of their father's occupation. Bechdel's father is not a loving figure in her memory; he required precision, neatness, and had fits of anger and rage when things were amiss. The house where the family lived stuck out in the town for its ornately decorated exterior and interior. Bechdel knew from an early age that her family was different from the others in town, that there was something fundamental about the way her father acted and interacted with her mother, her siblings, and his daughter. She also realized that there was something different about her own identity. She was not interested in dressing up and playing with toys that were considered appropriate for girls. Though she did not have the words to describe it as a child, her gender identity and expression were more masculine than other girls. She relates how she later came out as a lesbian and how her parents reacted to this news. *Fun Home* plays with the visuality of gender expression for the author and her father. Bechdel represents her knowledge of her father as being somehow different from very early on in her life. "In fact, we were unusual, though I wouldn't appreciate exactly how unusual until much later" (p. 5). Her father was hanging curtains, fixing molding in the house, obsessed with restoring found pieces into ornate riches that stood out in their neighborhood. Many of the panels in the beginning of the book illustrate Bechdel's father working on the house with no shirt and wearing cutoff jean shorts. The author's representation of her own gender identity shows a clear lack of conformity to the stereotypical norms for young girls. She refused to wear dresses and had very short hair. In fact, Bechdel plays the more stereotypically masculine child to her father's more feminine parent. "I was Spartan to my father's Athenian. Modern to his Victorian. Butch to his Nelly. Utilitarian to his Aesthete" (p. 15).

The visually available codes of difference in the book are modes of gender expression; sexual orientation, though too often conflated with gender, is not necessarily related in any way to one's place on the gender spectrum from masculine to feminine. Bechdel situates the gender roles of her family in their sexuality: "It's imprecise and insufficient, defining the homosexual as a person whose gender expression is at odds with his or her sex. But in the admittedly limited sample comprising my father and me, perhaps it *is* sufficient" (p. 97). She describes their gender as "inversions" of each other, the more precise and fussy about fashion and decoration her father, the more tough and masculine Bechdel became as a form of unconscious compensation. While the gender expression of the author is visually marked and sets her apart from other girls her age, the difference of her father is less visually apparent. Though Bechdel's masculinity is outwardly visible, with her short hair and traditional boyish clothes, her father's gender expression is more privately visible. On page 124, her father is sunbathing in his tiny underwear in the backyard, as the rest of the family is off to church: "yet my father did possess a certain radiance." The peeks at her father's sexuality are easier to decipher in hindsight for Bechdel, due to the relationship as parent and his outward denial of his sexual orientation. Children generally prefer to think of their parents as asexual, but Bechdel is confronted by incriminating signs of her father's sexuality and his attraction to young men. Over the course of the book, she becomes increasingly comfortable with her identity as a lesbian and open with her conflicted memory of and relationship with her dead father. Toward the end of the book, Bechdel illustrates a few awkward and emotionally fraught scenes between her father and her young adult self. In a pivotal scene riding in a car from pages 219 to 221, her father admits to having some physical relationship with an employee at the funeral home at age 14 and another in college. He then tells his daughter, "When I was little, I really wanted to be a girl. I'd dress up in girls' clothes," to which Bechdel responds, "I wanted to be a boy! I dressed in boys' clothes!" (p. 221). This car ride remains the only time that their "inversion" of gender roles is explicitly discussed, and it provides an important moment of connection but not the breakthrough that Bechdel had hoped for with her father. The gender and sexual visual difference of the text is realistically portrayed; the codes of gender nonconformity are subtle and almost an undercurrent, especially in her father.

Maus: A Survivor's Tale: My Father Bleeds History and the follow-up volume, *Maus: A Survivor's Tale: And Here My Troubles Began* by Art Spiegelman (1986, 1992) are classics in the medium of the graphic narrative that represents difference in visually interesting ways. The books tell the story of the author's father and mother and their time before and during World War II. One of the most important decisions that Spiegelman made in crafting the books was to draw different groups of people as different animals. He drew his father, mother, and other Jews as mice; the Germans were cats, Americans were dogs, and the French were frogs. He decided to create visually different groups of people where the difference is not visible. All of the characters in the book have certain animal characteristics, heads and tails related to the animal paired with their national and/or religious identities. However, they all wear human clothing, hats, and carry purses, briefcases, and so forth. They all walk upright and appear to be a visual cross between species. In one of the most interesting examples of visually depicting the invisible differences of the book, Spiegelman draws his parents in hiding, pretending to be German to hide from the Nazi soldiers. He draws them as mice in cat masks with their mouse tails peeking out from underneath their coat and dress. They are in disguise, but it is one that can never completely cover their identities. The image speaks to the concept of code switching and wearing masks to "pass" for another, often less marginalized or oppressed group. For Spiegelman, the decision to draw difference by using different animal species was an intuitive way to confront the horrifying atrocities of the Holocaust. The animal figures gave a surreal and less than serious veneer to a story that was very real and deadly serious. It is also a way to imagine human difference in a nonthreatening way; there is great peril in depicting ethnic, racial, or religious differences in human form. It too often falls into the realm of stereotypical visual code and assumption.

Epileptic

Epileptic by David B. (2006) shares some of the visual codes for difference made iconic by Spiegelman. In addition to creating visual dragons and monsters that serve as codes for his brother's epilepsy, the author represents the Japanese gurus that his family works with as different cats (though dressed and shaped otherwise like humans). David B. introduces us to "Master N." (p. 45), a Japanese master who teaches aikido and places the family on a macrobiotic diet based on the concepts of balancing the energy of Jean-Christophe and controlling his epilepsy. The master is a tiger, though walking upright and dressed in human clothing, much like all of the characters in *Maus* (Spiegelman, 1986, 1992). Unlike the visualization of human differences in *Maus,* Master N. is one of only three living human characters in the book that are consistently depicted as animal/humans. Jilau is the next cat/human in the text; he is the son of Master N. and attempts to take his place after Master N. was indicted for practicing medicine without a license. The powerful and healing presence of Master N. took the form of a large yet smiling tiger with a very long, striped tail. The son is described as "more like a playboy than a healer. Yet he's quite self-assured when he talks about macrobiotics and medicine" (David B., 2006, p. 70). The son is not the large, powerful tiger figure of his father but is slender and laid-back, with an almost silly grin on his face. The other living human/animal we meet is another Master N., not a tiger but another sleeker form of cat/human. This figure is powerful and skilled at aikido but does not have the time or energy to devote to Jean-Christophe. Other than these potentially healing Japanese figures, the other humans depicted as animals are the dead, especially the author's grandfather, who dies during his childhood. His grandfather takes on the form of an exaggerated bird-human who serves as a protector of Pierre-François. Why does David B. use animal/human figures to depict a handful of characters in the book? The use of the cat figures for Japanese masters could reflect racial difference, a way to represent the other without using stereotypical ethnic facial features. However, all of the figures have in common a connection to a world beyond the visible world of humans, with varying levels of spiritual connection. The animal features of the characters leave them closer visually to the ghosts, monsters, and soldiers of Pierre-François's imaginary world than to the human world of his family. Visualizing difference through the use of animal/human hybrids is an instant way to set up more foundational differences between people. Rather than using paragraphs of text to describe difference in detail, the images of Master N., Jilau, and the second Master N. require the reader to take immediately recognizable visual difference and then work to decode the difference.

As the narrative continues and Jean-Christophe is more consumed by his epilepsy, the drawings become more complex, darker, and the monsters and ghosts fill a growing importance in the narrative. At one point, on page 191, David B. (2006) wrote, "I can no longer distinguish my brother's illness as separate from him. Epilepsy has merged with his body." One panel shows the dragon-like monster that is the visual manifestation of epilepsy in the book and the next shows Jean-Christophe, his face darkened and features simplified and almost difficult to distinguish. The image of his brother has merged with the image of the monster. After this merger, his brother has several bouts of unexplainable violence and anger. It is unclear whether this anger and violence is a result of the epilepsy or of other psychological issues related to being defined as sick and outside of the norm. The violence is directed at all members of his family; he punches his father, throws a scalding pot of soup at his mother, and wields a knife in the middle of the night at his brother's bedroom door. During these violent episodes, David B.

illustrates the internal difference of temperament visually through the size, shape, and shade of Jean-Christophe's body and face. As he grows scarier, he literally grows on the page, glowering over his tiny family members, helpless against the rage. In one sequence, he burns himself with a match trying to light the oven and spins into rage (pp. 256–257). His body is at least twice as big as normal when he kicks his mother off her chair and stomps on her with his now giant foot. His face and body are crosshatched with thick black lines. The dark patterns covering his body and face, along with his sheer size, make visible the invisible processes of rage. The reader understands that David B. used these codes to show a change in mood, tone, and temperament. The most extreme example of this visual language is on pages 264–265, when Jean-Christophe begins to keep kitchen knives around his belt. In two panels, when confronted about hurting his father, he says, "Good! He had it comin'! I'm glad!" (p. 264). His face is monstrous in size and appearance. It fills the entire panel and now is mostly black with white crosshatching. His rage visually transforms him into someone or something else. David B. is masterful in his own visual language, creating codes that the reader must interpret as the narrative moves along. The codes evolve as readers become more ready to interpret them. The lines, shapes, and shading become increasingly more intense, and the use of animal stand-ins for humans, ghosts, and monsters increases until David B. begins to find his own professional success and moves emotionally away from his complex and troubled attachment to his brother and the disease. The visual quality of this text is intensely patterned and stylized, reflecting the inner world of David B. and his fight to save his brother and himself in the process. The dream world of battles, monsters, and creatures of his imagination and the actual sleeping dreams that he illustrates seem more real than the scenes of daily life. It is fitting that the author ends the text with an epilogue that offers another imagined dream sequence, a conclusion that lacks closure. In this final waking dream, David B. and his brother are riding on horses through the drawings of their childhood, discussing their complex relationship with greater clarity than they did anywhere else in the book. This conversation offers emotional clarity only because it is an imagined one, a dialogue that David B. constructs to make sense of their disjointed and troubling interactions. Jean-Christophe says, "Your drawings of battles piled up, and so did my seizures," to which David B. replies, "I could picture life only as a series of confrontations" (p. 358). It is fitting that the final page of the book includes a small panel where David B. imagines his own face on his brother's body; the whole story has really been about the author's battles and fear. He was horribly afraid of becoming his brother, more concerned about how he was affected by the seizures and his brother's seclusion from the world than about the well-being of his brother.

Pyongyang and *Burma Chronicles*

Pyongyang: A Journey in North Korea, a graphic travelogue by Guy Delisle (2007), is a narrative that follows Delisle on an extended stay in North Korea to work on a French animated television show. Though this is a nonfictional account of a different country and culture, it is not graphic journalism per se because Delisle did not travel to Pyongyang to investigate the political, cultural, or human conditions in the country. He travelled to the country to work in an animation studio and while there captured a unique portrait of the strange state. The book is an interesting visual window into a country that is the most closed off from the rest of the world. The illustrated panel of a close-up map of the Korean peninsula is an elegant metaphor for the isolation of the country; Delisle draws a basic map with a tall brick wall outlining the country of North Korea. Images that the outside world sees of the country are highly censored and controlled by the regime; cameras and photographs are closely monitored. Therefore, the drawings of Delisle offer a unique opportunity to see what (some of) the country looks like. As a foreigner, he is assigned a guide and a translator, two men who follow him very closely. He is not allowed to leave his isolated hotel for foreigners without his handler, who must approve of all destinations. The differences that Delisle illustrates in this narrative are ethnic and racial, but they are also the vast differences in levels of transparency, openness, and control between North Korea and the rest of the world (particularly with Canada, the author's home country). He manages to bring a copy of George Orwell's (1949) *1984* in his suitcase and he quotes Orwell throughout the text; the similarities between the dystopia of Orwell's London and of Kim Jong-il's Pyongyang are striking. Delisle does fall back on the stereotypical ethnic visual cues to portray the difference between himself and other Westerners and the North Koreans. His own eyes are small circles, sometimes growing to larger, open circles to express shock or surprise. Other Westerners have variations on the circular theme. The North Koreans, however, are given horizontal, slanted lines for eyes, playing on the stereotypical visual code of narrow, slanted eyes that Western visual culture has created for those of various Asian ethnicities.

Delisle (2007) manages to convey the strange and unique atmosphere of this country in image/text in ways that words alone could never accomplish. On page 33, he draws a full panel of a dinner he has in his hotel (the three restaurants are named Restaurant One, Restaurant Two, and Restaurant Three). In a large and seemingly opulent banquet hall, the author is alone, one seat filled in an otherwise eerily silent hall. In another full-page panel on page 49, Delisle draws a dark image of Pyongyang at night, where the only lights are from the few cars on the empty roads and spotlights brightly illuminating huge images of the "Dear Leader." Without the accompanying text on other pages, these images would be difficult to decode, but after reading the descriptions of the strange environment, these freestanding panels, devoid of text, speak volumes. A wind-up toy man is one visual metaphor for the mental containment that takes place in the country; it repeats in key locations of the text and symbolizes Delisle's sense of the strange brainwashing that creates unflinching admiration for a regime that is all powerful and controls its people in every way. When we first see this image, on page 59, it is a smiling man wearing a basic suit with a wind-up mechanism on his back. It is presented in a small panel with no text directly after a panel that reads, "With a six-day work week, one day of 'volunteer' work and preparations for the big events, the average citizen has almost no spare time. Body and soul serve the regime" (p. 59). Then, there is the image of the wind-up toy, moving only because some outside figure winds the mechanism; without a winder, this toy is useless and immobile. The wind-up toy appears again on page 75, in the context of Delisle questioning whether his translators and guide really believe the fabrications and intricate lies constructed by the regime. This image of the wind-up toy is instantly familiar to the reader, yet there is an important difference. This toy now has one mechanism on its back to control its ability to move, and it has a second mechanism on the back of its head. The newly added mechanism controls the ability to think and speak. For this toy, movement and thought are fully under the control of an outside party; individual or free thought is impossible. Delisle frames the question of thought: "Do they really believe the bullshit that's being forced down their throats?" (p. 74). Do the people in Pyongyang, some of whom have even travelled to Europe for work, really believe that the North Korean regime is infallible and righteous? Or, are they aware of the supreme control and scary implications for those who even hazard a negative thought against the regime?

As the narrative moves forward, the visual representation of the completely isolated and controlled country reinforces Delisle's (2007) discomfort. One powerful image of the strange conformity and veneer of happiness and prosperity in North Korea is from the author's planned and chaperoned excursion to the Children's Palace, a training ground for gifted children. The palace is filled with children working intently on various tasks, using their gifts to focus on ritualistic and uniform training in music, technology, and calligraphy, all done in the name of the Dear Leader. "You can just imagine the training needed to achieve such robotic results" (p. 157). The lasting image of conformity Delisle creates of this palace is a full-page panel on page 144. Row upon row of uniformly dressed, smiling girls sit and play the accordion. The smiles are artificially broad, straining to convey utter joy. "As though the thin veneer of their smiles were proof that these young prodigies are flourishing here. It's all so cold . . . and sad" (p. 157). Delisle draws the smiling accordion players as another visual metaphor for the country. The regime and its people put so much concentration and energy into creating the appearance of happiness and good fortune, but it is a strain to maintain such a façade. The achingly broad smiles of the girls at the Children's Palace are reminiscent of another façade that Delisle illustrates, an unfinished monster of a hotel in pyramid form that towers over the city: "...designed to host part of the 1988 Olympic trials, it would have been the tallest hotel in Asia with its 105 floors, 5 revolving restaurants and 3,700 rooms" (p. 124). This monumental building project, funded with French money, was abandoned once the concrete shell was built, leaving an impressive façade that is totally empty on the inside. Although Delisle knows that the few North Koreans he meets are certainly not empty on the inside, he is never sure of what is happening inside the brains of his translators and guides.

The overall effect of *Pyongyang* is that it offers up more questions than answers about North Korea, though it gives a glimpse into the daily life of foreigners in the country in what they are allowed to see, do, and eat. Delisle (2007) presents the characters in the book as living in tension, caught up in a melodramatic play that is performed on a national scale. Those who do not participate in the play are sent to prison camps or reeducation camps. He illustrates the constant threat of not conforming to the patriotic standard in a series of lineups he places throughout the narrative. As we travel through the book, North Koreans are removed from the lineup for various traitorous infractions. On page 66, we have our first lineup quiz, which asks us to identify the "vile imperialist spy in the pay of South Korea's puppet government" from a line of six North Korean men. Delisle writes the "answer" underneath and upside down, that number 6 is the spy because he is not wearing his official Dear Leader pin. We return to the quiz on page 92, (number 6 has now disappeared) to identify the "vile anti-party element corrupted by the imperialist bourgeoisie" from the remaining five men. This time, the offender is number 2 because his pin is smudged and he has no way to clean it off. The third and final lineup quiz asks us to identify the "conspirators who seek to destabilize our glorious nation" (p. 152). The answer is that numbers 1, 3, 4, 5, and 7 are all traitors due to either letting their portraits of the Dear Leader gather dust, not showing the proper enthusiasm at the last patriotic demonstration, or because their grandfathers fought with the South Koreans in the 1950s. So, at the end of the quiz, we find that all six men were disloyal to the regime in some way and therefore removed to some form of camp or prison. This series of recurring panels gives the reader a sense of how arbitrary and ominous the sentencing and punishment can be and how easily one can be labeled as a traitor, spy, or conspirator.

Delisle (2010) wrote about a different form of brutal dictatorship in his *Burma Chronicles*. The regime in Burma has different forms of control over the people; the government's power is nowhere near as absolute and unquestioned as the Dear Leader in North Korea. In the first few pages of the book, Delisle (now traveling for his wife's career with Médecins Sans Frontières [MSF, or Doctors Without Borders] rather than for his own animation work) and his family make the very long trip to Burma. The first sign that they are going to be living in a different, more repressed society is when he finds that pages of *Time* have been taken from the magazine by the country's censors, who painstakingly remove any negative references to the regime. The control is present but less all-consuming than in North Korea, where every movement is tracked and monitored. In Burma, Delisle is free to walk the streets with his young son, Louis, who draws adoring attention from the Burmese. The other major indicator of the political situation is the street in the family's new neighborhood that is blocked off due to the presence of Nobel Peace Prize winner, Aung San Suu Kyi. "In fact, she's not really a prisoner, she can't leave her home, but she's free to leave the country. Except she has chosen to stay and, by her simple presence, resist one of the most oppressive regimes in the world" (p. 33). Delisle illustrates the imprisonment of Suu Kyi by drawing her street, her house an empty white shell existing between fully drawn houses. The small woman stands inside her home, unable to leave and unwilling to give in. Aside from these references to the difference of living under an oppressive regime, the author focuses his attention on the little daily differences that fascinate him. He spends several pages drawing the shelves in the local grocery store. The local practice of chewing betel nut, which turns teeth a reddish-black shade, fascinates the author. He also notes with wonder the practice of spitting the remnants of one's betel nut chew into corners of stairways. Through his chronicling of subtle and daily differences, he brings his Western lens to Burmese culture with openness and ease. The visual differences are noted, especially in the clothes of the Burmese, generally worn for their ability to keep one cool in the sweltering heat. While one notes the differences, Delisle does not highlight these differences. They are accepted and viewed as interesting but not fundamental in character. Rather than differences between the author's Western upbringing and the Burmese culture, the most important human difference that he highlights is between the military elite and the rest of the people. The generals who rule the country control and have access to resources and opportunities that the Burmese people do not.

Many of the minor, daily differences in Burma are related to the larger repression of the military junta. For example, one day the junta decides to ban all foreign films. This directly affects the author because he suddenly loses access to pirated copies of Hollywood films. Reactions from the Burmese are quite different than those Delisle illustrated in North Korea; in Burma, no one believes the official propaganda from the regime; they know that they are being denied access to information and resent it. Delisle (2010) returns to the idea of censorship in a section titled "Cens-o-rama" (p. 66). The most potent visual representation of the censor's work in Burma, to allow some Western publications into the country but remove anything possibly negative, is a panel on page 67. This panel shows Delisle holding up a newspaper with articles cut out of every page, an empty shell, and a newspaper with no news. He uses the censorship as a mechanism to discuss the propaganda of official government publications: he lists the four "People's Desires" that the regime posts all around, including "Crush all internal and external destructive elements as the common enemy" (p. 68). The rhetoric of the Burmese military junta is very similar to the paranoid dictates of the Dear Leader, but the effects are quite different. If the image of North Korea with a tall brick wall built around it is the quintessential image from *Pyongyang* (Delisle, 2007), the one that speaks to a different level of isolation in Burma is a panel on page 70 that shows two speech bubbles filled with image rather than text. In the left bubble, a man with eyes blacked out and mouth taped firmly shut is coming from the official Burmese newspaper, and a man with no encumbrances is speaking loudly and freely from a radio playing a Burmese-language broadcast from Thailand. In this small panel, a main distinction between the two regimes of Delisle's books becomes clear: in North Korea, the control over access to information is complete; therefore the government's narrative is the only one. In Burma, the control over access to information is partial; therefore the people can critically compare and sift information for themselves.

In a visit to an elderly woman's bedside, she opens up to Delisle (2010), offering her true feelings about her country and the regime's effect—she has nothing to fear at her age. "What a horrible country this is. In my state, I've no one to fear. I can speak my mind" (p. 95). The Burmese that Delisle gets to know are much more open about criticizing the regime than the North Koreans he met. He also has more freedom to travel to certain areas of the country and meet locals around Rangoon. Delisle and wife Nédege form close relationships with their housekeeper/babysitter Sagn Nan and guard/playmate Maung Aye during their yearlong stay. Delisle also meets regularly with a group of three cartoonists whom he teaches about the basics of computer animation. In an important reminder of the oppressiveness of the regime, a journalist friend of the author visits Rangoon and illustrates a piece about his trip with a critique of the regime and an image of Delisle. The paper leads to trouble for one of the cartoonists, who works in a low-level government position; his association with a foreigner who could be critical of the regime is a serious offense. The man leaves the class without answers about the consequences of his association. Happily, at the end of the text, the missing student returns after a mysterious absence to join the group in a farewell dinner.

Delisle (2010) illustrates the complex situation for nongovernmental organizations (NGOs) in Burma through several of the short chapters. His wife is a manager for MSF-France, which operates several clinics in the field, mostly diagnosing and providing free treatment for malaria patients far from other care. However, at the end of the book, MSF-France is closing the doors to its mission in Burma. In one complex and interesting conversation, titled appropriately, "Conversation," Delisle discusses the departure with the MSF program manager Asis. The mission of MSF-France in Burma was to provide needed care for ethnic minority groups who are persecuted by the junta and living in warzones. The regime, however, will not allow any foreigners to pass through the regions where these persecuted groups live, including MSF. "MSF's mandate is to help the most disadvantaged. In our case, we've targeted a population, the Karens, who live in the mountains near the Thai border," Asis explained (p. 233). The military leaders do not want witnesses to the attacks, oppression, and conditions of the Karens; therefore they allow MSF-France to provide free care and medicine to Burmese who should be covered by the government. "At some point, if we agree to stay, we end up abetting the government's actions, and in the process, we become an instrument of discrimination" Asis said (p. 233). It is a difficult situation for many NGOs who set up in Burma wanting to help the most marginalized populations but inadvertently providing aid to the government through the tight control of movements and actions. Delisle visits the missions of several other Western NGOs while in Burma. The MSF-Holland mission works around Burma to help the growing number of HIV/AIDS patients, including working on prevention and education measures. The mission employs Delisle to write and illustrate an educational comic book for kids on the importance of taking their retroviral drugs. MSF-Holland also gives out free needles and condoms in an attempt to stem the tide of HIV/AIDS among heroin addicts and prostitutes serving gemstone miners in the northern region of the country. Poppy cultivation and heroin are major sources of income for the Burmese regime and many Katchin (a minority group in the north) are addicted to heroin. "In Hpakant, miners are paid in shots of heroin. There are also so-called shooting galleries, where $1 will get you a fix" (p. 239). It is a very difficult decision for NGOs to leave their posts providing needed medical care to protest the regime's repressive policies and discriminatory actions.

There are similar issues for NGOs in North Korea, although these groups are only allowed in very limited number and with limited missions. One of the major distinctions between the suffering of Burmese and North Koreans, in Delisle's illustrations, is that the world knows of the suffering and repression of certain groups in Burma. In North Korea, there are educated guesses about the number of people starving to death, sent to prison camps, and otherwise tortured and oppressed, but because of the complete vacuum of information, it is impossible to know for sure. In 1995, North Korea faced an extreme famine and the regime opened up a tiny door for food assistance from foreign aid agencies and governments. "In this highly stratified society, the regime uses rationing to consolidate power. A national public distribution system gives citizens portions based on their loyalty and usefulness to the regime" (Delisle, 2007, p. 47). The second sentence accompanies an illustrated grid of the North Korean population, divided first into the "Useful Population" and the "Useless Population." The "Useful" are divided further into "the core" of the regime command that receives the most rice; "the lukewarm" are those citizens that toe the line and conform to expectations and receive a subsistence level of rice. The "Useless" are divided into "the hostile," who are political prisoners, children of dissidents, and laborers; these people are given a starvation diet of 250 grams per day of rice. The final category of the "Useless" are unnamed, an estimated 6 million people, "ignored by the regime, [they] are left to fend for themselves" (Delisle, 2007, p. 47). The chart is a stark example of the profound inequality in the country and the greed and corruption of the regime. Given this reality, many NGOs (including Oxfam and Doctors Without Borders) left the country, determined not to contribute to such an unjust system of aid distribution. The calculations are similar in Burma and North Korea; the foreign aid, though full of good intentions, ended up contributing to the power of the repressive regimes and to the misery of ordinary people.

The structures of the two texts are quite different, leading to a difference in tone. *Pyongyang* (Delisle, 2007) is written in long sections that are unnamed but preceded by a full-page panel that illustrates an important iconic or strange image of North Korea. While there are certainly moments of humor in the text, the overall effect of the structure is a more serious focus on the utter isolation of the people and total control over every facet of life under the regime. In *Burma Chronicles,* Delisle (2010) structures the book into quite short (often a single page) anecdotes, each titled with an introductory frame and image at the upper left-hand corner of the first page in the section. The quick change of focus in the book leads from a more serious section, like one that focuses on Nobel Prize winner Aung San Suu Kyi or the disappearance of his student and friend, into a short and tender section about a family trip to a baby's birthday party. The effect of these transitions gives this text a lighter tone; the short sections have the feel of a series of comics, rather than a long, flowing graphic narrative. There is also a focus on daily Burmese life that is missing from the text on North Korea, necessitated by the author's much shorter stay in Pyongyang and the inability to travel freely and meet locals and form relationships. Another fundamental structural difference in the two texts is the use of recurring key and metaphorical images in *Pyongyang*. There are recurring images that are metaphors created by Delisle to illustrate the psychological effects of the isolation and control (the aforementioned wind-up toy, the loyalty lineup of North Koreans). Delisle (2007) also repeats two other visual themes: monumental objects (giant sculptures of the Dear Leader, buildings, monuments) and scenes of darkness devoid of human presence. The giant monuments overenthusiastically support the regime through patriotic slogans like "Forging ahead into the 21st century!" (p. 17) and "Advancing gladly despite the hardships!" (p. 99). The enthusiasm of the slogans juxtaposed with the scenes of emptiness and darkness bring a sense of Delisle's dislocation, of the strangeness of being a foreigner in a land where the surface illusion of prosperity and happiness so easily falls away to show the despair and isolation. There are no such recurring metaphors in *Burma Chronicles*. The images evolve throughout the text, generally filled with lively interaction and daily life. The most raucous illustrations are of the water festival, marking the Buddhist New Year celebration. The celebrations, water, and chaos-filled streets are a direct contrast to the vast emptiness of Pyongyang. Delisle drew the panels of *Pyongyang* in graphite pencil, with all shading and atmosphere added with pencil. The softness of the pencil line helps set the somber, thoughtful tone of Delisle's time.

In both texts, *Pyongyang* (2007) and *Burma Chronicles* (2010), Delisle plays the role of self-reflexive outsider. The differences that he illustrates in his work are clearly filtered through the author's lens and Western perspective. He draws both subtle and major cultural differences with a sympathetic eye for the local population. In both texts, he is highly critical of the dictatorial regimes while showing a great deal of care for the people he encounters. By making this a memoir with his own experiences and perspective at the center of the narrative, Delisle frames his representations of difference as obviously subjective. He does not pretend to be a cultural insider or expert in these books; he attempts to show a balanced, yet consciously biased, view of complex societies.

CHAPTER ELEVEN

Conclusion: Lessons of Critical Visual Literacy

As technological advances change the way we communicate and view the world through apps and mobile devices, the centrality of the image/text creates a dire need for visual literacy. Reading the world is no longer limited to reading the word; students need to be able to read images as they read text to decode for meaning, intention, and effect. Educational policy is moving away from teaching about the visual as arts budgets are cut and focus continues to be on the standardized assessment of reading and math skills. In this globalized world, students need greater instruction in critical textual, media, and visual literacy that engages with representations of difference in race, ethnicity, gender, sexuality, class, and location. Postcolonial theory provides an analysis of global relationships of power and displaces the West as center of all knowledge and creativity. Critical multicultural education focuses on school as a social and political institution that functions to marginalize certain groups and privilege others. Border theory is in many ways a contemporary form of pragmatic philosophy that roots ambiguity in the traveling between cultural and geographic borders. Border theory is the connection between postcolonialism and critical multicultural education; it celebrates uncertainty and the doubting of assumptions that are embedded in imbalanced relationships of power and privilege. My focus on the use of contemporary, border-crossing graphic authors necessitates a form of critical multicultural pedagogy that questions Eurocentric, modern myths that are entrenched in traditional pedagogy. The combined efforts of these approaches help me create pedagogy that can reform how we educate about difference and the way we see others and ourselves. The Visual Orientalist discourse, which has helped enforce the stereotypical Western views about Islam and Muslim women, can be used in conjunction with the graphic memoirs of Satrapi and Bashi, for example, to create a form of pedagogy that honestly analyzes stereotypes and works toward more complex understandings of difference.

A (Very) Brief History of Difference in American Education

American schools have historically served as battlegrounds on how difference was taught to kids and how kids who were different fought to be educated equally. Common School reformers of the early 19th century, like Horace Mann, developed a system of public schools to provide opportunities for rich and poor. Through the mid-1800s, African American children were either barred from receiving any education due to slavery or were segregated in separate schools in cities in the North. The late 1800s and early 1900s were a time of evolving policy in the education of Native Americans by the American government. Led by the efforts of Richard Henry Pratt and the Bureau of Indian Affairs (BIA), the government shifted from a policy of removal and extinction of Native tribes to overt and official forms of assimilation and indoctrination into the Anglo-Protestant American culture. Pratt infamously said that rather than killing the Indians, the government should, "Kill the Indian in him and save the man" (Adams, 1997, p. 53). Pratt believed that education could remove the "savage" Indian ways of knowing and living from young people and replace these with "civilized" ways of mainstream White Americans. Though this view of complete cultural assimilation appears very harsh through the current educational ideologies of multiculturalism and tolerance of difference, Pratt's idea that Indians could become like White Americans if given the proper education was radical for its time. In the most extreme examples of educational policy used as a tool for indoctrination and assimilation, the off-reservation boarding schools of the late 1880s took young boys and girls away from their families and transported them to schools far from home where they were educated in English, Christianity, and values such as punctuality and order. The Native

American students who arrived at these schools were accustomed to collective property and being connected with their tribe; they organized space and time around nature and the movements of the sun and moon. These schools were designed around the idea that there was a superior culture and difference was a problem to be done away with through education.

The struggle to legally desegregate American public schools by race began in Boston with the case of Sarah Roberts in 1855 and continued through the Supreme Court decision of *Brown v. Board of Education* in 1954. This landmark decision ended de jure segregation, though de facto segregation in the South continued into the late 1960s and to this day in urban centers throughout the country. Though racial segregation ended legally in 1954, the process of desegregation in the Deep South was painfully slow. There were many painful examples of angry crowds blocking young Black children from entering still-segregated White schools, though two examples garnered national media attention. In 1957, nine African American students in Little Rock, Arkansas, gained national attention when their attempts to integrate Little Rock's Central High were met with armed resistance. In addition to the angry crowd of citizens voicing their disapproval and anger, National Guard troops, called up by Governor Faubus, blocked entrance to the school. In 1960, six-year-old Ruby Bridges became the first African American student to enter William Frantz Elementary School in New Orleans, Louisiana. There were protesters lining her route to school and she had to be escorted to school by federal marshals. Once enrolled in the first grade, all of the other (White) children were removed from the classroom by their parents, leaving Ruby and her teacher Barbara Henry alone for the school year. Mrs. Henry was the only teacher in the school willing to teach a Black child.

American curriculum was actually linguistically diverse until World War I in the early 20th century. Until the United States was embroiled in a massive war in Europe, many European groups taught school in languages other than English. In Chicago, Illinois, and the Midwest, German Americans received their primary instruction in German. Once the United States entered World War I, then-President Theodore Roosevelt argued against instruction in any language other than English. To be patriotic in the war effort, schools purged books written in other languages and instituted English-only instruction. As part of the sweeping civil rights legislation of the 1960s and 1970s, the Bilingual Education Act of 1968 provided federal attention and funds for public school curriculum that attended to the specific needs of students who were nonnative English speakers. The pendulum of support for the speaking and learning of languages other than English in public schools began to swing again in the 2000s when several states, including Texas and California with high English as a Second Language (ESL) populations, stripped funding and access to bilingual education programs. Despite the fact that the United States does not have a national language, many politicians and citizens argue for English-only instruction in schools. With all of the progressions and regressions for the equality of access and opportunity of American students, there has been movement toward a general agreement about the value of at least tolerating difference in the classroom. There is an important distinction to be made between accepting students who are different from each other and from the norm and creating curriculum that honors the experience of these students and challenges injustice and oppression. I argue that we do not have a true critical multicultural curriculum without overt instruction in how to identify and fight against racism, sexism, heterosexism, able-ism, xenophobia, Islamophobia, and so forth. Tools for critical literacy in text, image, and the media need to be created and used in classrooms to allow for long-term systemic changes to the system.

Individuals and Curriculum of Isolation

The increasingly narrow focus of educational policy in the United States on standardization, quantifiable results, and competition represents a retreat from the engaged, critical multiculturalism that is needed to counteract toxic xenophobia. The No Child Left Behind (NCLB) Act, pushed through Congress by President George W. Bush in 2002, required state testing of all third through eighth graders in math and reading and once in Grades 10 through 12. The results of this testing regimen were used to determine Adequate Yearly Progress (AYP) for different subgroups of students with the stated goal of closing the achievement gaps. Critics of NCLB decried the hyper focus and narrowing of the curriculum to reading and math and the billions of dollars spent on creating or revising state standardized tests. Several states labeled NCLB an unfunded federal mandate and a handful, including Vermont, Idaho, Kentucky, and South Dakota, refused to comply and risked losing federal education funding.

Though many progressive educators were hopeful for a change in educational policy with the election of President Barack Obama, the federal policy moved further down the road of test and punish that began with No Child Left Behind (NCLB) under President Bush. The Obama administration, with Secretary of Education Arne Duncan at the helm, shifted a portion of federal education funding to a competitive grant process that awarded points to states "choosing" to rush the implementation of several controversial reforms, including Common Core State Standards, linking teacher evaluation to student test results and raising or lifting caps on the number of charter schools. Under the twin goals of producing high school graduates ready for college and career and being globally competitive, the administration moved forward major reforms by having states compete for funding through Race to the Top grants. The results so far are greater emphasis on standardized testing, more pressure for teachers to narrow their curriculum and to focus instruction on preparation for tests, and critique from both left- and right-wing activists against the Common Core State Standards. Diane Ravitch (2014), an educational historian and scholar, is one of the most vociferous critics of the standards. "Setting national academic standards is not something done in stealth by a small group of people, funded by one source, and imposed by the lure of a federal grant in a time of austerity" (para. 6). Conservatives have started to derisively call the Common Core "Obamacare for Education" and critique the standards as a federal over-reach into states' rights (Lord, 2014, para. 2).

All of this educational reform in the past decade and a half has a net result of isolating American students in several ways. "The nature of competition is that there are designated winners and losers" (Fertakis, 2011, para. 11). The student is isolated in her classroom, competing with her classmates for grades, test scores, and knowledge. She is isolated in her school, competing against other schools for the most qualified and effective teachers and valuable, scarce resources. She is isolated from the world, being groomed to be globally competitive while learning less and less about the rest of the world and how to collaborate across differences and borders for positive change. This increasing and all-encompassing isolation can foster xenophobia and a distrust of difference in all forms. Competition can lead to this fear of difference and encourage the creation and reification of hierarchies, so that being different is not just scary but also a deficit. In the face of this dehumanizing focus on isolation and standardization, the work of progressive, postcolonial, postmodern educators is increasingly needed as an antidote. Greene (1995) argued against isolation and for the importance of collaboration in education. "Speaking with others, working with others, playing with others, and making things with others, the young may attain some reciprocity of perspectives as they try to create networks of relationships within and among themselves" (p. 58). If students are not encouraged to engage with those around them as human beings worthy of respect, how can we expect them to expand notions of community to those outside of their real and imagined communities?

Current attempts at multicultural education are flawed in their approach and produce further marginalization of difference through the structure and form of curriculum. "Indeed, multicultural education has become the new metadiscipline that is most often deployed to address the current eruption of difference and plurality in social life now invading the school" (Dimitriadis & McCarthy, 2001, p. 113). The visualizing of difference in curriculum generally relies on stock images of difference that highlight exotic location, dress, and activity. In response to the Eurocentric forms of art education, I propose using pragmatic doubt, border theory, and postcolonial pedagogy to create a polycentric form of multicultural education, a pedagogy that breaks apart the traditional center/periphery binary to centralize the creative possibilities of uncertainty. I detail an extended sample lesson that is an example of how the postcolonial, pragmatic, visual pedagogy can function to shift our relationship to the representation of difference. The sample lesson that utilizes media images and graphic memoir is meant to be taught as part of an interdisciplinary curriculum that extends the visual beyond the art classroom, teaching lessons of visual literacy alongside more traditional textual literacy. This example is at the end of the chapter and applies the theoretical analysis of previous chapters into a concrete form of instruction. I believe that the work in the field of visual culture expands the notion of the visual to include daily encounters with images and the relationship among technology, images, text, and culture.

In looking into official curricula on difference, I found current textbooks making good faith efforts at multiculturalism in general, but quite limited in their presentation of certain types of difference. The complex and varied histories of Muslim women are given very little space and from one perspective. A popular global studies textbook for ninth and tenth graders, *World History: Patterns of Interaction,* by Robert Beck (2005), is an example of this effort. In the two paragraphs in the entire volume devoted to the lives of women in Islam, the book attempts to show a balanced vision. For instance, Muslim women are described historically to have many rights under the Qu'ran: "The shari'a gave Muslim women specific legal rights concerning marriage, family, and property" (p. 274). The conclusion of this short paragraph is that, "Nonetheless, Muslim women were still expected to submit to men" (p. 274). The second and final paragraph describing Muslim women brings us up to the contemporary era with this thought, "However, over time, Muslim women were forced to live increasingly isolated lives. When they did go out in public, they were expected to be veiled" (p. 274). The text describes Muslim women as a single, unified category and implies that they share exactly the same fate regardless of geographical or cultural context. While not overtly xenophobic in tone, the global studies textbook freezes Muslim women in a nebulous past and creates a flattened picture of one, uncontested identity. The book adds elements about differences between groups of people, but it does not devote the space to the diversity among these groups. If these two paragraphs are all of the information that students are receiving in their official education, then most of the ideas about difference must come from the unofficial education of the media.

Pedagogy Post-9/11

The task of critical educators is vitally important in the wake of the terrorist attacks on September 11, 2001. For many Americans who did not have experience or direct contact with the wider world, the events of that day brought the world into their living rooms. We needed guidance about how to understand the place of the United States in the world. Many of us received very little formal schooling about Islam or the history of Islam and the Middle East and did not have the knowledge or mental structures in place to make sense of the events. How do we reconcile the fear of terrorist acts (which are coded foreign, Islamist, radical, different) with honest desires to understand difference and not view the other as innately dangerous? Formal guidance about how to react to and deal with the attacks came from our political leaders and the media. President George W. Bush made calls for religious tolerance while at the same time drawing clear distinctions between "us" and "them." In just a sample of his speeches from the weeks after 9/11, Bush (2001) said the following:

> We fight the evil people. It's important for the boys and girls of Thurgood Marshall
> to know that we're fighting evil with good. (Bush, 2001a, para. 3)

> We believe that the country must stay on alert, that there is—that our enemies still
> hate us. Our enemies have no values that regard life as precious. (Bush, 2001b, para.
> 17)

The mass media coverage of the attacks reinforced the call for patriotism and unity against the outsiders and terrorists. Brian Monahan's (2011) presentation, "Mediated Meanings and Symbolic Politics," detailed his sociological research into the media coverage of 9/11 and how the media shaped the meaning of the terrorist attacks. His central question is how the various events of September 11, 2001, turn into the concept of 9/11. The rate of news media consumption on that day and the following weeks was much higher than usual, indicating that Americans were struggling to make sense of the events and the changing realities and were looking to the news media for answers. Monahan examined the coverage to locate patterns, and for 9/11, he found that network news created a news "story" out of a series of events. In creating a story, the coverage did not include complex historical analysis of possible causes and future implications. The story needed to have "dramatic amplification," which means that producers had to determine a central storyline and organize available information to fit into that narrative. The story relied on "cultivating emotionality," which means that the news had to focus on "highlighting sorrow, personalizing agents, injecting identifiability, and nationalizing the narrative" (slide). To craft this sorrowful, emotionally charged story that Americans could relate to, news organizations narrowed the meaning of the events of the day into a coherent narrative of attack and trauma, evil and good. Monahan argued that this narrative shut down other possible interpretations of the events and created shared memory that reflected the representation of that day rather than memories of the day itself. The collective memory of 9/11 is still being constructed, as meaning is constructed and contested, but it is impossible for most Americans to think of 9/11 without calling upon images shown on television news. In a comment on the website for the "9/11 TV News Archive Conference," artist Scott Blake (2011) wrote that on September 11th, "CNN showed the plane crash 109 times from 9am to midnight . . . the BBC showed the planes crashing into the towers 240 times" (para. 1). Though the horrifying events needed to be recorded and shown, the choice of these networks to play and replay the planes crashing into the World Trade Center forces the viewer to relive the horrifying moment, and this leaves a lasting mental picture of horror. "My primary goal is to remind everyone how the mainstream media broadcast the violent attacks over and over, giving power to the very people that wanted to frighten us" (para. 1). Blake argued that the media increased the level of trauma and fear by the incessant replaying of the plane crashing, the people's bodies falling from the top floors, and the buildings crashing to the ground.

Since September 11th and the continuing military offenses in Afghanistan and Iraq, Americans have been besieged with news stories, images, and visions of Islam and Muslim women that are not as nuanced as the short entry in the textbook. In a *Washington Post* poll conducted in March 2006, 58% of those polled felt that "there are more violent extremists within Islam than in other religions." Forty-six percent of the respondents said that they have a generally unfavorable opinion of Islam. Both of these figures increased dramatically from a similar poll taken directly after the attacks of September 11th (Cohen, 2006). Media stories focusing on terrorists, suicide bombers, and violence in regard to Islam have played on American fears. In the vast majority of news stories and accompanying photographs, Muslims are shown to be either "terrorists intent on doing us harm" or "victims in need of our rescuing." Both representations are historically based ethnocentric stereotypes that need to be deconstructed and analyzed. The veil, a cultural symbol deeply embedded with stereotypical meanings, is the ultimate visual signifier of the oppression, violence, and fear that has been enacted in the Western popular imagination. In examining this unofficial curriculum based on assumptions about those who are different, I argue that our official education in classrooms needs to more fully and responsibly engage with difference in all of its complexity. My work suggests one possible form that this curriculum could take, using the graphic narratives by authors who engage with difference in a self-conscious manner that embraces complexity and uncertainty.

In the text, *Teaching Against Islamophobia*, Kincheloe, Steinberg, and Stonebanks (2010) presented a series of chapters that discuss the rising tide of anti-Islam representations in politics and media in the post-9/11 era. The final section of the text introduces pedagogical approaches to confronting this Islamophobia through curricular interventions. One such intervention or possible intervention is the use of the Canadian young adult novel *Bifocal* (Ellis & Walters, 2007) analyzed by Riley (2010) for its pedagogical usefulness in the classroom to counteract Islamophobic representations. Two of the main characters of the novel are Haroon and Zana, Muslim brother and sister, who react quite differently to acts of intolerance and violence in their high school. Police wrongly arrest Haroon as a suspect in a terrorist plot, setting off acts of anti-Muslim vandalism and hatred in the school and the community. Jay is a White, Christian member of the football team who takes part in the vandalism and is torn between confronting the hatred and participating in it to go along with his teammates. The actions and the resulting discussion of the novel in two high school classrooms of predominantly White, non-Muslim students are the central focus of the chapter. While marketed and praised as a young adult novel that could be used in the classroom to confront and disrupt Islamophobia, the text has the possibility of reinforcing negative stereotypes if not specifically taught through a critical lens. The representation of a strong Muslim feminist in the character of Zana is an interesting point of analysis. Zana chooses to begin wearing the niqab (face covering veil) after the Islamophobic attacks start at her school. Against the wishes of her family, she expresses a desire to embrace her religious identity and to present an image of a strong Muslim woman to her peers. Her choice to cover and her powerful voice confront the stereotype of the silent, oppressed Muslim woman that Western media outlets promulgated in abundance post-9/11. Though stereotypically pre-sented as forcibly veiled and silenced, Zana is a self-proclaimed feminist who reacts to Islamophobia by embracing her difference, and she marks her difference visually. By presenting a character that so purposefully challenges a stereotype, the novel forces students to reexamine their previously constructed worldviews.

Riley (2010) suggested important pedagogical strategies for teachers implementing the novel with students: lead students to talk back to the text, look critically at the meaning of difference, and problematize the elements that seem natural to "expose the existing systems of power that inform the social relationships in the story" (p. 307). Riley also cited Sensoy's (2007) two strategies from "Pedagogical Strategies for Disrupting Gendered Orientalism," which suggest asking students to first critically examine their own biases and reactions to the text and then to become "perspective detectives" by asking whose views are represented, who and what are valued in the text, and whose perspective and voice are absent or marginalized. All of these teaching strategies ask teachers and students to engage more deeply with *Bifocal* (Ellis & Walters, 2007) and any text that deals with difference and, therefore, issues of power and privilege. Simply reading texts that include characters from diverse racial, religious, and economic backgrounds is not sufficiently critical and will not disrupt stereotypes and assumptions. Without interrogating their own reaction and how difference and power are positioned in texts, students will read through their experience and relate new information to their existing framework of representations. The racial profiling of Haroon by police officers who arrest him because he is brown and Muslim are not shocking if representations of Islamist extremist terrorists in the media are the readers' only reference point for Muslim men.

Sensoy (2007) wrote of pedagogies of difference and the importance of engaging students with complex discussions of identity. She argued that one's identity is a combination of how we think of ourselves and how others perceive and construct representations of us. We generally are taught to focus on identity as an individual and singular idea rather than a complex and shifting landscape that includes both individual and group identities. "Enhanced understanding of others means helping students to develop accurate, nuanced understanding of others by appreciating that their definitions of others may not match how others see themselves and that people will identify with and attach importance to different beliefs and practices" (p. 124). Any form of critical literacy must be paired with the work of understanding the multiple and shifting identities of self and other. Sensoy provided a useful framework for the importance of critical visual literacy in her chapter entitled, "'Madman Hassan Will Buy Your Carpets!': The Bearded Curricula of Evil Muslims." She explained three ways that representations of difference must be engaged to create meaningful pedagogy: studying the accuracy of a representation, studying the context of a representation, and studying the motivations/interests for a representation. These three areas of study ask students to move beyond analyzing the content of a representation and think deeply about context and possible effects. Accuracy of representation asks us to examine the image/text for a basic factual relationship to the historical, cultural, and geographical realities of the subject. For example, does the clothing of people in an image match the type and amount of clothing worn by people in a particular region, of a particular class, and cultural group? The context of representation asks us to consider when, by whom, how, and for whom the representation was produced. In looking at Marc Garanger's photographs of Algerian women from 1960 (Estrin, 2010), we must ask whether the photographer was French or Algerian, why the photographs were taken, and who was meant to use and look at the images. The answers to these questions are very important: the images were taken by a French photographer working for the colonial authority, the women were forcibly unveiled, and the images were to be used by the French authorities for identity cards to track their movements. "Unused to showing their full face and hair to anyone outside their family, they stood before Mr. Garanger's camera as if they were naked" (para. 5). The reading of these photographs would necessarily be quite different if the Algerian forces had taken them as a way to confront and resist colonial occupation. The context of a representation leads to the final question for analysis that asks students to investigate the motivations and intentions for creating the representation. This final layer is more complex and less clearly connected to the facts and content of the image and more about the political, cultural, and social implications of the image or text.

Problems with Multicultural Education

In the post-September 11th era, increased attention has been placed on the relationship of Islam and the West. Muslim women have been visualized in the American media as stereotypically oppressed and voiceless. What role can education play in addressing the issues raised by the historical and cultural construction of the Muslim woman as Western object/subject? Is there a way to create a responsible pedagogy of difference that could allay fear and avoid isolationism? Historically, American schools have been locations of nationalist indoctrination. Joel Spring (2004) emphasized how our schools create a unified national sentiment. "In the shared experience of schooling, students engage in the rituals of statehood through flag salutes, anthems, nationalist songs, and marches" (p. 10). Schools have been the natural breeding grounds of xenophobic, nationalist feelings that are extreme versions of everyday nationalism. The West has represented Muslim women historically as either exotic, sexualized objects of desire or exotic, covered objects of pity. The veil has been, and continues to be, the central visual code that carries the meaning of this exoticized difference; it is the piece of cloth that separates and marks the unbridgeable divide between "us" and "them." With renewed focus on everything Muslim since the attacks of September 11th, there is an urgent need for a postcolonial pragmatic pedagogy that can honestly address the relationship between stereotypical, biased media images of difference and the exclusionary feelings of fear that have controlled the popular discourse on Islam in the United States. Students need to engage with difficult questions about why the vast majority of media images of Muslim women involve the same visual codes and the same underlying theme of voiceless oppression. Using visual and media literacy tools of analysis, students can critically analyze the dominant media discourse that creates the object of our fears and pity. Once identified, the flattened visual images of the Muslim woman in the West need to be countered with more complex representations of experience created by artists and authors who travel between borders and cultures. The image/text of these works can open up new, uncertain, hybrid spaces for students to think about identity. Their art is not a panacea and cannot change behavior or perceptions without analysis and discussion. My hope, in using contemporary art as pedagogy, is to provide the seeds of doubt and uncertainty about assumptions that lead students to a curiosity about the representation of difference and the formation of identity. Reading and analyzing graphic narratives comprise a form of experience, of seeing multiple perspectives that can challenge and break apart the assumed, Western media image of what it means to be a Muslim woman and what it means to be in our own cultural location as well.

Graphic Narratives and Expanding Literacy

The graphic narrative is experiencing a level of popular and critical success and attention that creates new opportunities for educators to explore and discover how to use these narrative forms in complex ways. The form can teach traditional, textual literacy, but it can also teach visual and cultural literacies through the unique combination of image/text. Scholars of the graphic narrative are situated across traditional disciplinary boundaries and extend beyond the departments of English literature into areas of gender studies, graphic design, and literacy. One of the foundational texts in comics theory, *Understanding Comics* (McCloud, 1993), does a lot of work to legitimize the form as a viable and important source of information, art, and narrative. McCloud's (1993) work is unique because it lays out the language and function of comics in comic form, giving meaning and sense to the images and text that make up graphic novels and comic strips. The visual detail (or lack thereof) in comics and the transitions from one panel to the next mean that the reader has to be actively engaged in reading both text and image relationships to understand the narrative. He creates a system to describe the level of detail and abstraction in comic form as a three-pronged continuum from realistic to iconic on the x-axis and the level of non-iconic abstraction on the y-axis. It is a complex way to map the visual language of comics, but McCloud explains the meaning through visual charts and maps well-known comic figures along this continuum. "By de-emphasizing the *appearance* of the **physical** world in favor of the **idea** of the form, the cartoon places itself in the world of *concepts*" (p. 41). Comics artists do not use iconic form because of a lack of skill or for considerations of speed; the more iconic a human face, the more likely the reader is to identify with the face. Iconic comics ask the reader to bear more of the burden of closure, the mental work of connecting abstracted images, with little realistic detail, to objects and figures in real life. Different comics artists approach the use and level of visual icon in their work, using the level of detail to affect the experience and meaning of the reading. McCloud describes how some Japanese comics artists use the visual play of detail: "while *most* characters were designed *simply*, to assist in reader-identification—other characters were drawn more *realistically* in order to *objectify* them, emphasizing their difference from the reader" (p. 44). The juxtaposition of different visual codes and styles gives readers cues about their relationship to the characters and contexts of the narrative. McCloud tackles the relationship between images and text in comics; both are language systems that convey meaning, and their common element is the ease of decoding. The more iconic the image, reduced to lines and shapes, the more the image becomes symbolic and read in ways more similar to words. "When pictures are more abstracted from 'reality,' they require greater levels of *perception, more like words*. When words are bolder, more direct, they require *lower* levels of perception and are received *faster, more like pictures*" (p. 49). Analysis of graphic narratives that engage with these representations of difference offers ways to use the traditional textual literacy in English Language Arts classes to expand notions of literacy and engage with visual and textual texts. Teachers and districts are beginning to use these graphic texts in their classrooms.

Graphic Narratives in the Classroom

There has been a recent resurgence of interest in the pedagogical possibilities of comics to engage students of all ages in acts of literacy. Berninger (2010) wrote that comics were excluded from the classroom in the 1950s with the publication of *Seduction of the Innocent* (Wertham, 1954), which linked comics to delinquency and rebellion in youth. Wertham (1954) leveled many questionable criticisms on comics, notably that Batman and Robin were representations of a gay relationship and that Wonder Woman's strength and independence made her a lesbian. "They were accused of both reducing literacy by replacing 'proper reading' and of morally endangering children and teenagers through the themes of violence, sex, and crime, which they address" (p. 246). Comics were viewed as a distraction to "real" reading of texts rather than a tool for literacy. Thus, from the 1950s through the early 2000s, comics were generally not included in official curriculum of schools. With the recent interest in bringing comics into the classroom, they are often seen as a means to a different pedagogical end rather than an end in and of themselves. "Comics have thus again come to be seen in a reductive way, this time as the proverbial lump of (motivating) sugar that makes the medicine of (serious) content go down" (p. 247). Bringing comics into the classroom is often used to entice apprehensive or reluctant readers into (textual) literacy by starting with a format considered engaging and fun. Once the students have been brought into the literacy fold, comics are often removed and give way to serious works of literature or textbooks that relegate images to illustrative and secondary features. Comics can be used for students to learn to read, but they can also be used for students to read to learn. Academic content in many fields, literary precepts, and diversity can all be taught using comic texts in curriculum. However, if comics are brought into the classroom with little regard of how to read comics and instruction in the language of comic forms, opportunities for engagement are limited. Yang (2008b) drew his argument for bringing comics into the classroom in a short comic entitled, "Graphic Novels in the Classroom." In this comic, Yang reiterated many points made in other books and articles on why we should include graphic novels in schools. He argued that comics are intrinsically motivating for young people, due to the appeal of visual media to students who spend increasing amounts of free time on social media sites and watching streaming video on the Internet. He argued that, "by combining image and text, graphic novels bridge the gap between media we watch and media we read" (p. 187). The graphic novel includes visual elements that can enable visual literacy with the text that allows for traditional textual literacy. He made this argument to appeal to and motivate struggling readers. Yang's other primary argument for graphic novels is the fact of their visual permanence. The images/text on the page do not move through time and space at a fixed rate, as opposed to film and animation, which proceed in time at a fixed rate without intervention from the viewer. In comics, readers determine the pace at which the narrative proceeds and can go backward or forward in the narrative as they wish. Yang discovered the benefits of this distinction when he was teaching high school algebra and wrote his substitute notes as a comic lecture for students. "It doesn't matter how quickly I 'say' the lecture. What matters is how fast you choose to read it! The rate of information-transfer is firmly in your control!" (p. 188).

Berninger (2010) detailed strengths and challenges in bringing comics into the classroom for meaningful learning and engagement. Many of the challenges involve the public image of comics that retains the stigma of being lowbrow, low art, childish, and comical. Other challenges speak to the lack of preparation teachers receive in their own education about how to teach with comics and where comics fit in the school day that is fragmented into disciplinary blocks. In middle and high schools, English teachers may regard comics as not serious enough to count as literature, and the art teachers may regard comics as not real works of art. Without an academic home and teachers trained and willing to engage with the material, can the strengths and opportunities outweigh the challenges? Berninger argued that comics in the classroom can act as a bridge between traditional notions of literacy and new media literacy and can mediate the dichotomy of canonical texts and popular culture. He called for specific attention to using comics in the classroom as part of teacher education programs so that teachers understand the complexity of comic form and content and how to teach that complexity to provide both engagement and insight.

There are certainly many resources available in print and on the Internet, including teacher-produced blogs and materials. An initial read of these resources supports Berninger's (2010) assertion that comics and graphic novels are often used in classrooms to motivate reluctant readers and as a way to ease students into text-heavy books and traditional notions of literacy. This is certainly a vital use for comics, but it limits their usefulness to the service of reading words. The following books were published in 2013: *Teaching Graphic Novels in the Classroom: Building Literacy and Comprehension* (Novak, 2013); *Wham! Teaching with Graphic Novels Across the Curriculum* (Brozo, Moorman, & Meyer, 2013); *Teaching Graphic Novels: Practical Strategies for the Secondary ELA Classroom* (Monnin, 2013). The focus of these texts is on developing textual literacy through teaching with graphic novels, with Novak's text advertising that it "aligns with the Common Core State Standards" as a selling feature of the book. Novak's (2013) book focuses mainly on comic books and superheroes as a way to entice students who have watched and enjoyed Hollywood versions of superhero fables to read.

In one of the other texts published in 2013, Monnin presented a more detailed and diverse selection of graphic novels for consideration in the English Language Arts classroom. In her charts, entitled "Three Types of Content Panels" and "Eleven Types of Story Panels" (p. 5), Monnin offered a way for students to understand basic comics theory. Her content panels chart is very basic and limits content to word panel, image panel, and word and image panels. The types of panels the author delineates are all related to narrative flow rather than visual elements. She names these the plot, character, setting, conflict, rising action, climax, resolution, symbols, theme, foreshadowing, and combination story panels: "…based in the elements of story familiar to ELA teachers when teaching traditional literature, story panels develop or detail the story/text" (p. 5). These categories of panels align with the analysis of word-based texts and traditional notions of literacy rather than instructing teachers to read the particular language of comics. The use of graphic novels in the classroom seems to conform to traditional notions of literacy because that is what is tested and required by the standardized tests and the Common Core State Standards. Monnin also offers more specific instruction for teachers on McCloud's (1993) groundbreaking work on the language of comics, specifically detailing his six types of gutters and transitions.

In *The Graphic Novel: POWerful Teaching and Learning with Images*, Bakis (2012) wrote of visual literacy in reading instruction and therefore connected graphic novels to the classroom in a more complex way. Part of her pedagogy involves learning how to read images and text while also working to create images and text to communicate ideas. "I soon realized that in order for students to truly understand and appreciate comics as a storytelling and communications medium that I had to let them try their hand at composing sequential art" (p. 6). Bakis's approach is unique in the way that she engages students with consuming and producing comics; although she also discusses the usual focus of using comics to motivate reluctant readers into textual literacy, she adds production and direct instruction in visual literacy skills. Frey and Fisher (2008) edited a text that focuses on teaching visual literacy using comics. While the focus is not on critical literacy, in the introduction, the editors used Hobbs's (1998) precepts of critical literacy to frame the book: "All messages are constructions; messages are representations of social reality; individuals negotiate meaning by interacting with messages; messages have economic, political, social, and aesthetic purposes" (p. 2). Messages in the form of graphic novels include combined image and text that must be analyzed through these frames. By focusing on critical visual literacy, the editors asked readers to engage with the political implications and impact of identity of image/text represent-ations. "The emphasis of critical literacy is less about acquisition of skills and more about questioning the author's purpose, searching for alternative meanings, and considering the role identity plays" (p. 2). The lens of critical literacy must include critical visual literacy to fully capture the unique combination of image and text in graphic narratives. Thus, asking students to engage fully with the tools of critical visual and textual analysis is a more complex form of reading rather than simply an intermediary step between reluctance and motivation or illiteracy and literacy. Teachers engaged in the complex work of critical visual/textual literacy must ask students to consider the context of the creation of the work: who is the author, where and when was the author working, and what was the purpose of writing the text? Students also must consider the context of the publication: who and where was the publisher and what was the intended market for the book? And, students must consider the context of reception: who was the intended audience for the book, for what age was it intended, how was it received, who purchased and read it, and how?

Sample Curriculum

In this sample of curricular material, I attempt to utilize the theoretical foundations described earlier in this chapter to create concrete educational activities. I hope to realize a critical postcolonial lesson that involves students in the questioning of assumptions and the critical analysis of Eurocentric and Orientalist media representations of difference. The purpose of this lesson is to increase a student's ability to critically question and analyze stereotypical media images of difference and to analyze contem-porary works of art that subvert the stereotypical codes to use their understanding of visual codes to design a creative visual project that addresses the representation of difference. Though the subject for this lesson is the Western representation of Muslim women, the critical visual literacy used in this context can be applied to the visualization of difference in multiple forms. By beginning the lesson with uncovering and analyzing stereotypical visual codes, the goal is to create a critical sense of doubt and uncertainty in the truth claims of the media images. Student experience with the media and American reaction to Islam and Muslim women in the post-September 11th era are important components of connecting the material in the lesson to the relevant extracurricular student knowledge. Students will research stereotypical images of Muslim women to critically explore how we (in the West) view them (Muslim women, different). In bringing up stereotypical views and deciphering the visual codes that are historically and culturally based, students will examine how they have formed their views of difference.

This visual analysis will be accompanied by historical and cultural texts that could give context for the representation of Muslim women in the Western media. Students will learn about the basic events of European colonialism in countries such as Egypt and Algeria, including original texts by Lord Cromer describing his views of the Egyptian people. The social Darwinism of the colonial enterprise that placed Europeans at the pinnacle of evolution can be identified within these historical texts, and the students would be encouraged to draw connections to more contemporary views and representations of Islam. American foreign policy interests in the Middle East will be studied, particularly relating to the CIA's role in the overthrowing of the democratically elected leader in Iran and its support for the authoritarian Shah. The readings that will accompany the visual analysis would not attempt to construct an alternate objective "truth" about the relationships of difference; they can reveal the multiplicity of readings of historical and cultural events and expose the bias and interests behind Western reporting about other cultures from one particular viewpoint. Hopefully, through reading texts that contextualize and complicate the relationship of the United States and the "Muslim world," students will be better able to see and analyze the repetition of certain derogatory visual codes in the media images.

At the beginning of the lesson, students will start a journal with an entry about all of the assumptions and previously held ideas they have about Muslim women and about the practice of Islam. As the process of analyzing media representations and reading historical and cross-cultural texts evolves, students will keep a daily written journal to keep track of impressions, new observations, and any alterations or doubts that they might have about their previously held views. The journal writing is to be shared in small groups of students to discuss similar impressions and differing interpretations of images or texts. As a class, students will create a display of the stereotypical media images that they have researched and add to the board as new images are discovered. Even after the "official" lesson is completed, the analysis and discussion of the visual codes can continue, as new images and observations are brought in and posted.

Bringing in the Graphic Representations

After the contingent historical context and stereotypical visual codes are established through analysis, readings, writings, and discussions, the work of graphic artists, engaging with more complex representations of difference, will be brought into the classroom to complicate the assumptions and biases that have been discovered. The class will begin the second phase of this extended lesson by reading/viewing Satrapi's (2003) *Persepolis: The Story of a Childhood*. Students will reflect on how Iran was/is portrayed in American media as part of the "axis of evil" and how that compares to the story of Satrapi and her family. In their journals, students will identify illustrations that are of particular interest or connection to the visual codes that were identified in the media images. In small discussion groups about the text, students will share the images that stood out and how the meaning of visual codes shifts in this alternate perspective of Islam and Muslim women.

Throughout the time that the class takes to absorb *Persepolis* (Satrapi, 2003), I will bring in contemporary images created by Iranian artists to compare to Satrapi's visions of Iranian life and the roles of Iranian women. Students will view *Speechless* by Iranian artist Shirin Neshat, write down initial reactions to the image, and then read selected critical responses to the piece. The relationship between this image and the media images that show Muslim women oppressed in their veils will need to be debated. Questions that acknowledge the complexity of global power relationships will help frame student response and discussion. How can we read about real suppressions of women's freedoms in postrevolutionary Iran without denying agency and voice to Iranian women as a group? What is the relationship of Western colonial power in Iran to the way that the media and these artists represent Iranian women? The work of graphic artists can engage students in analysis of image/text, using the intrinsic motivation that young people have to read comics in order to address stereotypes. Graphic narratives that represent traditionally marginalized voices through self-representation or self-as-other representation open doors to lived experience that is much more complex than the flattened media images of difference. If we ask students to engage with multiculturalism at a surface level, learning of food, dress, and holidays, without reference to past and present injustices and imbalances of power, educators miss a vital opportunity.

BIBLIOGRAPHY

9/11 Political Cartoons. (2011). Retrieved from http://www.cagle.com/topics/holiday/911/ page/2/

9/11 Volume 1: Artists Respond. (2002). New York, NY: DC Comics.

9/11 Volume 2. (2002). New York, NY: DC Comics.

Abirached, Z. (2012). *A game for swallows: To die, to leave, to return*. Minneapolis, MN: Graphic Universe.

Abu El-Haj, T. R. (2010). "The Beauty of America": Nationalism, education, and the war on terror. *Harvard Educational Review, 80*(2), 242–275.

Adams, D. W. (1997). *Education for extinction: American Indians and the boarding school experience 1875–1928*. Lawrence: University Press of Kansas.

Ahmed, L. (2011). *A quiet revolution: The veil's resurgence, from the Middle East to America*. New Haven, CT: Yale University Press.

Ahmed, M. (Director). (2008). *The Muslims I know* [Motion picture]. USA: Neelum Films.

———(2009). Additional questions & answers with Mara Ahmed. http://interactive. wxxi.org/chats/mara-ahmed/moreqa

Al-Mutawa, N. (2006). *The 99*. Kuwait: Teshkeel Comics.

Alloula, M. (1986). *The colonial harem*. Minneapolis: The University of Minnesota Press.

Alsultany, R. (2012). *Arabs and Muslims in the media: Race and representation after 9/11*. New York: New York University Press.

Amir, S., & Khalil. (2011). *Zahra's paradise*. New York, NY: First Second.

Anderson, B. (1991). *Imagined communities: Reflections on the origin and spread of nationalism*. New York, NY: Verso.

Appiah, K. (1998). Cosmopolitan patriots. In P. Cheah & B. Robbins (Ed.), *Cosmopolitics: Thinking and feeling beyond the nation* (pp. 91–114). Minneapolis: The University of Minnesota Press.

Astier, H. (2006, October 30). Suburban gangs defy French police. Retrieved from http://news.bbc.co.uk/2/hi/europe/6096706.stm

Bailey Jones, R. (2011). *Postcolonial representations of women: Critical issues for education*. New York, NY: Springer.

Bakis, M. (2012). *The graphic novel: POWerful teaching and learning with images*. Thousand Oaks, CA: Corwin.

Barber, B. (1995). *Jihad vs. McWorld: How globalism and tribalism are reshaping the world*. New York, NY: Random House.

Barthes, R. (1972). *Mythologies*. New York, NY: Hill and Wang.

Bashi, P. (2009). *Nylon road*. New York, NY: St. Martin's Griffin.

Barzegar, L. (2012). *Persepolis* & orientalism: A critique of the reception history of Satrapi's memoir. Unpublished manuscript, Department of English, Colorado State University, Fort Collins, Colorado.

Bauman, Z. (2000). *Liquid modernity*. Cambridge, UK: Polity Press.

Bechdel, A. (2007). *Fun Home: A family tragicomic*. New York, NY: First Mariner Books.

Beck R. (2005). *World history: Patterns of interaction*. Boston, MA: McDougal Littell.

Berlatsky, N. (2014). What makes the Muslim *Ms. Marvel* awesome: She's just like everyone else. Retrieved from http://www.theatlantic.com/entertainment/archive/2014/03/what-makes-the-muslim-em-ms-marvel-em-awesome-shes-just-like-everyone/284517/

Berninger, M. (2010). Workshop II: Comics in school. In M. Berninger, J. Ecke, & G. Haberkorn (Eds.), *Comics as a nexus of cultures: Essays on the interplay of media, disciplines and international perspectives* (pp. 245–252). Jefferson, NC: McFarland.

Bhabha, H. (1994). *The location of culture*. New York, NY: Routledge.

bin Laden, O. (November 3). *Bin Laden rails against crusaders and UN*. Retrieved from http://news.bbc.co.uk/2/hi/world/monitoring/media_reports/1636782.stm

Blake, S. (2011). 9/11 TV news archive conference. Retrieved from https://blog.archive.org/2011/08/03/upcoming-911-tv-news-archive-conference-from-internet-archive-and-new-york-university/

Blumenbach, J. F. (1865). *Treatise on the natural variety of mankind*. London: Longman, Green, Longman, Roberts & Green.

Braxton, K. (Producer). (2011). All-American Muslim [*Television series*]. Dearborn, MI: Shed Media.

Brozo, W., Moorman, G., & Meyer, G. (2013). *Wham! Teaching with graphic novels across the curriculum*. New York, NY: Teachers College Press.

Burgas, G. (2011). Review time! With *Habibi*. Retrieved from http://goodcomics.comic bookresources.com/2011/12/21/review-time-with-habibi/

Burka Avenger. (2013). Retrieved from http://www.burkaavenger.com/about

Bush, G. (2001a). Text: President Bush on pen pal campaign. Retrieved from http://www.washingtonpost.com/wpsrv/nation/specials/attacked/transcripts/bushtext_102 501.html

———(2001b). Remarks by the President in photo opportunity with Homeland Security Council. Retrieved from http://avalon.law.yale.edu/sept11/president_079.asp

Butler, J. (1990). *Gender trouble: Feminism and the subversion of identity*. New York, NY: Routledge.

Chute, H. (2010). *Graphic women: Life narrative and contemporary comics*. New York, NY: Columbia University Press.

Clark-Flory, T. (2009). Feminists face off over the veil. Retrieved from http://www.salon.com/2009/09/05/veil_debate/

Clifford, J. (1988). *The predicament of culture: Twentieth century ethnography, literature, and art*. Cambridge, MA: Harvard University Press.

———(1997). *Routes: Travel and translation in the late twentieth century*. Cambridge, MA: Harvard University Press.

Clements, R., & Musker, J. (Producers), & Clements, R., & Musker, J. (Directors). (1992). *Aladdin* [Motion picture]. USA: Walt Disney Pictures.

Cohen, J. (2006). Poll: Americans skeptical about Islam and Arabs. Retrieved from http://abcnews.go.com/US/story?id=1700599

Cromer, E. (1908). *Modern Egypt, vol. II*. New York, NY: Macmillan.

Curry, N. & Soffel, J. (2013). The 99: Islamic superheroes going global. Retrieved from http://www.cnn.com/2013/06/11/showbiz/comic-book-heroes-the-99-write/

Damluji, N. (2011). A conversation about Habibi's Orientalism with Craig Thompson. Retrieved from http://hoodedutilitarian.com/2011/11/a-conversation-about-habibisorient alism-with-craig-thompson/

Danes, K. (2010). *Beneath the pale blue burqa: One woman's journey through Taliban strongholds*. Sydney, Australia: Ligare.

Darnell, S. & Barta, H. (2002). What's important. In *9/11 Volume 1: Artists Respond* (pp. 69-70). New York, NY: DC Comics.

David B. (2006). *Epileptic*. Paris, France: L'Association.

Delisle, G. (2007). *Pyongyang: A journey in North Korea*. Montreal, Quebec: Drawn & Quarterly.

————(2010). *Burma chronicles*. Montreal, Quebec: Drawn & Quarterly.

Demrdash, D. (2013). Egypt's new hijab-clad superheroine. Retrieved from http://www.bbc.com/news/world-middle-east-25254555

Denson, G. R. (2011). From victim to victor: Women turn the representation of rape inside out. Retrieved from http://www.huffingtonpost.com/g-roger-denson/facing-the-interior-and-t_b_1073672.html

de Saussure, F. (1972). *Course in general linguistics*. Paris, France: Editions Payot.

Dimitriadis, G., & McCarthy, M. (2001). *Reading and teaching the postcolonial: From Baldwin to Basquiat and beyond*. New York, NY: Teachers College Press.

Disney, W. (Producer), & Geronimi, C., Jackson, W. & Luske, H. (Directors). (1953). *Peter Pan* [Motion picture]. USA: Walt Disney Productions.

Donnell, A. (2003). Visibility, violence and voice? Attitudes to veiling post-11 September. In D. Bailey & G. Tawadros (Eds.), *Veil: Veiling, representation and contemporary art* (pp. 120–135). London, UK: Institute of International Visual Arts.

"Egypt 'worst for women' out of 22 countries in Arab world." (2013). BBC News Middle East. Retrieved from http://www.bbc.com/news/world-middle-east-24908109

Ellis, D. & Walters, E. (2007). *Bifocal*. Brighten, MA: Fitzhenry & Whiteside.

Ellsworth, S. (2012). *Habibi*. Retrieved from http://www.intergalacticmedicineshow.com/cgi-bin/mag.cgi?do=columns&vol=spencer_ellsworth&article=053

El Rassi, T. (2007). *Arab in America*. San Francisco, CA: Last Gasp.

Estrin, J. (2010). Unwilling subjects in the Algerian War. Retrived from http://lens.blogs.nytimes.com/2010/05/14/showcase-161/?_php=true&_type=blogs&_r=0

Ewen, E., & Ewen, S. (2006). *Typecasting: On the arts & sciences of human inequality*. New York, NY: Seven Stories Press.

Facing History and Ourselves. (2002). *Race and membership in American history: The eugenics movement*. Brookline, MA: Facing History and Ourselves.

Faludi, S. (2007). *Terror dream: Fear and fantasy in post-9/11 America*. New York, NY: Metropolitan Books.

Fanon, F. (1967). *Black skin, white masks*. New York, NY: Grove Press.

————(2003). Algeria unveiled. In D. Bailey & G. Tawadros (Eds.), *Veil: Veiling, representation and contemporary art* (pp. 74–85). London, UK: Institute of International Visual Arts. (Original work published 1959)

Femen. (n.d.). Retrieved from http://femen.org/about

Fertakis, M. (2011). Should children have to compete for their education?" Retrieved from http://www.washingtonpost.com/blogs/answer-sheet/post/should-children-have-to-compete-for-their-education/2011/08/16/gIQAR8XJKJ_blog.html

Florida Family Association (FFA) Letter. (2012, December). Retrieved from http://www.huffingtonpost.com/asher-huey/complaints-against-allame_b_1153216.html

Follain, J., & Cristofari, R. (2002). *Zoya's story: An Afghan woman's struggle for freedom.* New York, NY: HarperCollins.

Ford, P. (2001, September 19). Europe cringes at Bush "crusade" against terrorists. Retrieved from http://www.csmonitor.com/2001/0919/p12s2-woeu.html

Foucault, M. (1972). Truth and power. In P. Rabinow (Ed.), *Foucault reader* (pp. 51–75). New York, NY: Random House.

Fox, D. (1993, June 10). Disney will alter song in "Aladdin": Changes were agreed upon after Arab-Americans complained that some lyrics were racist. Retrieved from http://articles.latimes.com/1993-07-10/entertainment/ca-11747_1_altered-lyric

Frey, N., & Fisher, D. (2008). *Teaching visual literacy: Using comic books, graphic novels, anime, cartoons, and more to develop comprehension and thinking skills.* Thousand Oaks, CA: Corwin.

Galton, F. (2001). *Inquiries into human faculty and its development.* Online reissue (originally published in 1883): http://galton.org/books/human-faculty/text/galton-1883-humanfaculty-v4.pdf

Glidden, S. (2011). *The waiting room.* Retrieved from http://www.cartoonmovement.com/comic/10

Globalization. (2007). Retrieved from http://en.wikipedia.org/wiki/Globalization

Goldberg, J. (2011, June). Danger: Falling tyrants. Retrieved from http://www.theatlantic.com/magazine/archive/2011/06/danger-falling-tyrants/308493/

Gomez-Pena, G. (2001). *The new world border: Prophecies, poems, and loqueras for the end of the century.* San Francisco, CA: City Lights.

Goodwin, J. (2003). *Price of honor: Muslim women lift the veil of silence on the Islamic world.* New York, NY: Penguin.

Greene, M. (1995). *Releasing the imagination: Essays on education, the arts, and social change.* San Francisco, CA: Jossey-Bass.

Groensteen, T. (2007). *The system of comics.* Jackson: University Press of Mississippi.

Guilbert, E. (2009). *The photographer: Into war-torn Afghanistan with Doctors Without Borders.* New York, NY: First Second.

Hall, S. (Ed.). (1997). *Representation: Cultural representations and signifying practices.* Thousand Oaks, CA: Sage.

Haroon. (2013). *Burka avenger.* Retrieved from http://www.burkaavenger.com/

Harris, B. & Ruth, G. (2002). Which one is real? In *9/11 Volume 1: Artists Respond* (pp. 94-95). New York, NY: DC Comics.

Hatfield, C. (2011). A *Habibi* roundtable. Retrieved from http://www.tcj.com/a-habibi-roundtable/

Hicks, E. (1991). *Border writing: The multidimensional text.* Minneapolis: Regents of the University of Minnesota.

Hirsi Ali, A. (2012, September 17). Ayaan Hirsi Ali on the Islamists' final stand. Retrieved from http://www.newsweek.com/ayaan-hirsi-ali-islamists-final-stand-64811

Hobbs, R. (1998). Literacy for the information age. In J. Flood, S. B. Heath, & D. Lapp (Eds.), *Handbook of research on teaching literacy through the communicative and visual arts* (pp. 7–14). New York, NY: Simon & Schuster.

hooks, b. (1984). *Feminist theory: From margin to center*. Cambridge, MA: South End Press.

Huntington, S. (1996). *The clash of civilizations and the remaking of the world order*. New York, NY: Touchstone.

Hussein, K. A. (2011). *The Tunisian awakening*. Publisher: Author.

Jacobson, S., & Colón, E. (2006). *The 9/11 report: A graphic adaptation*. New York, NY: Hill and Wang.

Janks, H. (2000) Domination, access, diversity and design: A synthesis model for critical literacy education. *Educational Review, (52)*2, 175-186.

Kellner, D. (2004). September 11, terror war, and blowback. In J. Kincheloe & S. Steinberg (Eds.), *The miseducation of the west: How schools and the media distort our understanding of the Islamic world* (pp. 25–42). Westport, CT: Praeger.

Kincheloe, J., & Steinberg, S. (1997). *Changing multiculturalism: New times, new curriculum*. Bristol, PA: Open University Press.

———(2010). Why teach against Islamophobia: Striking the empire back. In J. Kincheloe, S. Steinberg & C. Stonebanks (Eds.), *Teaching against Islamophobia* (pp. 3–27). New York, NY: Peter Lang.

Klein, N. (2002). *Fences and windows: Dispatches from the front lines of the globalization debate*. New York, NY: Picador.

Knowles, D. (2011). All-American Muslim: TV Review. Retrieved from http://www.holly woodreporter.com/review/all-american-muslim-tv-review-258770

Kukkonen, K., & Haberkorn, G. (2010). Workshop I: Toward a toolbox of comics studies. In M. Berninger, J. Ecke, & G. Haberkorn (Eds.) *Comics as a nexus of cultures: Essays on the interplay of media, disciplines and international perspectives* (pp. 237-244). Jefferson, NC: McFarland.

Landridge, R. (2002). Clown's day off. In *9/11 Volume 1: Artists Respond* (p. 52). New York, NY: DC Comics.

Legum, J. (2012, September 17). Joe Scarborough on the entire Muslim world: "They hate us because of their religion." Retrieved from http://thinkprogress.org/media/2012/09/17/856741/joe-scarborough-on-the-entire-muslim-world-they-hate-us-because-of-their-religion/#

Leslie, M. (2000). The vexing legacy of Lewis Terman. *Stanford Magazine*. Retrieved from: http://alumni.stanford.edu/get/page/magazine/article/?article_id=40678

Lippard, L. (1995). *The pink glass swan: Selected essays on feminist art*. New York, NY: The New Press.

———(2000). *Mixed blessings: New art in a multicultural America*. New York, NY: The New Press.

Lord, J. (2014). Common Core: Obamacare for education. Retrieved from http://spectator.org/articles/59227/common-core-obamacare-education

Lorde, A. (1984). *Sister outsider: Essays and speeches*. New York, NY: Ten Speed Press.

Maalouf, A. (1984). *The Crusades through Arab eyes*. New York, NY: Schocken.

———(1996). *In the name of identity: Violence and the need to belong*. New York, NY: Penguin.

Macan, D. (2002). An expert opinion. In *9/11 Volume 1: Artists Respond* (p. 40). New York, NY: DC Comics.

MacKinnon, C. (1989). *Toward a feminist theory of the state*. Cambridge, MA: Harvard University Press.

Madden, T. F. (2014). *The concise history of the Crusades*. Lanham, MD: Rowman & Littlefield.

Mann, S. (2011). A visual heartbreak: A review of Craig Thompson's Habibi. Retrieved from http://witandfancy.com/2011/12/09/a-visual-heartbreak-a-review-of-craig-thompsons-habibi/

Martin, M. (2002). Untitled. In *9/11 Volume 1: Artists Respond* (p. 32). New York, NY: DC Comics.

McCarthy, C. (1998). *The uses of culture: Education and the limits of ethnic affiliation*. New York, NY: Routledge.

McClintock, A. (1995). *Imperial leather: Race, gender, and sexuality in the colonial conquest*. New York, NY: Routledge.

McCloud, S. (1993). *Understanding comics: The invisible art*. New York, NY: HarperCollins.

Mernissi, F. (1992). *The veil and the male elite: A feminist interpretation of women's rights in Islam*. New York, NY: Basic Books.

Mirzoeff, N. (1999). *An introduction to visual culture*. New York, NY: Routledge.

———(2011). *The right to look: A counterhistory of visuality*. Durham, NC: Duke University Press.

Mitchell, T. (1998). Orientalism and the exhibitionary order. In N. Mirzoeff (Ed.), *The visual culture reader* (pp. 495–505). New York, NY: Routledge. (Original work published 1992)

Mohamed, D. (2014). Answers and responses. *Qahera*. Retrieved from http://blog.qaherathe superhero.com/tagged/anonymous

——— (2013a). Part I: Brainstorm. *Qahera*. Retrieved from http://qahera.tumblr.com/post /64031330049

———(2013b). Part II: On Femen. *Qahera*. Retrieved from http://qahera.tumblr.com/post/61173083361

———(2013c). Part III: On sexual harassment. *Qahera*. Retrieved from http://qahera.tumblr.com/post /60081962515

———(2013d). Part IV: On protests. *Qahera*. Retrieved from http://qahera.tumblr.com/post/68110255239

Monahan, B. (2011). Mediating meanings and symbolic politics. Retrieved from https://archive.org/details/911conferenceBrianMonahan

Monnin, K. (2013). *Teaching graphic novels: Practical strategies for the secondary ELA classroom*. Gainesville, FL: Maupin House.

Montellier, C. (1979). *Blues*. Paris, France: Kesselring.

Mulvey, L. (1989). *Visual and other pleasures*. Bloomington: Indiana University Press

Murray, C., & Herrnstein, R. (1994). *The bell curve: Intelligence and class structure in American life*. New York, NY: Free Press Paperbacks.

Musu, A. & Saadi, Y. (Producers) & Pontecorvo, G. (Director). (1966). *The battle of Algiers* [Motion picture]. Algeria: Casbah Films.

Neel, A. (2013). Burka Avenger, Pakistan's new superhero. *The Washington Post Blog*. Retrieved from http://www.washingtonpost.com/blogs/she-the-people/wp/2013/08/01/burka-avenger-pakistans-new-superhero/

Novak, R. (2013). *Teaching graphic novels in the classroom: Building literacy and comprehension*. Waco, TX: Prufrock Press.

Nunez, V. (2010). Pocahontas. *Disney Movies and Racism*. Retrieved from http://disneyand movies.pbworks.com/w/page/17905676/1%20Pocahontas

Orwell, G. (1949). *1984*. London, UK: Secker & Warburg.

Pajaczkowska, C. (2001). *Feminist visual culture*. New York, NY: Routledge.

Peagler, S. (2011). Review: Craig Thompson's *Habibi. The Heroes Online Blog*. Retrieved from http://www.heroesonline.com/blog/2011/09/19/review-craig-thompsons-habibi/

Peeters, B. (1998). *Case, planche, récit: Lire la bande dessinée*. Paris, France: Casterman.

Pentecost, J. (Producer), & Gabriel, M., & Goldberg, E. (Directors). (1995). *Pocahontas* [Motion Picture]. USA: Walt Disney Pictures.

Pocahontas trivia. (n.d.). Retrieved from http://www.imdb.com/title/tt0114148/trivia

Quijano, A. (2000). Coloniality of power, Eurocentrism, and Latin America. *Nepantla: Views from South 1*(3). 533-580.

Ravitch, D. (2014). The fatal flaw of the Common Core Standards. Retrieved from http://www.huffingtonpost.com/diane-ravitch/common-core_b_5016877.html

Reilly, M. (2007). Introduction: Toward transnational feminisms. In M. Reilly & L. Nochlin (Eds.), *Global feminisms: New directions in contemporary art* (pp. 14–45). New York: Merrell Publishers Limited.

Riley, K. (2010). A *Bifocal* lens on Islamophobia: Using young adult fiction as a teaching tool. In J. Kincheloe & S. Steinberg (Eds.) *Teaching against Islamophobia* (pp. 297–308). New York, NY: Peter Lang.

Robelen, E. (2011, August 30). Majority of states' standards don't mention 9/11. *Education Week*. Retrieved from http://www.edweek.org/ew/articles/2011/08/31/02sept11_ep.h31.html

Rodriguez, R., Weinstein, K., Hanson, V. D., & Mead, W. R. (2003). *Terrorists, despots, democracy: What our children need to know*. Washington, DC: Thomas B. Fordham Institute.

Rose, G. (2001). *Visual methodologies*. Thousand Oaks, CA: Sage.

Ross, L. (2002). Untitled. In *9/11 Volume 1: Artists Respond* (pp. 71-73). New York, NY: DC Comics.

Runciman, S. (1951–1954). *A history of the Crusades, Vol. I–III*. Cambridge, UK: Cambridge University Press.

Sacco, J. (2001). *Palestine*. Seattle, WA: Fantagraphics Books.

Said, E. (1979). *Orientalism*. New York, NY: Random House.

———(1993). *Culture and imperialism*. New York. NY: Knopf.

Satrapi, M. (2003). *Persepolis: The story of a childhood*. New York, NY: Pantheon.

———(2004). *Persepolis 2: The story of a return*. New York, NY: Pantheon.

———(2006). *Embroideries*. New York, NY: Pantheon.

Scheinberg, M., & Khan, F. (2013). Hey! That's my hummus! [Audio podcast]. http://www.heythatsmyhummus.com/

Sensoy, Ö. (2007). Pedagogical strategies for disrupting gendered Orientalism: Mining the binary gap in teacher education. *Journal of Intercultural Education, 18*(4), 361–365.

Shahin, T. (2011). *Rise: The story of the Egyptian revolution as written shortly before it began*. Cairo, Egypt: Al Khan Comics.

Shohat, E. (1998). Introduction. In E. Shohat (Ed.), *Talking visions: Multicultural feminism in a transnational age* (pp. 1–64). Cambridge, MA: The MIT Press.

Shohat, E., & Stam, R. (1994). *Unthinking Eurocentrism: Multiculturalism and the media*. New York, NY: Routledge.

———(1998). Narrativizing visual culture: Towards a polycentric aesthetics. In N. Mirzoeff (Ed.), *The visual culture reader* (pp. 27-52). New York, NY: Routledge,

Small, D. (2010). *Stitches*. New York, NY: W. W. Norton.

Smith, T. (1998). Visual regimes of colonialism: Aboriginal seeing and European vision in Australia. In N. Mirzoeff (Ed.), The visual culture reader (pp. 483-494). New York: Routledge.

Soueif, A. (2003). The language of the veil. In D. Bailey & G. Tawadros (Eds.), *Veil: Veiling, representation and contemporary art* (pp. 110–119). London, UK: Institute of International Visual Arts.

Spiegelman, A. (1986). *Maus: A survivor's tale: My father bleeds history*. New York, NY: Pantheon Books, Inc.

———(1992). *Maus: A survivor's tale: And here my trouble began*. New York, NY: Pantheon Books, Inc.

Spiegelman, A. (2001). *In the shadow of no towers*. NY: Pantheon.

Spivak, G. (1994). Can the Subaltern Speak? In P. Williams & L. Chrisman (Eds.), *Colonial discourse and post-colonial theory: A reader* (pp. 66-111). New York: Columbia University Press. (Original work published 1988)

Spring, J. (2004). *How education ideologies are shaping global society: Intergovernmental organizations, NGO's, and the decline of the nation-state*. Hillsdale, NJ: Lawrence Erlbaum.

Stamaty, M. A. (2010). *Alia's mission: Saving the books of Iraq*. OK: Dragonfly Books.

Steyn, M. (2006). *America alone: The end of the world as we know it*. Washington DC: Regnery.

———(2008). The future belongs to Islam. Retrieved from http://shariaunveiled. wordpress.com/2013/11/27/the-future-belongs-to-islam/

Stoskopf, A. (1999). The forgotten history of eugenics. Retrieved from http://www.rethinking schools.org/archive/13_03/eugenic.shtml

Stotsky, S. (2004). *The stealth curriculum: Manipulating America's history teachers*. Washington, DC: Thomas B. Fordham Institute.

Stoddard, J., & Hess, D. (2011). *9/11 and the war on terror in curricula and in state standards documents*. Medford, MA: Center for Information and Research on Civic Learning and Engagement.

Sulima & Hala. (2002). *Behind the burqa: Our life in Afghanistan and how we escaped to freedom*. New York: Wiley.

Thompson, C. (2004a). *Blankets*. Marietta, GA: Top Shelf Productions.

———(2004b). *Carnet de voyage*. Marietta, GA: Top Shelf Productions.

———(2011). *Habibi*. New York, NY: Pantheon.

Timeline: French riots. (2005, November 14). Retrieved from http://news.bbc.co.uk/2/hi/ europe/4413964.stm

Vaught, L. A. (1902). *Vaught's practical character reader*. Retrieved from http://archive. org/stream/vaughtspractical00vaug#page/n5/mode/2up

Volkan, V. (1997). *Bloodlines: From ethnic pride to ethnic terrorism*. Boulder, CO: Westview Press.

Walker, A. (1983). *In search of our mothers' gardens: Womanist prose*. Orlando, FL: Harcourt Books.

We Shall Never Forget 9/11 Coloring Book—Graphic Coloring Novel. (2011). St. Louis, MO: Really Big Coloring Books.

We Shall Never Forget 9/11— Vol. II: The true faces of evil—terror. (2012). St. Louis, MO: Really Big Coloring Books. Retrieved from Coloringbooks.com

Wertham, F. (1954). *Seduction of the innocent*. New York, NY: Rinehart & Company.

Wiederhold, A. (2013). The 9/11 report: A graphic adaptation: Making meaning in the (gutter) spaces between word, image, and ideology. *International Journal of Comic Art, 15*(1), 419–434.

Willinsky, J. (1998). *Learning to divide the world: Education at empire's end*. Minneapolis: The University of Minnesota Press.

Wilson, G. W. (2014). *Ms. Marvel #1*. New York, NY: Marvel.

Yang, G. (2008a). *American born Chinese*. New York, NY: First Second.

———(2008b). Graphic novels in the classroom. *Language Arts, 85*(3), 185–192.

INDEX

minding the media

CRITICAL ISSUES
FOR LEARNING AND TEACHING

Shirley R. Steinberg & Pepi Leistyna
General Editors

Minding the Media is a book series specifically designed to address the needs of students and teachers in watching, comprehending, and using media. Books in the series use a wide range of educational settings to raise consciousness about media relations and realities and promote critical, creative alternatives to contemporary mainstream practices. *Minding the Media* seeks theoretical, technical, and practitioner perspectives as they relate to critical pedagogy and public education. Authors are invited to contribute volumes of up to 85,000 words to this series. Possible areas of interest as they connect to learning and teaching include:

- critical media literacy
- popular culture
- video games
- animation
- music
- media activism
- democratizing information systems
- using alternative media
- using the Web/internet
- interactive technologies
- blogs
- multi-media in the classroom
- media representations of race, class, gender, sexuality, disability, etc.

- media/communications studies methodologies
- semiotics
- watchdog journalism/investigative journalism
- visual culture: theater, art, photography
- radio, TV, newspapers, zines, film, documentary film, comic books
- public relations
- globalization and the media
- consumption/consumer culture
- advertising
- censorship
- audience reception

For additional information about this series or for the submission of manuscripts, please contact:

Shirley R. Steinberg and Pepi Leistyna
msgramsci@gmail.com | Pepi.Leistyna@umb.edu

To order other books in this series, please contact our Customer Service Department:

(800) 770-LANG (within the U.S.)
(212) 647-7706 (outside the U.S.)
(212) 647-7707 FAX

Or browse online by series:
www.peterlang.com